CONFIDENTIAL ECOMMERCE STRATEGY AND TACTICS FOR SUCCESS - PART 1

E-COMMERCE MASTERY: STAKEHOLDER'S SECRET SAUCE TO ACHIEVING SUCCESS

RAVNEESH DHANESHWAR

Made with ♥ on the Notion Press Platform
www.notionpress.com

Contents

Contents

Preface

"Confidential Ecommerce Strategy and Tactics for Success" invites you on an illuminating exploration of the dynamic and ever-evolving landscape of e-commerce. This groundbreaking guide transcends the saturated discourse of performance marketing, digital marketing, and social media, offering a fresh perspective on distinguishing your brand in the fiercely competitive marketplace. Beyond conventional discussions, the guide focuses on essential sales and marketing skills, recognizing them as linchpins for success in the digital realm.

In the digital space, where brands armed with excellent products and services navigate complexities in sales and marketing, the struggle for survival often overshadows the journey toward building a sustainable and scalable business. The playbook, "Confidential Ecommerce Strategy and Tactics for Success," emerges as a reliable compass, navigating the intricate maze of digital commerce. It not only uncovers critical factors that set your brand apart but also addresses overlooked gaps in your business model, particularly the challenges of inconsistent sales and differentiation. Moreover, it places a significant emphasis on the crucial issue of alignment within your organization. Alignment, beyond being a buzzword, demands a profound understanding and articulation of objectives, ensuring that every team member works in harmony towards common goals. The playbook serves as a beacon, guiding stakeholders to gain insightful comprehension of the factors shaping the business model. It illuminates the intricate considerations that form the lifeblood of a company, empowering recognition of gaps and opportunities.

In the relentless pursuit of success, the playbook underscores the paramount importance of being aware of the competition. It emphasizes a laser-sharp focus on customer needs as the cornerstone of competitors' achievements. The customer, the raison d'être of your business, is positioned as the North Star, consistently guiding decisions in the intricate landscape of digital commerce. The journey initiated with a noble intent—to solve problems for customers, fitting perfectly into the market, and building a business not merely surviving but thriving. "Confidential Ecommerce Strategy and Tactics for Success" unfolds as an indispensable roadmap, guiding towards precisely that destination.

Welcome to the realm of direct-to-consumer success, where guiding principles are not mere buzzwords but the bedrock of a thriving e-commerce venture. The playbook beckons you to embark on a transformative journey towards a more prosperous and customer-centric future. As the pages unfold, they illuminate the path to differentiation and sustainable growth, redefining the narrative of your e-commerce venture.

Acknowledgements

I wish to express my deep and heartfelt gratitude to the industry professionals whose unwavering support and invaluable guidance have significantly influenced my journey right from its inception. These remarkable individuals have not only shaped my thought processes but have also imparted the profound importance of maintaining a clear vision and embracing strategic and tactical prowess.

My sincere thanks extend to:

Suku Murti (Group M): Your are someone i looked up to and your insights and counsel during the nascent stages of my career have been nothing short of invaluable. Your guidance provided me with the tools to navigate the intricate terrain of our industry.

AL Sriram (The Times of India Group): Your wisdom and experience have been a wellspring of inspiration and knowledge. The enriching interactions we shared have left an indelible mark on my journey. I soaked up every morsel of wisdom we discussed, much like a sponge absorbing water.

Manmohan Shetty and Pooja Shetty: I extend my heartfelt appreciation for your audacious spirit and determination to venture into the unknown. Your ability to persevere through uncharted territories and emerge triumphant is a true source of inspiration.

Anup Jalan (Laqshya): Your mentorship and unwavering support have been instrumental in propelling my vision and professional journey to new heights. Your sage advice and encouragement continue to drive my growth and success.

I am also indebted to my esteemed professors at IIM Calcutta, Prof. Biswatosh Saha and Prof. Kaushik Roy. Your teachings and profound wisdom have illuminated my path and significantly contributed to my growth and perspective.

A special tribute is owed to two extraordinary individuals:

Suresh Bharadwaj (Adlabs Films Ltd): Your unparalleled insights, expertise, and mentorship have been instrumental in my personal and professional development. Your contributions have left an indelible imprint on my journey.

Rishubh Satiya (Plix Life): Your innovative approach and unorthodox methods have demonstrated that conventional norms can be challenged and overcome. Your pioneering spirit has been a wellspring of inspiration.

Collectively, your influence has indelibly marked my journey towards success. I am profoundly thankful for your mentorship and steadfast support.

Last but by no means least, I wish to offer a heartfelt tribute to my wife, Geetika Kohli Dhaneshwar. Your unwavering support and enduring presence through thick and thin have been my greatest blessing and a wellspring of strength.

CHAPTER ONE

Brands are Engaging Directly with Consumers. Here's Why?

Manufacturers take pride in their brands and have control over them until the moment of distribution. They often have detailed expectations for in-store displays, online marketing, and product presentation, which are laid out in supplier agreements. However, the execution of these expectations can often be varied and not reflect the original intentions. This is where D2C can be advantageous, as it allows manufacturers to have complete control over the entire customer experience, from product presentation to marketing and sales. By going direct to consumers, manufacturers can ensure that their brand is presented and marketed in the way they intended, without any variation or misinterpretation from third-party retailers.

The supplier/retailer relationship has been dependent on the account managers' ability to achieve the required expectations through persuasion or contractual agreements. However, as retail margins continue to fall, retailers are looking for ways to cut costs, which can result in fewer staff, less frequent store refits, and lower stock cover. These factors can create a divide between brand expectations and reality, making it difficult for manufacturers to ensure that their products are presented and marketed in the way they intended. This is where D2C can be beneficial, as it allows manufacturers to have complete control over the customer experience, from product presentation to marketing and sales. By going direct to consumers, manufacturers can ensure that their brand is presented and marketed in the way they intended, without any variation or misinterpretation from third-party retailers.

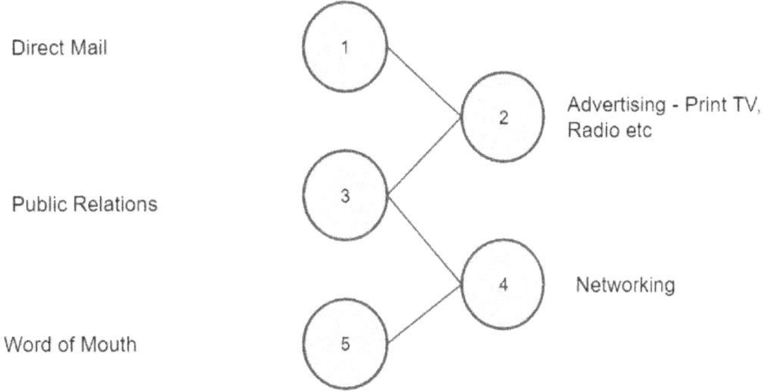

The D2C digital-first brand journey enhances market agility and fosters direct consumer relationships.

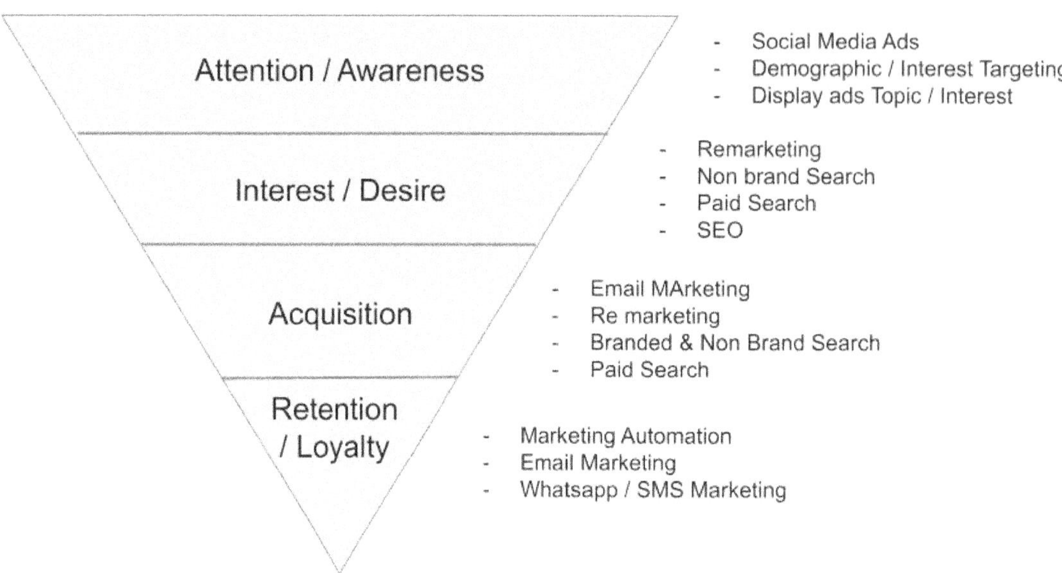

The digital consumers purchase journey is complex

There are numerous benefits of a direct-to-consumer strategy for brands, as well as for customers. One of the benefits for brands is that owning the entire distribution stream from end-to-end enables manufacturers to deliver the ultimate brand experience. By going direct to consumers, manufacturers can control every aspect of the customer experience, from product presentation to marketing and sales, ensuring that their brand is presented and marketed in the way they intended. This can lead to better brand recognition, increased customer loyalty, and higher customer satisfaction levels.

Customers also benefit from a direct-to-consumer strategy, as they can enjoy a better brand experience. By purchasing directly from the manufacturer, customers can be assured of the authenticity of the product, and can also enjoy a more personalized shopping experience. In addition, direct-to-consumer brands often offer more competitive pricing, as they don't have to factor in the costs of third-party retailers. consumers are demanding an ever-improving shopping experience, and brands that focus on the whole customer experience, rather than just the product, are more likely to meet and surpass customer expectations. By going direct to consumers, manufacturers can offer a more personalized and seamless shopping experience, which can lead to increased customer satisfaction and loyalty. Direct-to-consumer brands have the ability to collect data on their customers'.

In addition, direct-to-consumer brands often offer more competitive pricing, as they don't have to factor in the costs of third-party retailers. This can lead to cost savings for customers, which can also contribute to a better overall shopping experience.

Knowing your customer is the first step to satisfying them, both today and in the future. By going direct to consumers, manufacturers can establish a direct brand relationship with their customers, allowing them to collect valuable data on their preferences, behaviors, and buying patterns. This data can be used to tailor marketing and sales strategies to meet the unique needs and preferences of each customer, leading to increased customer satisfaction and loyalty.

In addition, by establishing a direct brand relationship with their customers, manufacturers can also gain valuable insights into product performance and customer feedback. This information can be used to improve products and services, and to develop new products that meet the evolving needs and preferences of customers. A direct-to-consumer strategy can help manufacturers build stronger and more meaningful relationships with their customers, leading to increased customer satisfaction, loyalty, and long-term success.

- Brand Vision: Achieving our initial goals for the brand can be attained only when each part of the brand is managed thoroughly. Selling directly aids in preserving the integrity of the brand.
- Consumer Data & Insights: Getting access to customer data is more worthy than any other commodity. With the introduction of GDPR, customers' information is safeguarded and can only be retrieved with authorization.

Companies that have a connection to their consumers can quickly respond to the market and make changes such as releasing new products, launching promotions, etc. This gives them an advantage that less direct companies do not necessarily have. Also by granting customers direct access to the manufacturer, there's an opportunity to share unfiltered and uncensored feedback. Footfall in high streets is diminishing, and more and more retailers are struggling, presenting a sales challenge to brands. By going D2C (direct-to-consumer) brands can make up for lost sales. Bypassing traditional retail distribution partners with a direct strategy enables manufacturers to save significantly up to 10-15% from wholesale distribution and 15-40% from retailers. Speed to Market is a direct-to-consumer (D2C) strategy that provides brands with swift access to selling possibilities of new items, discounts, trials, and customer remarks on extensive brand understanding. D2C brands have the ability to bring the entirety of their product line to life on their own website, allowing customers a full view of what they have to offer.

Many brands require that their retail partners provide a dedicated shopping experience, but they still cannot replicate the unique brand experience like those of Apple, Adidas and NIKE stores. Though every effort is made, it is still simply a shop situated within another store and not quite the same thing.
Moving from traditional sales channels to direct-to-consumer is going to be quite monumental for manufacturers who have previously concentrated on developing their products and building their brands. Several things should be considered before embarking on a D2C strategy, in short, are your staff & partners ready, and can your infrastructure support the change? Systems and operations must be concentrated on order management; while they may already have this in place for B2B customers, D2C operations involve additional components. These include payment options, gateways, taxes, one-off delivery of goods and individual item returns; all of which require careful strategizing and clear communication to personnel. Once your strategy is ready and you have the necessary support structure in place to facilitate its execution, make sure that your existing retail partners are also ready. Do you intend to take a soft approach and incorporate the existing sales channels, or does Nike's Direct to Consumer strategy prevail as your priority? Such boldness could come with its own risks, though it is likely you have assessed them within your plan.

"*Strategy without tactics is the slowest route to vistory. Tactics without strategy is the noise before defeat. - San Tzu*"

CHAPTER TWO

WHO IS 1ST THE BRAND OR THE CONSUMER

In the current marketing climate, both large and small companies are having difficulty staying up-to-date with the latest trends and techniques. Everywhere is feeling the strain of trying to be successful, modern and incorporating fresh forms of media into their strategies. Assessing a marketing strategy's effectiveness is essential, and the foremost method of doing this is to gauge how successfully it attains the company's primary objectives. Understanding what you are attempting to accomplish is absolutely key to your venture's success. In order to fit a marketing opportunity into their daily agenda, it's necessary to first test and evaluate its potential it other words Spot, evaluate, and engage in emerging opportunities:. To remain at the forefront of new trends and technologies, marketers must be selective in the strategies they take on, since many won't turn out to be worthwhile investments. It is essential to have a creative team assess opportunities and decide if they are beneficial. Most won't be taken advantage of, but the ones able to make an impact can drastically affect the business.

Rather than viewing strategy and innovation as one, it is important to disassociate them in terms of marketing. Breaking the two apart can help to create a successful plan and ensure a more effective outcome. Achieving success in marketing requires taking a look at each concept separately. In order for a strategy to be considered good, it must effectively achieve the objectives that have been set. On the other hand, innovation is all about creating something that is new and different. Unfortunately, new things often fail as standard solutions. Combining these two elements could lead to mismanagement within an organization as it complicates things for both investors and new marketers. This is why businesses tend to put their best people, such as directors and senior executives, on innovation projects to minimize the chances of failure.

In the past, the main focus of marketing campaigns was to acquire customers' attention and generate awareness through exciting advertising campaigns. However, in today's digital age, promotional campaigns are more likely to result in an internet search rather than a sale. This is why brands have shifted into communities where people feel a sense of wholeness and purpose when interacting with the brand. To grow your customer base in the digital age, you must inspire them to purchase and participate.

In the digital age, customers appreciate the convenience of digital marketing. Companies can easily reach their audiences through email, social media, and other online methods. Personalized messages can be used to target specific consumer groups, ensuring that content is relevant and engaging for each customer segment. Companies can use email campaigns or social media posts to reach out to their target audiences while providing timely updates about their products or services at no extra cost. Using personalized content, tailored messaging, and community engagement activities helps to build customer relationships. Brands can interact with customers in real-time to answer queries or provide guidance on product usage. With digital media marketing techniques such as SEO strategies, PPC advertising, email campaigns, video content, and influencer marketing programs, brands can reach out to their desired target audiences effectively.

CHAPTER THREE

NUANCES OF SCALING A BRAND

Building a successful brand is not a sprint; it's a marathon. In this chapter, we will explore the key principles and strategies for building and scaling a brand that stands the test of time. We'll emphasize the importance of laying a strong foundation, setting clear goals, and adopting a long-term perspective in brand building. In the initial stages of brand building, the focus should be on cultivating a loyal customer base with healthy repeat purchase rates.Building a Strong Foundation. This foundation provides stability and a steady source of revenue that can sustain your brand over the long term. Customer loyalty is the bedrock of brand success.

To build a brand is a Mid to Long-Term endeavor: It is not a quick-fix solution. It's a process that unfolds over time, and the fruits of your labor may not be immediately visible. Embrace the idea that your brand's true potential will manifest in the mid to long term. To effectively scale your brand you must planning for growth:, by establishing clear, well-defined goals. These goals should serve as a compass, guiding your brand-building efforts in the right direction. Whether it's expanding your market share, entering new markets, or increasing brand recognition, your goals should be specific and achievable. Distinguish between strategy and tactics. Strategy involves the overarching plan that outlines how you intend to achieve your goals. It's a long-term, high-level plan that sets the direction for your brand. Tactics, on the other hand, are the specific actions you take to execute your strategy. They operate on a smaller scale and often have a short-term focus.

Strategy: A blueprint for long-term success.

Tactics: The actionable steps to execute the strategy.

Building Brand-Latching Properties:

Instead of chasing immediate growth, focus on creating brand assets that have lasting value. These brand-latching properties could include a strong online presence, a loyal customer community, or proprietary technology. These assets will continue to benefit your brand as it grows. Take the time to immerse yourself in your industry or category. Understanding the nuances, trends, and customer behavior within your niche is essential for making informed decisions. This knowledge will help you identify your unique selling proposition and plan for expansion strategically. Every successful brand endeavours to finds its niche to achor itself and build a strong foundation. It's the segment of the market where your brand can excel. By focusing on your niche and understanding it intimately, you can tailor your brand-building efforts to cater to the specific needs and preferences of your target audience.

Successful brand building and scaling require a methodical and strategic approach, devoid of quick fixes or shortcuts. It involves the careful cultivation of a robust customer base, the definition of clear objectives, and the embrace of a long-term vision. Rather than chasing immediate gains, the focus should be on sustained growth and resilience in a competitive market. The key lies in meticulous planning, staying attuned to the overarching goals, and recognizing that the journey of brand building is continuous. This perspective fosters adaptability, resilience, and the ability to navigate the dynamic challenges of the market, ensuring that the brand not only survives but flourishes over time.

CHAPTER FOUR

Get the Strategy you need now

As a business owner & stakeholder it is imperative to grasp that strategy serves as the linchpin for shaping a prosperous future. Through strategic formulation, an organization takes proactive strides towards future planning, mitigating the pitfall of short-term reactivity to potential threats. This deliberate approach steers the course away from mere goal attainment, fostering enduring impacts. A strategic vantage also liberates resources from mundane day-to-day troubleshooting, allowing them to be channeled into visionary pursuits.

Furthermore, a meticulously devised and effectively communicated strategy serves as a compass, guiding decision-making across the organizational spectrum. This harmonization ensures a unified trajectory, synchronizing the collective efforts of leadership and employees. With a shared sense of direction, resources are judiciously directed towards pivotal projects, while key metrics become the focal point of measurement. Strategic investment is pinpointed, fortifying critical domains, and adaptive shifts are seamlessly orchestrated in response to emerging competitors and stakeholder dynamics. It's paramount to recognize that the essence of strategy transcends organizational boundaries. Not limited to corporations, strategic fundamentals cascade into business units, fortifying their operational frameworks. Mastery over the intricacies of conceiving, communicating, and executing a novel strategy is a hallmark of effective leadership, regardless of hierarchy. A sagacious business luminary comprehends that the nexus of strategic prowess is a quintessential attribute for steering an organization towards sustained success.

In the ever-evolving landscape of strategic approaches, this book offers a comprehensive guide to navigating the dynamic terrain of business strategy. Rather than adhering to a singular school of thought, the book is centered around the practical art of devising strategies that synchronize seamlessly with your leadership team's vision. It places paramount emphasis on tailoring your strategy to align with your distinct capabilities, prevailing circumstances, and industry nuances. Within this playbook, you'll find the tools to craft a strategic masterpiece, defining the tactical underpinnings that will propel your organization forward. By delving into fundamental principles and providing a robust framework, it lays the bedrock for fostering strategic discussions. The guide seamlessly shepherds you through the nuanced thought processes involved in formulating, stress-testing, communicating, and ultimately executing a strategy that reverberates throughout your workforce. Distinguishing between the pivotal elements of strategy, tactics, implementation, and execution, the book beckons you to grasp the essence of each, fostering an ecosystem where clarity prevails. It extols the virtues of a deep-seated comprehension of one another's objectives, nurturing a synergy that permeates every facet of your strategic endeavors.

Embarking on a journey of innovative thinking, the book urges you to sculpt strategies and tactics that transcend convention. By deftly weaving elements of contrast, combination, constraint, and context, you're prompted to construct a tapestry of value that resonates profoundly. With the accelerated pace of growth in modern enterprises shaping industries, the book underscores the inherent need for a dynamic strategy. This entails integrating purpose into your strategic blueprint, cementing a bedrock upon which lasting success can be built. Rooted in self-awareness, the book facilitates an exploration of cognitive biases that might inadvertently influence your decision-making. It beckons you to discern the steps required for triumph in your competitive landscape, all while acknowledging the necessity for tailored adaptations based on your organizational capabilities. Scrutinizing the alignment of your team with your strategic compass, it ensures your workforce becomes an effective conduit for executing tactics that bear direct revenue implications.

The tome isn't limited to formulating and executing strategy; it's equally devoted to the intricate dance between articulation and action. Communicating your intentions and actions effectively assumes a pivotal role, and the book imparts wisdom on accomplishing this feat harmoniously. While it champions a novel approach, it resonates with the inevitability of change that accompanies such a journey. Embedded within its pages are the scaffolds of skills, processes, and practices that elucidate the contours of executing a strategy, thereby elevating your prospects of success.

Notably, this guide doesn't merely expound on strategy and execution in isolation; it elucidates their symbiotic relationship. It shines a spotlight on bridging gaps that emerge, offering practical insights into navigating them deftly. By emphasizing the perils of relying solely on metrics, it forewarns against veering off course into mediocrity, underscoring the indispensability of insightful perspectives. This book is a strategic compass that steers you through the labyrinth of modern business strategy. Its teachings extend beyond theory, permeating the realm of actionable insights that equip you to navigate uncharted waters with sagacity. It is a guide that empowers you to craft, execute, and refine strategies that not only thrive in the present but also lay the groundwork for a triumphant future.

Becoming a proficient strategist and technician is a gradual process that demands consistent practice. The sequence and methodology delineated within this compendium aren't rigidly sequential, yet each facet holds significance and should not be disregarded. Establishing a strong foundation is paramount; lacking it will render your endeavors mere survival tactics rather than growth pursuits.

Anticipate unforeseen hurdles along the way. Above all, bear in mind that strategic constancy is fallacious; your plans will necessitate frequent recalibration and enhancement. Rivals won't await your annual strategy cycle to mount an offensive, customers won't defer their preference shifts, and emerging technologies won't pause for your strategy cycle before surging ahead.

Pave the path for your company's future by engaging in continuous contemplation, commencing from this very moment. Overlooking or muddling strategy implementation and execution engenders muddled thinking and lackluster performance across all echelons of operation. In the pragmatic business sphere, aligning strategy implementation and execution, while remaining attuned to their nuanced differences, is indispensable for astute management. Furthermore, the topics explored in the book represent my endeavor to promote the democratization of marketing.The growing complexity of marketing has created a divide between what the biggest companies can achieve and what the average marketer can handle.

> *"The concept of democratizing marketing aims to bridge this gap. The essence of democratized marketing is to provide every business with the strategies, tools, resources, and tactics necessary, ensuring that everyone has an equal chance for success."*

In the realm of strategic management, we delve into two fundamental dimensions:

Corporate Strategy: At the pinnacle of corporate strategy lies the task of defining the unique capabilities that set a company apart. This involves identifying the essence of the company's competitive advantage – what makes it stand out in the marketplace. A critical aspect is determining the precise terrain in which the company should operate: what industries to engage in, how to orchestrate operations, what acquisitions to pursue, and which markets to venture into. This realm encompasses the overarching decisions that mold the company's identity and trajectory.

Business Unit Strategy: Within the domain of business unit strategy, the spotlight turns to the customers who shape our target market. It is imperative to discern the factors that differentiate our products and services from competitors – our distinct competitive edge. In crafting a compelling value proposition, we must pinpoint the unique value our offerings bring to the table. Furthermore, honing our capabilities to amplify the delivery of this value proposition sets the stage for business excellence. These strategic considerations reverberate across all facets of our operations, steering decisions in pricing, research and development, manufacturing, and more.

Adaptation is the lifeblood of strategy, given the ceaseless tides of market forces. A strategy with elasticity ensures our continued relevance and competitiveness. The journey from current standing to desired future is best navigated with parallel implementation efforts rather than sequential steps. Execution entails translating our meticulously crafted strategy into tangible actions and decisions, culminating in the realization of commercial success. This is the conduit through which strategy becomes palpable results. Achieving execution excellence is the cornerstone of optimizing outcomes. The synergy between strategy implementation and execution is not a mere coincidence; they are inextricably intertwined. The spheres of strategy formulation, implementation, and execution form an interwoven trinity, each influencing the others. To thrive in the dynamic business landscape, a comprehensive strategy that embodies both corporate and business unit elements, executed with precision, is essential. It is this orchestration that enables an enterprise to not only weather market forces but also to flourish.

The alignment between strategy implementation and execution is a critical nexus in the realm of business strategy. While often used interchangeably, these terms bear distinct nuances that merit attention. It is important to acknowledge that adeptly executing a flawed strategy poses challenges, and even more daunting is the task of achieving stellar outcomes when the strategy's execution is lacking. To embark on a course of action that begets success, our strategic planning must take root in a well-defined strategy replete with delineated tactics and initiatives. This framework serves as the bedrock upon which we can proficiently implement and execute, thus engendering the envisioned outcomes and fostering value generation for all stakeholders involved.

CHAPTER FIVE

DEFINE YOUR STRATEGY

As you would have understood by now a strategic plan doesn't just happen. It takes time, thought, and a lot of effort to get right. But once you're there, you'll have a blueprint for success—a clear path forward that all of your employees can follow. Strategic planning is integral for any business, whether it's a startup or even an established multinational organization. This allows businesses to prepare a well-defined roadmap for the future. This roadmap and a clear set of criteria help all stakeholders work toward a single strategic business goal. An organizational strategy is a business plan that outlines how a company will achieve its goals. It is a guide for how businesses can achieve their goals, and it works as a strategic roadmap for companies to take in order to be successful.

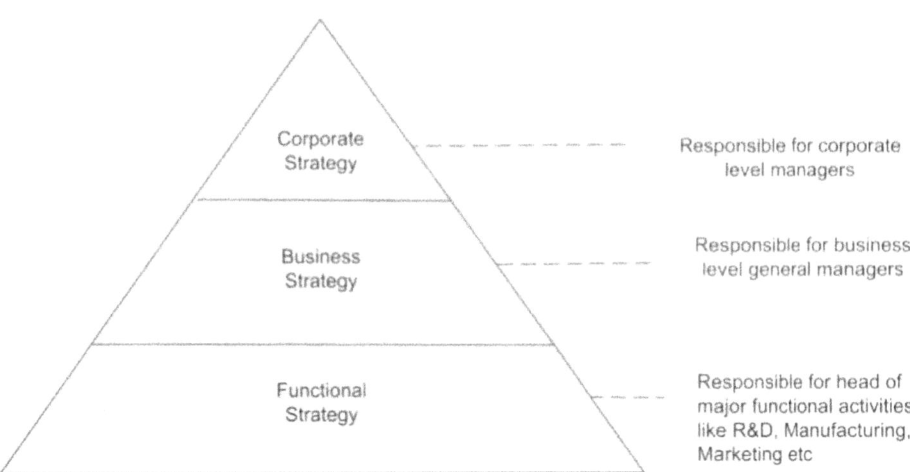

For an organisation to function seamlessly there should be clarity within the organisation on their role and what the whats the collective goal.

More often than not, organizational strategies outline overall business objectives that need to be achieved. An organization strategy is the best possible way to build credibility and trust with your customers. Companies can use different types of organizational strategies to fulfill their business goals and create a strategic roadmap. It's important to understand the difference between a strategy and its parts. Part of a strategy may be a low-cost provider, but it's not the whole thing. And being first-to-market with a new product or service is part of your strategy, but it isn't your entire strategy. It's also important not to confuse your mission statement with your strategies. Your mission statement is what drives your company and inspires you to do what you do, but it's not an actual plan for how you'll get there. Strategy is an integrated and externally oriented concept of how a firm will achieve its objective and how it will compete against its rivals. A strategy consists of an integrated set of choices. It is concerned not only with the current situation, but also with the future; not just with what a firm does, but also with what it does not do; not just with what resources are used, but also with which ones are not used. These decesion making process relates to five elements managers must consider when making decisions. Arenas.

1. Where will we be active?
2. Differentiators. How will we get there?
3. Vehicles. How will we win in the marketplace?
4. Staging. What will be our speed and sequence of moves?
5. Economic logic. How will we obtain our returns?

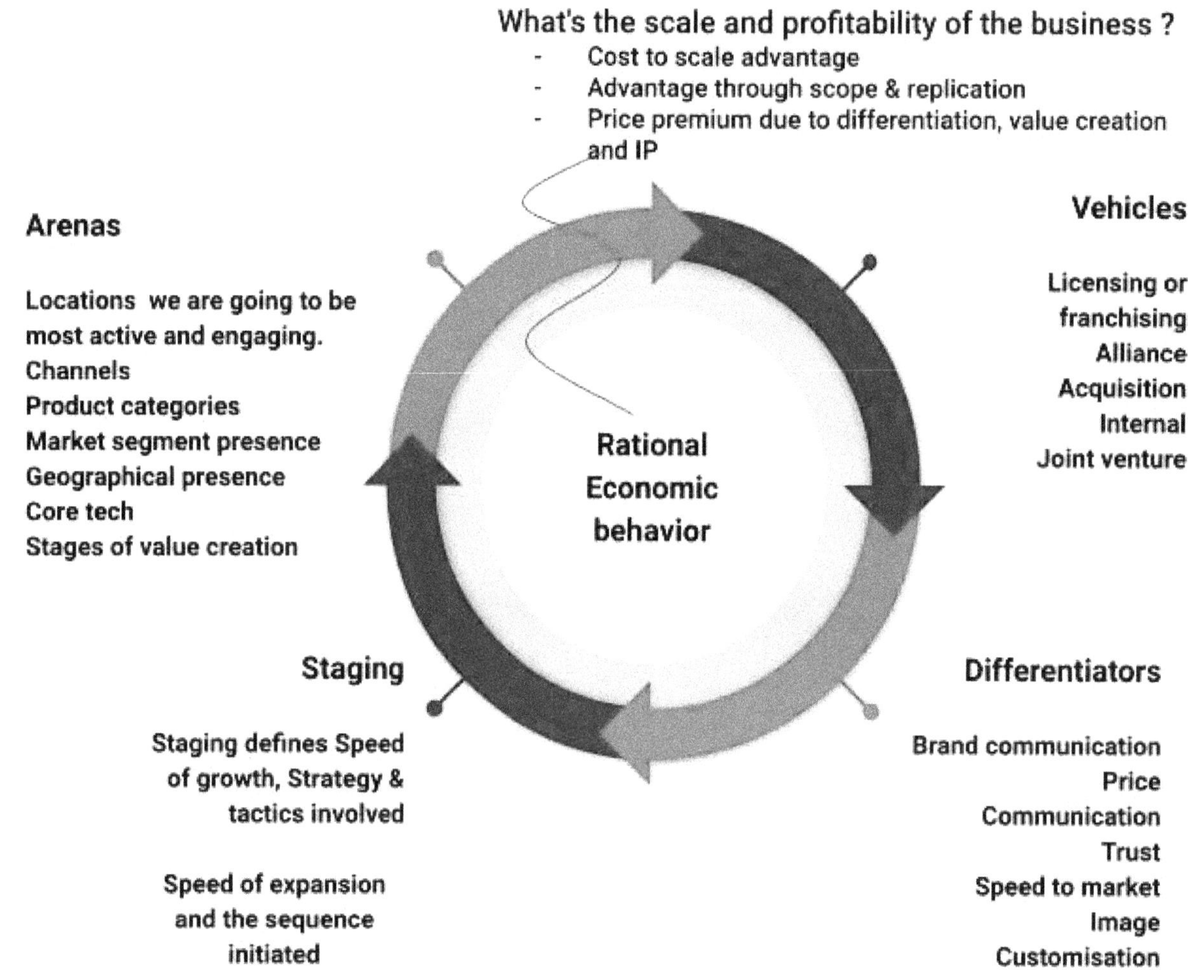

Decesion making needs to be aligned with the function and not loosing sight of what the outcome of the decesion will be across the organisation

Arenas: The arenas facet helps you answer questions about business strategy—that is, it helps you determine which particular industry or geographic segments are the firm's prime competitive arenas. The arenas facet also allows you to summarize corporate strategy—that is, it allows you to summarize which group of industry and geographic segments the firm competes in. The arenas facet starts by identifying the five arenas that a firm competes in:

- Industry (the most profitable or strategically important arena for a firm)
- Geographic Segment (the areas in which a company has competitive advantage)
- Customer Segment (the customer groups that provide the best opportunities for differentiation)
- Competitor Set (the other firms with which a company competes)
- Differentiators : are features and attributes of a company's product or service that help it beat its competitors in the marketplace. Firms can be successful in the marketplace along a number of common dimensions, including image, customization, technical superiority, price, quality, and reliability.

Differentiators are often used as part of a marketing strategy to build loyalty among current customers and attract new ones. They are often based on the unique characteristics of the offering or the company itself. Companies that want to win in the marketplace must use differentiators. Differentiators are the key to creating value for the customer, and they help you stand out from your competition.There are two critical factors in selecting differentiators. Decisions must be made early. Key differentiators rarely materialize without significant up-front decisions, and without valuable differentiators firms tend to lose marketplace battles.

Identifying and executing successful differentiators mean making tough choices and trade-offs. Managers who can't make tough decisions about trade-offs often end up trying to satisfy too broad a spectrum of customer needs; as a result, they execute poorly on most dimensions. Differentiators are what drive potential customers to choose one firm's offerings over those of competitors. The earlier and more consistent the firm is at driving these differentiators, the greater the likelihood that customers will recognize them. In today's business enviornment, it is critical for companies to create a brand identity for themselves that differentiates them from other companies in their industry. This does not mean that they should try to be different for its own sake; rather, they should try to be different because it will help them achieve their goals. The first step toward creating a strong brand identity is developing a clear understanding of who your customers are and what they want from you as a company. Once you know who they are and what they want, you can begin thinking about how to differentiate yourself from others in the market.

Its also important to understand the importance of vehicles for growth, They are the means for participating in targeted arenas. For instance, a firm that wants to go international can do so in different ways. It can buy an existing company that already operates in the desired market and then use it as a platform for expansion; it can build an entirely new subsidiary in the target country; or it can find local partners who will help it enter the new market. Each of these approaches has its own advantages and disadvantages, so it is important to understand what they are before deciding which one best suits your needs.

> "*The possible vehicles for entering a new arena include acquisitions, alliances, and organic investment and growth.*"

1. Staging & Pacing : Staging decisions are important because they help firms prioritize their opportunities and set the stage for a successful strategy. The key factors to consider when making staging decisions include resources, urgency, credibility, and the need for early wins.
2. Resources are critical to all companies: not every opportunity is worth pursuing, and not every opportunity can be pursued at the same time. Once you have identified your most valuable opportunities and those that match your available resources, you can consider how far along each opportunity is in its lifecycle. There may be some opportunities that can be implemented quickly or with little investment; others may require more time or investment before they are ready to launch.
3. Urgency matters as well—not all opportunities have permanent windows of opportunity. In some cases, timing is everything! In other cases, there may be more than one opportunity that could work for your company but only if it's donc now.
4. Reputation matters too: if you want to build your brand as an industry leader over time, it's important that you start off on the right foot with your first few moves into new arenas. This means making sure that any new products or services meet quality standards and are delivered on time so that customers' expectations are

met—and exceeded! A firm's economic logic is the "fulcrum" for profit creation. It refers to how the firm will earn a profit and how it will cover all fixed, variable, and financing costs. Earning normal profits requires that a firm meet all fixed, variable, and financing costs. Achieving desired returns over the firm's cost of capital is a tall order for any organization. In analyzing a firm's economic logic, think of both costs and revenues. When analysing economic logic you will be able to differentiate if it resides on the cost side or rests on the firm's ability to increase its customers' willingness to pay premium prices for products. If you are able the increase the customers willingness to pay then BINGO! you have hit the jackpot.

This playbook it is all about developing a Direct to Consumer (D2C) strategy. This approach can be very effective for brands and manufacturers who want to establish themselves as the primary point of contact with their customers. By bypassing traditional retail channels, you can gain more control over the customer experience and build stronger relationships with your audience. It's important to take a fresh approach when developing a D2C strategy, as traditional methods may not be the best fit for this unique approach to sales and marketing. By focusing on the specific needs and preferences of your target audience, and leveraging the latest tools and technologies available, you can create a D2C playbook that is tailored to your brand and audience. To develop a successful D2C strategy, there are a few key steps you should consider:

- Define your target audience: Who are your ideal customers, and what are their needs and preferences? Understanding your audience is crucial to creating a successful D2C strategy.
- Choose your sales channels: There are many different ways to sell directly to consumers, including eCommerce websites, social media platforms, and even physical retail locations. Consider which channels are most appropriate for your brand and audience.
- Develop your brand and messaging: To stand out in a crowded marketplace, you need a strong brand identity and messaging that resonates with your audience. This includes everything from your logo and website design to your product descriptions and marketing campaigns.
- Build relationships with your customers: One of the biggest advantages of a D2C strategy is the ability to build direct relationships with your customers. Make sure you're engaging with them regularly through social media, email marketing, and other channels.
- Measure and optimize your results: As with any marketing strategy, it's important to track your results and make adjustments as needed. Use analytics tools to monitor your sales, website traffic, and other metrics, and use this data to optimize your strategy over time.

Following and this structure and framework should help you get started with developing a successful D2C strategy!

To determine when to use D2C, companies should consider several factors including their product strategy, sales channel strategy, customer support, operational support, marketing strategy, and technical support.

- Product Strategy: Companies should assess whether their products are well-suited for direct sales to consumers. Products that have a high level of customization or are difficult to sell through traditional retail channels may be good candidates for D2C.
- Sales Channel Strategy: Companies should evaluate their existing sales channels and assess whether D2C can complement or replace these channels. Companies may choose to use D2C as a standalone channel or integrate it with existing channels to offer a seamless omnichannel experience.
- Customer Support: Companies must ensure that they have the necessary resources to provide high-quality customer support for D2C sales. This may include training customer service teams, providing online support resources, and establishing clear policies for handling customer issues.
- Operational Support: Companies should assess their operational capabilities to fulfill direct orders to customers. This may include inventory management, order processing, and shipping logistics.

- Marketing Strategy: Companies should evaluate their marketing strategies to determine whether D2C can help them reach their target audience more effectively. D2C allows companies to collect valuable customer data, which can be used to develop more targeted marketing campaigns.
- Technical Support: Companies should assess their technical capabilities to support D2C sales. This may include developing or integrating e-commerce platforms, establishing secure payment processing, and providing online support resources.

Companies should evaluate their product strategy, sales channel strategy, customer support, operational support, marketing strategy, and technical support to determine when to use D2C. By carefully considering these factors, companies can determine whether D2C is a viable option for their business and prepare accordingly.

Growth Strategy

Boost existing customer markets

Move Into adjacent customer markets

Create new markets

Cultivate R reframe existing products, offerings, revenue streams & competencies

Cultivate & collaborate with external partners for products, offerings, revenue streams & competencies

Sustaining Growth (Short term planning horizon, mining the core)

Transformative Growth (Intermediate term planning horizon, advancing into adjacencies)

Disruptive Growth (Long term planning horizon, incite breakthroughs)

Build your growth strategies with a clear vision of resources in hand

Manufacturers have several options when it comes to distribution, and the right choice often depends on the specific needs of the business. Some suppliers choose to distribute their products through multiple channels, such as selling directly to consumers through their own website, selling through retailers, or partnering with distributors. This allows them to reach a wider audience and potentially increase sales. On the other hand, some manufacturers may choose to focus on just one channel, such as selling exclusively through a specific retailer or distributor. This can help to build a strong relationship with that partner and streamline the distribution process. Ultimately, the best route to market for a manufacturer will depend on a variety of factors, including the product itself, the target audience, and the resources available to the business.

CHAPTER SIX

Start Early Shape your "Competitive Advantage"

A word of caution before we begin this journey. It's important to differentiate strategy from tactics or visa versa. Before you begin to map out your strategy its important to understand your business environment by answering two questions.

Q1. How unpredictable or predictable is your environment ?
Q2. What's the power you or your competitors have to change an environment?

Once you have answered both the questions, you can then define your strategy styles from the 4 methods below.

Strategy Style 1: Classical Strategy. This type of strategy is majorly taught in various business schools and this works well in predictable and immutable (unchanging over time or unable to be changed) business environments. Classical strategy, also known as traditional strategy, refers to the foundational approaches and principles of strategic management that have been widely used and studied in the field of business strategy. It encompasses the core concepts and frameworks that have shaped the understanding of strategy development and implementation. The classical strategy is rooted in the work of prominent scholars and practitioners such as Michael Porter, Igor Ansoff, and Henry Mintzberg, among others. It is characterized by a systematic, analytical, and structured approach to strategy formulation and execution. Classical strategy emphasizes the significance of understanding the external environment in which an organization operates. This involves assessing industry structure, competitive forces, market dynamics, and identifying opportunities and threats. The widely used analytical tools in this context include Porter's Five Forces framework, PESTLE analysis (examining political, economic, social, technological, legal, and environmental factors), and SWOT analysis (analyzing strengths, weaknesses, opportunities, and threats). Classical strategy recognizes the importance of assessing an organization's internal capabilities and resources. This involves analyzing the firm's strengths and weaknesses, core competencies, value chain activities, and competitive advantage. Techniques like resource-based view (RBV) and value chain analysis help in understanding the firm's internal dynamics and identifying potential areas of competitive advantage. Once the external and internal analyses are conducted, classical strategy provides a structured approach to strategy formulation. It involves setting clear objectives, identifying strategic alternatives, evaluating options, and selecting the most appropriate course of action. This process often includes the development of mission and vision statements, goal setting, and the formulation of strategies at the corporate, business unit, and functional levels. Classical strategy places a strong emphasis on achieving and sustaining a competitive advantage in the marketplace. Competitive advantage refers to the unique attributes or capabilities that enable an organization to outperform its competitors and deliver superior value to customers. Strategies for attaining competitive advantage may involve cost leadership (achieving low-cost production and operations), differentiation (creating unique and desirable products/services), or focus (concentrating on specific market segments or niche markets). Classical strategy recognizes the importance of effectively executing the chosen strategy and monitoring its progress. This involves translating strategic plans into action, aligning organizational resources, establishing performance measures and targets, and regularly evaluating performance against set objectives. It also includes the need for adjusting strategies when necessary and adapting to changes in the competitive landscape. It's important to note that while classical strategy has been influential, the field of strategic management has evolved over time, and alternative perspectives and approaches have emerged. For example, contemporary strategies like the resource-based view, dynamic capabilities, and disruptive innovation theories have expanded the understanding of strategy beyond the traditional boundaries. Nonetheless, classical strategy continues to provide a solid foundation for strategic thinking and remains relevant in many business contexts.

Strategy Style 2: Adaptive Strategy. Adaptive strategy in business refers to an approach that allows an organization to respond effectively and flexibly to changes in its internal and external environments. It emphasizes the need for continuous monitoring, learning, and adjustment to ensure long-term success and sustainability. Adaptive strategies are particularly valuable in dynamic and uncertain business landscapes, where traditional static strategies may become obsolete or ineffective. The core idea behind adaptive strategy is to foster organizational agility and resilience by actively sensing and responding to emerging trends, market shifts, customer demands, competitive forces, technological advancements, regulatory changes, and other relevant factors. Rather than adhering rigidly to a fixed plan, an adaptive strategy embraces ongoing experimentation, learning, and adaptation. There are several key elements that contribute to the meaning and implementation of adaptive strategy. Adaptive strategies require organizations to develop robust systems and processes for gathering and analyzing information about their operating environments. This involves monitoring industry trends, customer behavior, competitor activities, technological advancements, and other relevant data sources. By keeping a pulse on the external and internal factors impacting the business, organizations can identify emerging opportunities and threats. Adaptive strategies prioritize learning as a fundamental component of business success. This involves promoting a culture of curiosity, experimentation, and knowledge sharing within the organization. Learning can take various forms, such as conducting market research, engaging in pilot projects, seeking customer feedback, conducting experiments, and fostering cross-functional collaboration. The insights gained through these activities help refine and adjust business strategies in response to changing circumstances. Adaptive strategies emphasize the importance of flexibility and agility in responding to changing conditions. This may involve developing modular or scalable business models, agile project management methodologies, or flexible organizational structures that can quickly adapt to new circumstances. By being nimble and responsive, organizations can seize emerging opportunities and mitigate risks more effectively. Adaptive strategies embrace an iterative approach, where plans are continually refined and adjusted based on feedback and new information. This iterative cycle involves setting goals, testing assumptions, evaluating outcomes, and making necessary adjustments. This iterative process encourages organizations to be proactive in adapting their strategies as they learn from their experiences. They require careful consideration of resource allocation and risk management. By assessing the potential impact and feasibility of different strategic options, organizations can allocate their resources effectively. Additionally, risk management practices should be in place to identify, assess, and mitigate risks associated with adaptive strategies, ensuring that the organization can respond to unexpected challenges while minimizing potential negative consequences. Successful implementation of adaptive strategies relies on aligning various organizational components, such as culture, leadership, structures, and processes. Leaders must foster a culture that embraces change, experimentation, and learning. They need to promote open communication channels, empower employees to make decisions, and create a supportive environment for innovation and adaptation. Organizational structures and processes should be designed to facilitate the flow of information and decision-making across different levels and functions. Adaptive strategy in business is a dynamic approach that emphasizes continuous learning, flexibility, and responsiveness to change. It enables organizations to adapt their plans, products, services, and processes in alignment with evolving market conditions and customer needs. By embracing an adaptive strategy, organizations can position themselves to thrive in today's fast-paced and uncertain business landscape.

Strategy Style 3: Shaping Strategy. This style of strategy works well in an unpredictable environment where you have the power to change. Shaping strategy in business refers to a deliberate and proactive approach taken by companies to influence and shape their competitive environment, rather than simply responding to external forces and market conditions. It involves actively participating in shaping the industry dynamics, market trends, and customer preferences to create a more favorable business landscape. The underlying principle of shaping strategy is that companies should strive to become drivers of change rather than passive observers. Instead of solely reacting to market conditions and competitors‘ actions, shaping strategy empowers organizations to take a proactive stance and exert influence on various factors that impact their industry. Here are some key elements that contribute to the in-depth meaning of shaping strategy in business. Shaping strategy involves scanning the external environment to identify emerging trends, technological advancements, regulatory shifts, and changing customer needs. By anticipating these changes, companies can prepare themselves to adapt and even capitalize on new opportunities before their competitors. It often requires companies to aim for industry leadership or establish a dominant position within their sector. By becoming a leader, an organization gains the credibility and influence necessary to shape the direction of the industry, set standards, and define best practices. Shaping strategy may involve collaborating with other stakeholders, including customers, suppliers, industry associations, research institutions, and even competitors. By forming strategic partnerships, companies can collectively influence market dynamics and foster innovation that benefits the entire industry. This for of strategy emphasizes the importance of continuous innovation and disruption. By introducing new products, services, or business models, companies can redefine the competitive landscape and shape customer preferences. Innovation can involve leveraging emerging technologies, exploring new markets, or finding unique ways to solve existing problems. Companies pursuing shaping strategy actively engage in advocacy efforts to influence regulations and policies that impact their industry. By working closely with policymakers, businesses can help shape legislation that aligns with their objectives and creates a conducive environment for growth and innovation. Shaping strategy may involve creating new markets or expanding existing ones. Companies can influence demand by educating customers, promoting new use cases, and demonstrating the value of their offerings. This proactive approach allows businesses to shape customer preferences and stimulate market growth. The aim is to establish a sustainable competitive advantage by building unique capabilities, cultivating strong relationships, and actively shaping the business environment. It goes beyond short-term tactics and focuses on long-term success by positioning the company in a favorable and influential position. Shaping strategy in business signifies a proactive, forward-thinking, and influential approach that empowers companies to shape their industry rather than being solely influenced by it. It requires a deep understanding of market dynamics, continuous innovation, collaboration, and a willingness to challenge the status quo. By adopting a shaping strategy, businesses can create a more favorable competitive environment, unlock new growth opportunities, and secure long-term success.

Strategy Style 4: Visionary Strategy. "Build it and they shall come." A visionary strategy represents a bold, future-oriented approach that seeks to create transformative change and drive an organization towards a compelling vision. It requires a combination of foresight, innovation, strategic alignment, and adaptability. By pursuing a visionary strategy, businesses can disrupt markets, lead industry transformations, and achieve sustainable success in an ever-changing business landscape. An organisation mapping a visionary strategy looks beyond the present and takes a long-term perspective. It involves envisioning what the organization could become in the future and aligning all efforts towards that vision. This forward-looking approach helps leaders identify emerging trends, anticipate customer needs, and position the company for future success. This often requires significant transformation and change within the organization. It goes beyond incremental improvements and embraces radical shifts in business models, processes, and culture. This willingness to challenge the status quo and embrace innovation is crucial for achieving the desired vision. A visionary strategy begins with a compelling vision statement that captures the essence of what the organization aspires to achieve. The vision statement should be clear, concise, and inspiring, serving as a guiding light for employees, customers, and stakeholders. It should create a sense of purpose and direction, motivating people to rally behind the vision. The implementation often involve disruptive innovation, challenging established norms and creating new market spaces. It requires thinking outside the box, exploring uncharted territories, and leveraging emerging technologies or business models. By embracing innovation, visionary companies can differentiate themselves and gain a competitive edge. This form os strategy places a strong emphasis on understanding and meeting customer needs. By deeply understanding the target market and anticipating future demands, visionary organizations can develop products, services, and experiences that exceed customer expectations. This customer-centric approach drives loyalty, market growth, and sustained success. Successful roll out requires aligning all aspects of the organization, including people, processes, technology, and resources, towards the vision. This alignment ensures that every decision and action is directed towards achieving the desired future state. It involves communicating the vision effectively, fostering a culture of innovation and agility, and aligning goals and incentives throughout the organization. Visionary strategies acknowledge that the path to the future is uncertain and dynamic. Organizations must be agile, adaptable, and open to learning from both successes and failures. This iterative approach allows companies to continuously refine their strategies, pivot when necessary, and seize emerging opportunities. It often involves aiming for industry leadership or becoming a dominant player in the market. By leading the way and setting new industry standards, visionary companies can shape the competitive landscape and influence market dynamics to their advantage.

For beginners and early stage companies am going a step ahead to define - predictable & unpredictable environments and mutable & immutable environments.

The terms "predictable" and "unpredictable" refer to the degree to which the behavior or outcomes of the system can be foreseen or anticipated. A predictable environment is characterized by a high level of regularity, stability, and consistency in the behavior of the system. In such an environment, the cause-and-effect relationships are well-understood, and there is a high degree of certainty in predicting future outcomes based on past data or patterns. Key features of a predictable environment include:

- Stability: The system exhibits a relatively steady and unchanging state over time.
- Regularity: Events or phenomena occur in a repetitive and orderly manner.
- Linear Relationships: Cause-and-effect relationships are clear and easily identifiable.
- Historical Patterns: Past data and trends can be used to make accurate predictions about the future.
- Relatively Low Uncertainty: There is a reduced level of unknown factors or random variations.
- Examples of predictable environments include well-established industries with stable market conditions, manufacturing processes with standardized procedures, and predictable weather patterns in certain regions.

An unpredictable environment, on the other hand, is characterized by a high level of uncertainty, variability, and dynamism. In such an environment, it is difficult to accurately forecast or anticipate future outcomes due to the presence of numerous unknowns, complex interactions, and non-linear relationships. Key features of an unpredictable environment include:

- Instability: The system experiences frequent and significant changes or fluctuations.
- Randomness: Events or phenomena occur in an irregular or unpredictable manner.
- Non-linear Relationships: Cause-and-effect relationships are complex and may not follow a straightforward pattern.
- Lack of Historical Patterns: Past data or trends may not be indicative of future behavior.
- High Uncertainty: There are numerous unknown factors, external influences, or disruptions.
- Examples of unpredictable environments include emerging markets with rapidly changing consumer preferences, natural disaster-prone regions, financial markets with high volatility, and highly competitive industries with disruptive technologies.

It's worth noting that many real-world systems exhibit a combination of predictable and unpredictable elements. Additionally, the level of predictability or unpredictability can change over time due to various factors, such as technological advancements, regulatory changes, or shifts in societal dynamics. In business strategy, the terms "mutable" and "immutable" refer to the characteristics of the business environment and how they influence strategic decision-making. The mutable and immutable aspects of the business environment have distinct features and implications for organizations. Let's define and explain the difference between these two concepts: A mutable business environment is one that is subject to frequent and significant changes, both internally and externally. It is characterized by volatility, uncertainty, complexity, and ambiguity (VUCA).

	Drivers	Impact	Needs
Volatility	Change Nature Change Dynamics Change Speed Change Rate	Instability Loss of control Increased risk	Vision
Uncertainty	Unpredictability Potential Surprises Unknown impacts Unknown Outcomes	Indecisiveness Increased Analysis Delayed action	Understanding
Complexity	Task Correlation Interdependencies Interrelationships Interopratibility	Data overload Decline in productivity Mistakes Learning on the fly	Clarity
Ambiguity	Unclear cause Unclear action Unclear aims Unclear effect	Doubts Distrust Lack of confidence Delays	Agility

We operate in a very unpredictable and constantly changing business enviornment

Features:

- Rapid technological advancements: Technological innovations can quickly disrupt existing business models, markets, and industries.
- Changing customer preferences: Customers' needs, wants, and behaviors can evolve rapidly due to various factors, such as changing demographics, cultural shifts, or emerging trends.
- Dynamic competitive landscape: The market can experience intense competition, new entrants, mergers and acquisitions, changing regulations, and shifting power dynamics among competitors.

Implications for business strategy:

Organizations operating in mutable environments need to be flexible and responsive to change. They must continuously scan the environment, gather information, and adjust their strategies accordingly. And in order too stay ahead, businesses must foster a culture of innovation and be willing to experiment with new ideas, products, and processes. Preparing for multiple potential future scenarios and having contingency plans in place can help mitigate risks and seize opportunities in a mutable environment. An immutable business environment refers to a stable and relatively predictable business landscape where changes occur less frequently and are relatively gradual. Established industries and markets: Industries and markets in immutable environments have stable structures, established players, and well-defined rules and regulations. Customer needs and preferences remain relatively stable over time, allowing businesses to build and maintain long-term relationships. Disruptions to the industry or market are infrequent and may occur due to slow-moving factors such as regulatory changes or gradual technological advancements. Organizations operating in immutable environments can engage in more long-term planning and focus on building sustainable competitive advantages. With a stable environment, businesses can concentrate on improving operational efficiency, cost reduction, and process optimization. Rather than radical innovation, organizations can focus on incremental improvements to existing products, services, or processes. It's important to note that while mutable and immutable are two ends of a spectrum, most business environments exhibit elements of both. The degree of mutability or immutability may vary across industries, regions, and time periods. Successful business strategies take into account the characteristics of the specific environment and adapt accordingly. In today's competitive environment you need a thought through and systematic planning to execute a plan. You can tailor your strategy to match your style, industry, business environment, geography and competition. This way you can deploy your unique capabilities and resources to better capture the opportunities. To test bed or deploy any strategy its important to have adequate capital & resources.

Adding a caveat to the 4 strategies, if there is an economic downturn or you have suffered losses or in constraint of deploying capital or you do not have the capability to compete you need to be quick and deploy the 5Th strategy which is the Strategy of Survival. This style of strategy will not yield you any results in the long term and can only be deployed in a short period of time. The strategy requires a company to focus defensively. During this phase brands should look into the future and prepare themselves for the future with a definitive thought through growth strategy. Brands need to deep dive and access their industry well. While doing so they need to examine predictability and understand how far in the future and how accurately they can predict outcomes. It's also important to determine to what extent competition influences those factors. Strategists tend to use either the classical or the visionary styles of strategy. A brand should articulate a goal and then decide on the strategy style to follow. When you see an opportunity, make no two bones about it and seize it. When you are studying your competition you will find their economic moat and your moat as well. This is the part where you need to be smart and engage with competition in a way to eat into competition and protect yourself.

CHAPTER SEVEN

WHAT'S YOUR COMPETITIVE STRATEGY STYLE ?

As someone actively involved in commerce brand strategy and marketing, it's essential to grasp the four main competitive strategies, which can be categorized into the following types:

1. Adaptive Strategy
2. Shaping Strategy
3. Classical Strategy
4. Visionary Strategy

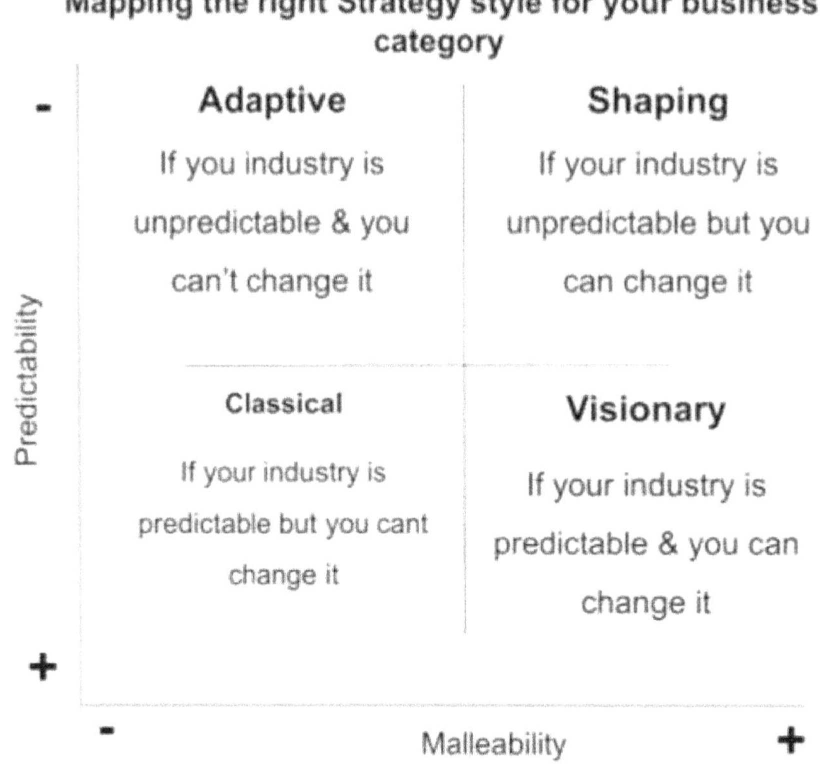

Choose a style relevant to you and your organisation

Each of these competitive strategies requires a unique approach to marketing, operations, and branding. Choosing the right strategy depends on your brand's strengths, the market you operate in, and the specific customer segments you aim to serve. Successful brands often adapt and combine these strategies as needed to stay competitive and achieve their goals. let's dive into the various strategy styles for different industries:

Understanding the appropriate strategy style for a given industry is crucial for the long-term success and competitiveness of a business. Adaptation, shaping, classical approaches, and visionary thinking are all valuable, depending on the specific industry dynamics and goals of the company. How do you choose your right strategy style? Selecting the right strategy style from the four types of competitive strategies - Adaptive, Shaping, Classical, and Visionary - depends on several factors, including your organization's goals, industry dynamics, and market conditions. Here's a brief overview of each and how to choose the right one:

Adaptive Strategy

When to Use: Choose an adaptive strategy when the business environment is uncertain or rapidly changing. It involves making adjustments as needed to respond to evolving conditions.

Key Characteristics: Flexibility, continuous monitoring, quick decision-making, and the ability to pivot.

Adaptive Strategy Style Industries

- Transportation & Infrastructure: These companies often adapt to market changes, regulations, and technological advancements, focusing on efficiency and sustainability.
- Biotechnology: Adaptation is crucial as scientific breakthroughs and regulatory shifts can affect the industry's landscape.
- Semiconductors: Adaptation is key in this rapidly evolving sector, with companies responding to market demands and technological advancements.
- Textile & Apparel: Staying adaptable helps navigate changing fashion trends, global supply chains, and sustainability concerns.

Shaping Strategy

When to Use: Opt for a shaping strategy when you want to actively influence the industry or market environment. It involves proactively creating favorable conditions for your business.

Key Characteristics: Market leadership, innovation, and setting industry standards.

Shaping Strategy Style industries

- Healthcare Technology: Companies in this sector shape strategies by innovating and setting industry standards, focusing on cutting-edge solutions.
- Internet & Catalog Retail: Shaping strategies involve defining e-commerce trends and customer experiences.
- Airlines: These companies shape their strategies by focusing on route networks, customer service, and industry partnerships.
- Trading & Distribution They influence markets by shaping distribution and pricing strategies.
- Professional Services: Shaping strategies involve delivering specialized expertise and setting industry standards.
- Hotels, Restaurants & Leisure: These companies shape strategies by providing unique experiences and catering to changing consumer preferences.

Classical Strategy

When to Use: Classical strategy is a traditional approach that focuses on optimizing current operations and maximizing efficiency. Use it when market conditions are stable and well-understood.

Key Characteristics: Efficiency, cost reduction, process improvement, and maintaining the status quo.

Classical Strategy Style Industries

- Automobiles: These companies often follow classical strategies focusing on quality, cost-effectiveness, and brand loyalty.
- Commercial Banks: Stability and risk management are classical strategy pillars in the banking industry.

- Tobacco: Established companies rely on classical strategies centered on brand reputation, regulation compliance, and market presence.
- Pharmaceuticals: Classical strategies emphasize research, regulatory compliance, and brand recognition.
- Beverages: These companies often use classical strategies, focusing on brand loyalty, marketing, and distribution.
- IT Services: Classical strategies involve delivering reliable and efficient services.
- Household Products**: Brands in this sector often emphasize quality, safety, and market presence in their strategies.
- Healthcare Equipment: Classical strategies involve R&D, regulatory compliance, and establishing a trusted brand.

Visionary Strategy

When to Use: A visionary strategy is suitable when you want to radically transform your industry or create a new market. It's about having a clear and ambitious vision and pursuing it relentlessly.

Key Characteristics: Innovation, disruptive thinking, risk-taking, and long-term vision.

To choose the right strategy style, consider the following steps:

- Assess Your Market and Industry: Analyze the current market conditions, competitive landscape, and industry trends. Determine whether the environment is stable, evolving, or in flux.
- Define Your Goals: Clearly outline your organization's goals and objectives. What do you want to achieve in the short and long term?
- Understand Your Strengths and Weaknesses: Assess your company's strengths, weaknesses, resources, and capabilities. Identify areas where you have a competitive advantage.
- Evaluate Risk Tolerance: Consider your risk tolerance as a business. Some strategies involve more risk than others. Ensure your chosen strategy aligns with your comfort level.
- Adaptability: Consider how adaptable your organization is. If you can quickly adjust to changing circumstances, an adaptive strategy may be more suitable.
- Long-Term Vision: If you have a clear long-term vision and the ambition to shape your industry, a visionary strategy could be the right choice.
- Industry Disruption: If your industry is ripe for disruption, and you have innovative capabilities, a visionary or shaping strategy may be ideal.
- Visionary Strategy Style Industries:
- Software: Visionary strategies focus on innovation, user experience, and staying ahead of the technological curve.
- Media: Companies in this sector set trends by shaping content consumption and delivery methods.
- Food Products: Visionary strategies involve creating unique and sustainable food products while considering consumer health and environmental concerns.
- Healthcare Providers & Services: Visionary strategies prioritize patient-centric care, digital health, and cost-effective solutions.
- Containers & Packaging: Visionary strategies focus on sustainable packaging solutions and innovative designs.
- Aerospace & Defense: Companies in this sector set the bar for innovation and security, shaping the industry's future.

In many cases, a combination of these strategy styles may be appropriate, depending on the different facets of your business. It's essential to periodically review and adjust your strategy as market conditions evolve to stay competitive and achieve your goals. The chapter below articulates the ways in which to find competitive moats and yours as well. The way to use the strategies may overlap and vary depending on the business, objective or geographic region. The intent of a well mapped out strategy is to find competitors moat or define and protect your own moat.

CHAPTER EIGHT

BUILD YOUR MOAT & PROTECT YOUR BUSINESS - START EARLY

How do companies stay ahead of competitors

Cost Advantage Moat
Company Producing goods at the **Lowest possible price**

High Switching Cost
Company making it very **costly for customers to switch to a competitor**

Regulation Moat
Regulations Make it **Lowest possible price**

Network Effect Moat
More Users = More Value

Intangible asset Moat
Branding, Patents and trademarks make it hard for others to copy

Digital Moats
Large engaged audience

Moats protect businesses and profitability from competetion. To sustain and grow your business ideally you should find and protect your business with the most relevant advantage. You can not always win on price advantage & or by giving discounts.

The company's moat is mainly reflected in intangible assets, network effects, user conversion costs, product provision costs and so on. When there is no moat, the better products will incur more fierce competition and when everyone's business models are similar, profit margins also act as barriers.

1. A brand moat or competitive moat, is a term used in business and marketing to describe a sustainable competitive advantage that a company possesses over its competitors. Just as a physical moat provides protection and makes it difficult for others to breach a fortress, a marketing moat creates barriers that make it challenging for competitors to replicate or surpass a company's market position.

2. A marketing moat is typically built through various strategic elements that differentiate a company's products or services, enhance customer loyalty, and establish a strong market presence. These elements can include:
3. Branding: A strong and recognizable brand helps create customer trust, preference, and loyalty. Companies with well-established brands often enjoy a marketing moat.
4. Customer Relationships: Building strong relationships with customers through exceptional customer service, personalized experiences, and ongoing communication can create a loyal customer base that is less likely to switch to competitors.
5. Distribution Channels: Owning or controlling efficient distribution channels, such as exclusive partnerships or an extensive network, can provide a competitive advantage by making it difficult for competitors to reach customers effectively.
6. Intellectual Property: Patents, trademarks, copyrights, or proprietary technologies can establish a moat by providing legal protection and preventing competitors from easily replicating a company's offerings.
7. Scale and Network Effects: Companies that achieve significant scale or have network effects, where the value of their product or service increases as more users or participants join, can build a marketing moat by creating high barriers to entry for competitors.
8. Switching Costs: If customers face significant costs, both monetary and in terms of time and effort, to switch from one product or service to another, it can create a marketing moat for the company with the existing customer base.

The concept of a marketing moat is closely related to the idea of a competitive advantage and is often used to assess a company's long-term sustainability and market position. By developing and nurturing a strong marketing moat, a company can protect itself from competitive threats and maintain a dominant market position over an extended period.

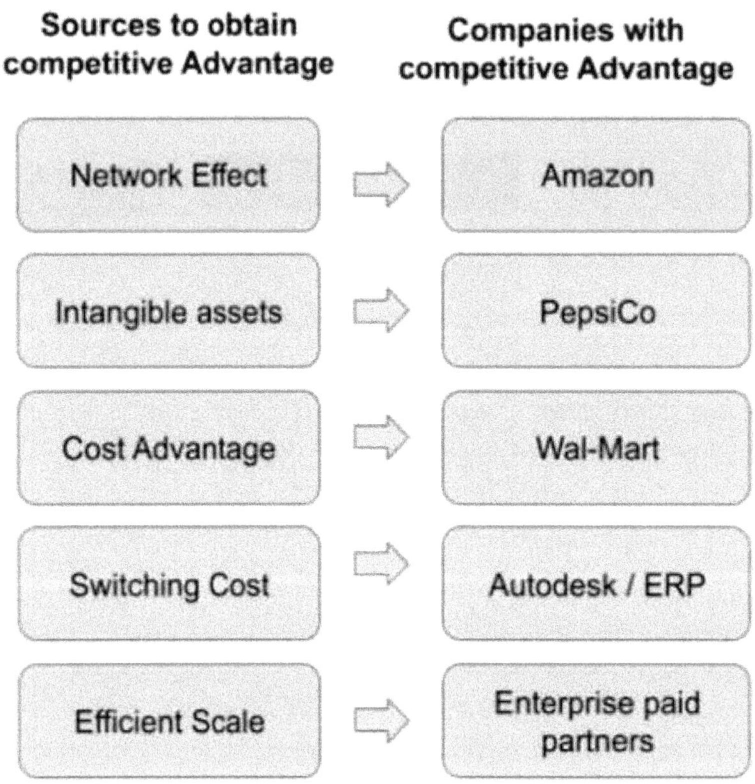

A few examples of the various kinds of moats.

By considering these factors, you can identify the key elements of your brand moat. By strengthening these elements, you can make it more difficult for competitors to challenge your market position.

Here are some additional tips for building a strong brand moat:

- Invest in marketing and advertising to build brand awareness and generate positive customer sentiment.
- Focus on customer satisfaction and loyalty by providing excellent customer service and offering high-quality products and services.
- Protect your intellectual property by registering patents, trademarks, and copyrights.
- Innovate and stay ahead of the competition by constantly developing new products and services.
- Build relationships with key stakeholders, such as suppliers, distributors, and customers.
- By following these tips, you can build a strong brand moat that will protect your business from competition and help you to achieve long-term success.

How do you find the company's moat? In the company's analytical framework, the most important thing is to see "do you have any elements that are not easy for competitors to imitate", which is called a "moat" in Buffett's framework. The moat theory is very classic, and the companies selected according to it have been repeatedly verified by Buffett's outstanding investment performance, so I will focus on the four points he emphasized. They are:

1. Intangible assets,
2. Network effect of business model,
3. User conversion cost and
4. Product cost.

Support your judgment with financial data.

When we analyze a company's moat, we must not take it for granted to subjectively judge whether a company has these moats. Financial data is an important argument to support the moat judgment! If you think a company's moat is a brand, you should see "whether this company's products have higher pricing and lower sales costs than similar products." If you think a company has economies of scale, you should look at "whether its revenue is growing faster than its cost, and whether its profit margin will increase with the increase of sales." If a company's products have a multilateral network effect, it usually has faster customer growth and marginal decreasing costs than the industry. If you think switching costs are a barrier to a company, look at "does it have a higher repurchase rate and lower marketing expenses?" If you judge that a company has a cost advantage, it should have a higher gross profit margin and a lower expense rate than its competitors. In addition, players who take the initiative to use low profit margins to gain more market share are worth paying attention to, and it is often a short-sighted behavior to pursue profits prematurely when the barriers are not clear.

Unveiling the Power of Defensibility with Scale

Defensibility with scale is a strategic concept wherein a company's competitive advantage strengthens as it grows and achieves a larger scale of operations. As a company expands and accumulates resources, customer base, and market influence, it gains distinct advantages that are difficult for competitors to replicate. Let's explore this concept further with examples: Network Effects: Network effects occur when the value of a product or service increases as more people use it. This creates a powerful defensible moat because the larger the user base, the more appealing the product becomes to new users. Competitors find it challenging to entice customers away from a well-established network. Example: Social media platforms like Facebook and LinkedIn exhibit strong network effects. As more users join, the platforms become more attractive due to increased connectivity and content sharing, making it difficult for new entrants to compete.

1. Economies of Scale: Economies of scale refer to the cost advantages a company gains as it produces more goods or services. As production increases, the average cost per unit decreases, allowing larger companies to offer competitive pricing and better margins. This cost advantage becomes a barrier for smaller competitors. Example: Amazon's vast scale enables it to negotiate lower prices with suppliers, operate efficient distribution centers, and provide cost-effective shipping options. This cost structure is difficult for smaller e-commerce startups to match.
2. Brand Loyalty or Latch-On Effect: As a company grows, it has more opportunities to build a strong brand and foster customer loyalty. This loyalty makes customers more likely to stick with the company's offerings, even when alternatives are available. Example: Apple's extensive product ecosystem encourages customers to stay within the brand. Once a customer invests in Apple devices, they are more likely to continue purchasing from Apple due to the compatibility and familiarity of the products.
3. Switching Costs: As a company's offerings become more integrated into a customer's processes or routines, switching to a competitor becomes more difficult and costly. These switching costs act as a deterrent to customer attrition. Example: Enterprise software companies like Salesforce create switching costs by providing complex solutions that require employee training and data migration. These costs make it challenging for businesses to switch to a competing software platform.
4. Market Access and Relationships: Large companies often have established relationships with suppliers, distributors, and partners. These relationships are difficult for competitors to replicate quickly, giving the company an advantage in terms of market access and resources. Example: Walmart's extensive supply chain relationships and distribution network allow it to stock a wide range of products at competitive prices. Competitors would need significant time and resources to match Walmart's market presence.

Defensibility with scale involves leveraging the advantages that come with growth to build strong barriers against competitors. Network effects, economies of scale, brand loyalty, switching costs, and established relationships all contribute to this defensibility. As a company scales, these advantages create a virtuous cycle where growth leads to more advantages, making it increasingly challenging for competitors to erode the company's market position.

Moat Myths

There are several common myths and misconceptions about moats. These myths can lead to misunderstandings about how moats work and their significance in evaluating a company's competitive advantage. let's delve into more detail about the common myths and misconceptions surrounding economic moats and how they can lead to misunderstandings about a company's competitive advantage:

1. **Myth: Moats Last Forever:** A prevailing myth is that once a company establishes a moat, it will remain impervious to competition indefinitely. Moats are not static. They can erode over time due to changes in technology, consumer preferences, or competitive dynamics. A strong moat requires continuous effort to maintain and adapt.
2. **Myth: Size Equals Moat:** Assuming that large companies inherently have a strong moat is a misconception. A company's size alone doesn't guarantee a competitive advantage. Smaller companies can possess unique products, innovative strategies, or efficient operations that constitute strong moats.
3. **Myth: Moats are Quantifiable Metrics:** Some might believe that moats are quantifiable metrics that can be easily measured. Moats often encompass qualitative factors that are harder to quantify, such as brand loyalty, customer relationships, and intangible assets. Evaluating these
4. **Myth: Moats Protect Against All Threats:** It's a common belief that moats safeguard companies from all competitive threats. Moats can mitigate certain types of competition, but they might not protect against unforeseen disruptions, changes in consumer behavior, regulatory shifts, or new technologies. Companies need

to remain adaptable and resilient.

5. **Myth: Moats are Obvious:** People often think that moats should be immediately visible and easy to identify. Some moats are not readily apparent. For instance, strong brand loyalty might not be immediately visible in financial statements but can significantly impact customer retention and pricing power.
6. **Myth: Moats Guarantee High Returns:** It's not uncommon to assume that a company with a moat will automatically generate high stock returns. While a moat can contribute to a company's success, other factors like management competence, market conditions, and execution are also critical to financial performance.
7. **Myth: Moats are All About Low Prices:** Believing that offering low prices is the primary indicator of a strong moat is a mistake. While cost advantages can be part of a moat, true competitive advantage involves factors like brand strength, network effects, and unique offerings.
8. **Myth: Moats Cannot be Replicated:** Thinking that once a moat is established, competitors cannot replicate it. Competitors can adapt, innovate, and find ways to overcome barriers. A true moat often requires ongoing innovation and strategic planning to maintain its effectiveness.
9. **Moats are Only for High-Tech Companies:** Moats are not limited to technology companies. They apply across industries, including consumer goods, finance, healthcare, and more. A moat can be based on factors specific to the industry and company.

These myths can lead to faulty assessments of a company's competitive position, potentially resulting in misguided investments or strategic decisions. To accurately evaluate a company's moat, it's crucial to consider a wide range of factors, both quantitative and qualitative, that contribute to its long-term competitive advantage. It's important to approach the concept of economic moats with a nuanced understanding and consider a variety of factors that contribute to a company's competitive advantage. Avoiding these common myths can lead to more accurate assessments of a company's long-term prospects.

False Moats or Weak Moats

False moats, often referred to as "illusory moats" or "weak moats," are factors that might appear to provide a competitive advantage at first glance but, upon closer examination, do not offer a sustainable, long-term barrier to competition. These factors might give a company a temporary edge but are not strong enough to withstand challenges from competitors or changes in the market. Here are some examples of false moats:

1. Temporary Cost Advantages: Cost advantages that can be quickly replicated or eliminated by competitors are often false moats. If a company's lower costs are due to short-term factors like favorable currency exchange rates, volatile commodity prices, or temporary supply chain efficiencies, these advantages might not last.
2. Price Leadership: If a company is only competitive because it offers the lowest price, it's not necessarily a strong moat. Competitors can easily engage in price wars, eroding profitability for everyone and potentially leading to a race to the bottom.
3. Product Imitation: A company might have a unique product or service for a short time, but if competitors can easily replicate it or create similar offerings, this is a false moat. True competitive advantage comes from offering something difficult to copy.
4. First-Mover Advantage: Being the first to enter a market doesn't automatically guarantee a moat. If competitors can quickly follow and catch up, the first-mover advantage might not provide a lasting barrier.
5. High Growth without Profitability: Rapid growth can be impressive, but if a company is not generating sustainable profits, it might be relying on external funding or unsustainable practices to fuel its expansion.
6. Excessive Marketing Spending: Relying solely on heavy marketing and advertising to attract customers is not a strong moat. Competitors can increase their own marketing efforts to compete, leading to escalating costs and diminishing returns.

7. Lack of Brand Loyalty: Assuming customers will stay loyal even without strong brand connections is a false moat. Brand loyalty requires ongoing effort to maintain, and if customers are easily swayed by lower prices or competitor offerings, it's not a reliable moat.
8. Limited Geographical Advantage: A company might have a strong presence in a particular region, but if it can't replicate its success in other areas or if competitors can enter that region easily, the advantage might not hold up.
9. Regulatory Protections Alone: While certain industries might have regulatory barriers to entry, relying solely on regulations to protect against competition is a false moat. Regulations can change, and competitors can find ways to comply.
10. Weak Intellectual Property Protection: Having patents, trademarks, or copyrights is valuable, but if they are easily circumvented or not enforced effectively, they might not provide a meaningful moat.

It's important for investors and businesses to critically evaluate the sources of a company's competitive advantage and consider whether they are truly sustainable over the long term. False moats can lead to misguided investments and strategic decisions, so a thorough analysis is crucial.

Short term moats or Transient Advantage

Transient advantage in strategy refers to a temporary or short-lived competitive edge that a company or organization possesses over its rivals. It is a concept often discussed in the field of strategic management and is contrasted with sustainable advantage.A transient advantage arises from various factors such as technological innovation, market dynamics, customer preferences, or regulatory changes, among others. These factors create a temporary window of opportunity that allows a company to outperform its competitors for a limited period. The key characteristic of a transient advantage is its impermanence. It is time-bound and can erode or disappear as circumstances change, rivals catch up, or new disruptive forces emerge. Unlike sustainable advantages, which are durable and can be maintained over the long term, transient advantages require constant adaptation and responsiveness to stay ahead. Companies with a transient advantage must capitalize on their lead by leveraging their strengths, innovating rapidly, and maximizing their market position during the limited timeframe. This could involve aggressive marketing, expanding market share, investing in research and development, or optimizing operations to maximize profits while the advantage lasts. However, it's important to note that relying solely on transient advantages is not a sustainable strategy. Organizations should also focus on developing sustainable advantages that provide long-term value and stability. These sustainable advantages can act as a foundation for future success while transient advantages come and go. Overall, understanding and effectively leveraging transient advantages is crucial for companies to navigate dynamic and competitive business environments. By recognizing and seizing these fleeting opportunities, organizations can stay ahead of the curve and create value in a rapidly changing world.

A few examples of transient advantages in the context of direct-to-consumer (D2C) brands:

1. Early Mover Advantage: Being one of the first brands to enter a specific market or industry can provide a transient advantage. For example, companies like Casper and Warby Parker were pioneers in the direct-to-consumer mattress and eyewear industries, respectively. By entering these markets early and disrupting traditional distribution channels, they were able to establish themselves as leading D2C brands and gain a competitive edge.
2. Social Media Buzz: Leveraging the power of social media platforms can provide a transient advantage to D2C brands. Brands like Glossier and Kylie Cosmetics effectively used social media marketing and influencers to generate significant buzz and create a direct connection with their target audience. This social media-driven popularity can translate into a competitive advantage, but it requires ongoing innovation and adaptability to maintain the momentum.

3. Limited Edition Releases: Offering limited edition or exclusive products can create a transient advantage for D2C brands. By creating a sense of scarcity and exclusivity, brands can generate increased demand and a sense of urgency among consumers. Examples include streetwear brands like Supreme, which frequently releases limited quantities of products, leading to high demand and rapid sellouts.
4. Product Innovation: Launching innovative products that meet evolving consumer needs can provide a transient advantage. For instance, Dollar Shave Club disrupted the shaving industry with its subscription-based model, offering affordable and convenient shaving products directly to consumers. This innovation allowed them to quickly gain market share and challenge established brands.
5. Cultural Relevance: Aligning with popular trends or cultural movements can give D2C brands a transient advantage. Brands like Outdoor Voices, with its focus on athleisure wear and wellness, capitalized on the growing interest in active lifestyles and gained traction among health-conscious consumers. Staying attuned to shifting cultural preferences and effectively positioning the brand can create a short-term advantage.

It's important to note that these examples of transient advantages may change over time as markets evolve and new competitors enter the scene. D2C brands need to continuously adapt, innovate, and identify new opportunities to maintain their competitive edge in a dynamic business landscape.

Lifecycle of a short term or transient moat

Brands must remain vigilant and not be seduced by the allure of short-term competitive advantages that often prove fleeting. Instead, they should anchor their strategy on three enduring propositions. First, a compelling value proposition that resonates with buyers, ensuring that the brand consistently delivers real value and addresses customer needs. Second, a robust profit proposition that aligns with the value proposition, allowing the company to generate sustainable revenues and profits, safeguarding its longevity. Lastly, the often underestimated people proposition - this motivates and engages the team within the company to passionately execute the strategy, recognizing that it's the people behind the brand who ultimately breathe life into these strategic positions. By focusing on these three strategic pillars, brands can build lasting moats that withstand the test of time and competition.

IIow to find a competitors MOAT

Finding moats in competitors refers to identifying the competitive advantages or barriers that protect a company's market share and profitability from potential rivals. Moats can be characterized by various factors such as brand strength, economies of scale, intellectual property, network effects, and switching costs. Here's a step-by-step guide on how to identify moats in competitors:

1. Research the industry: Start by gaining a thorough understanding of the industry in which the competitors operate. Study the market dynamics, key players, and trends shaping the sector. This knowledge will provide a foundation for assessing competitive advantages.
2. Analyze financial performance: Review the financial statements of the competitors, including their income statements, balance sheets, and cash flow statements. Look for consistent and sustainable profitability, high profit margins, and strong cash flows. A company with consistently strong financial performance may have a competitive advantage.
3. Assess the brand strength: Evaluate the brand reputation and recognition of the competitors. Strong brands often create customer loyalty, trust, and preference, acting as a moat against new entrants. Look for indicators like market share, customer reviews, and customer retention rates.
4. Evaluate economies of scale: Consider whether the competitors benefit from economies of scale, which can lead to cost advantages. Larger companies often enjoy lower costs per unit due to their size, efficient operations, and negotiating power with suppliers. Look for signs of cost leadership and efficient production processes.
5. Examine intellectual property and patents: Investigate whether the competitors possess valuable intellectual property (IP) or patents. Intellectual property can provide legal protection and exclusivity, making it difficult for competitors to replicate or enter the market. Look for patents, trademarks, copyrights, or proprietary technologies.
6. Look for network effects: Network effects occur when the value of a product or service increases as more users join the network. Assess whether the competitors benefit from network effects, such as social media platforms, marketplaces, or software platforms. Strong network effects can create significant barriers to entry.
7. Consider switching costs: Evaluate the costs or difficulties associated with customers switching from one competitor to another. Higher switching costs can create customer stickiness and loyalty, providing a competitive advantage. Look for long-term contracts, customer lock-ins, or complex integration requirements.
8. Study regulatory barriers: Assess any regulatory or legal barriers that may protect the competitors. Certain industries, such as pharmaceuticals or utilities, may have stringent regulations and high entry barriers. Understand the licensing requirements, compliance costs, and industry-specific regulations that may impact new entrants.
9. Monitor customer feedback and reviews: Stay updated on customer feedback, reviews, and complaints about the competitors‘ products or services. Positive customer sentiment and high customer satisfaction can indicate a competitive advantage, while negative feedback may highlight areas of vulnerability.
10. Stay informed about industry developments: Continuously monitor industry news, research reports, and market analyses to stay informed about the competitive landscape. Identify any emerging trends, disruptive technologies, or innovations that could potentially impact the competitors' moats.

Remember that identifying moats requires a combination of research, analysis, and ongoing monitoring. A comprehensive understanding of the competitors' strengths and weaknesses will help you assess their competitive advantages and inform your own business strategies. The moat maybe tough for an early stage company or startup to find and articulate but it's something you should work towards to build a profitable and strong company in the future.

CHAPTER NINE

INNOVATION

In the ever-evolving landscape of e-commerce, innovation is a critical factor for brands aiming to capture and sustain the attention of their target audience. The digital marketplace is characterized by intense competition and rapidly changing consumer preferences. To stand out amidst this crowded space, e-commerce brands must continuously introduce novel and inventive features, products, or services. Innovation not only attracts initial attention but also fosters brand loyalty by demonstrating a commitment to staying ahead of the curve. For instance, incorporating cutting-edge technologies like augmented reality for virtual try-ons, implementing personalized shopping experiences through machine learning algorithms, or adopting eco-friendly packaging solutions can set a brand apart, creating a distinct identity in the minds of consumers. An innovative business model is indispensable for the profitable growth of e-commerce brands. A forward-thinking approach allows companies to adapt to market dynamics, capitalize on emerging trends, and identify untapped opportunities. By constantly reassessing and refining their business models, e-commerce brands can optimize operational efficiency, reduce costs, and enhance customer satisfaction. Innovative strategies such as subscription-based services, gamified shopping experiences, or strategic partnerships with influencers can not only drive revenue but also generate positive word-of-mouth, expanding the customer base. In a digital landscape where consumer expectations are shaped by the latest advancements, a failure to innovate can lead to stagnation and ultimately result in diminished market relevance and profitability. Therefore, a commitment to innovation is not just a strategic choice for e-commerce brands; it's a necessity for survival and sustained success. Innovation in e-commerce extends beyond technology to encompass novel business models and marketing strategies. D2C brands often disrupt traditional distribution channels by selling directly to consumers, cutting out intermediaries. Subscription-based models, limited edition releases, and exclusive collaborations are innovative approaches to creating a sense of exclusivity and urgency among customers. Social media plays a crucial role in the marketing innovation of these brands, with influencers, user-generated content, and interactive campaigns fostering a sense of community and brand engagement. Innovation in e-commerce and D2C involves a harmonious blend of technology adoption, data-driven decision-making, and creative business strategies that resonate with the evolving preferences of the modern consumer.

Innovation is classified as innovation when it meets specific criteria and characteristics that set it apart from routine activities or incremental improvements. There is no universally accepted definition, but generally, innovation is considered as such when it exhibits the following traits:

- Novelty: An innovation introduces something new, whether it's a product, service, process, technology, or idea. It should represent a departure from the status quo.
- Value Creation: Innovation should create value for individuals, organizations, or society as a whole. It should address a problem, fulfill a need, or offer benefits that were not previously available.
- Market Implementation: True innovation is more than just a concept or idea; it must be implemented and adopted in the market. It has to make a real impact.
- Improvement or Change: Innovation can involve improvements to existing solutions or completely new concepts. It can be incremental (small changes) or disruptive (radical changes).

- Risk and Uncertainty: Innovation often involves a degree of risk and uncertainty. It may not be guaranteed to succeed, and there could be obstacles to overcome.
- Measurability: Innovations should be measurable in terms of their impact. This impact can be assessed in various ways, such as increased efficiency, cost reduction, revenue growth, or improved quality of life.
- Adoption and Diffusion: The innovation should be adopted and diffused in the market or within its target audience. It should gain acceptance and use over time.
- Sustainability: Sustainable innovation considers the long-term effects on the environment, society, and the economy. It should aim to be environmentally and socially responsible.
- Intellectual Property: In some cases, innovations may be protected by patents, copyrights, or other intellectual property rights.
- Problem Solving: Innovation often addresses specific problems or challenges, offering unique and effective solutions.

It's important to note that innovation is a dynamic and ongoing process. What was considered innovative at one point may become commonplace as technology and society evolve. Innovations can range from small, everyday improvements to groundbreaking discoveries and inventions. The classification of an innovation depends on its impact, context, and relevance to the specific field or industry in which it occurs. Innovation refers to the process of introducing something new, whether it's an idea, product, process, or service that creates value and addresses a particular need or problem. It involves transforming existing practices, concepts, or technologies into novel and impactful solutions. Innovation is crucial for businesses and societies as it drives growth, competitiveness, and progress.

Technology plays a significant role in fostering innovation. It provides tools, resources, and capabilities that enable individuals and organizations to explore new possibilities and develop groundbreaking ideas. Here are some ways technology facilitates innovation. Technology has democratized access to information and knowledge, allowing individuals and businesses to stay informed and learn from various sources. This access to vast amounts of information encourages creative thinking and the development of new ideas. Technology has revolutionized communication, making it easier for individuals and teams to collaborate and exchange ideas across geographical boundaries. Tools like video conferencing, instant messaging, and project management platforms enable seamless collaboration, fostering innovation through collective intelligence. Technological advancements, such as automation, artificial intelligence (AI), and machine learning, streamline processes and free up human resources. By automating repetitive tasks, businesses can focus on higher-value activities and allocate resources toward innovative endeavors. Technology enables the collection, storage, and analysis of vast amounts of data. By leveraging data analytics and business intelligence tools, organizations can gain valuable insights into customer behavior, market trends, and operational inefficiencies. These insights inform the innovation process, helping businesses identify opportunities and develop tailored solutions. In addition to technology, the adoption of new business models can also drive innovation. A business model encompasses the way a company creates, delivers, and captures value. By rethinking and redesigning their business models, organizations can unlock new avenues for innovation. Here are some examples:

- Disruptive business models: Disruptive business models challenge established norms and introduce new ways of delivering value to customers. Companies like Uber and Airbnb disrupted the transportation and accommodation industries respectively, by leveraging technology platforms and peer-to-peer networks.
- Subscription-based models: Subscription-based models offer products or services on a recurring payment basis, providing customers with convenience and businesses with predictable revenue streams. Companies like Netflix and Spotify have revolutionized their respective industries through subscription models.
- Platform ecosystems: Platform-based business models create ecosystems that bring together multiple stakeholders and facilitate interactions and transactions. Examples include app stores like Apple's App Store and digital marketplaces like Amazon, which foster innovation by enabling third-party developers to create and offer new

products and services.

- Sharing economy models: Sharing economy models promote the efficient use of resources by enabling individuals to share or rent out their underutilized assets. Companies like Zipcar and TaskRabbit have embraced this model, encouraging sustainability and innovation through resource optimization.
- Overall, innovation is achieved through the integration of technology and the adoption of new business models. By leveraging technology tools and platforms and reimagining traditional business practices, organizations can unlock new possibilities, create value, and drive meaningful change.
- Direct-to-Consumer (D2C) brands have experienced significant innovation in recent years, leveraging technology and new business models to disrupt traditional retail and deliver products and services directly to consumers.

Analyzing innovative brands in both the Indian and international markets is essential for several reasons. Firstly, it provides valuable insights into emerging trends and consumer preferences, allowing businesses to stay ahead of the curve and adapt their strategies accordingly. Understanding the success stories of innovative brands can offer a blueprint for others, revealing the key factors that contribute to their growth and resilience. Additionally, a comparative analysis between Indian and international brands can uncover unique cultural nuances and market dynamics, helping businesses tailor their approaches to specific regions. Learning from successful brands on a global scale fosters a cross-pollination of ideas, encouraging creativity and strategic thinking. By dissecting innovative brands in diverse markets, businesses can gain a comprehensive understanding of the evolving landscape, enabling them to make informed decisions, foster innovation, and ultimately thrive in an increasingly competitive and dynamic business environment. Here are examples of innovative brands in the domestic and international market we can learn from.

- Ola : revolutionized the transportation industry in India by introducing a convenient, app-based ride-hailing service. They provided a platform that allowed users to book rides with just a few taps on their smartphones, offering various vehicle options, including auto-rickshaws and electric vehicles.
- Patanjali Ayurved : disrupted the FMCG (Fast-Moving Consumer Goods) sector with its focus on natural and Ayurvedic products. They emphasized the use of traditional Indian ingredients and holistic wellness, attracting consumers looking for healthier alternatives.
- Paytm:Innovation : a pioneer in digital payments and mobile wallets in India. They made digital transactions accessible to millions of Indians, facilitating cashless payments for a wide range of services, from mobile recharges to bill payments and online shopping.
- Zomato : redefined how Indians explore and order food. They combined restaurant discovery, reviews, and online food delivery into a single platform. Their innovative approach streamlined the dining and food delivery experience.
- Maggi (Nestlé India): adapted to Indian tastes and preferences by introducing regional flavors and instant noodles that were quick and easy to prepare. This innovation resonated with the Indian market and made Maggi a household name.
- Reliance Jio : disrupted the telecom industry by providing high-speed 4G data services at incredibly low prices. They offered free voice calls and data for a significant period, democratizing access to the internet and digital services in India.
- Infosys : one of India's leading IT services companies, played a pivotal role in bringing software services outsourcing to India. They introduced innovative software development and project management practices, making India a global hub for IT services.
- ISRO (Indian Space Research Organisation) : has consistently innovated in space exploration and technology. They achieved remarkable milestones, such as the Mars Orbiter Mission and launching numerous satellites, while keeping costs relatively low, setting a new standard in the global space industry.
- Mahindra Electric : introduced electric vehicles (EVs) to the Indian market. They've developed EVs for both personal and commercial use, contributing to India's sustainable mobility solutions.

- MakeMyTrip : transformed the travel industry in India by providing an online platform for booking flights, hotels, and holidays. They streamlined the travel planning process and offered a wide range of options to consumers.
- Warby Parker: revolutionized the eyewear industry by offering affordable, stylish prescription glasses online. They introduced the try-at-home concept, allowing customers to order multiple frames to try on before making a purchase. This disrupted the traditional brick-and-mortar eyewear retail model, making it more convenient and cost-effective for consumers.
- Dollar Shave Club: disrupted the shaving industry by providing high-quality razors and grooming products at an affordable price through a subscription-based model. They combined convenience, affordability, and a quirky marketing campaign to challenge established brands and acquire a loyal customer base.
- Casper: disrupted the mattress industry by offering premium-quality mattresses directly to consumers. They introduced the concept of the "bed-in-a-box," providing a convenient and affordable way to purchase mattresses online. Casper's innovative marketing, risk-free trial periods, and hassle-free return policies have reshaped the way people buy mattresses.
- Glossier: a beauty brand that has achieved success by building a strong online community and leveraging user-generated content. They have created a direct line of communication with their customers, actively involving them in product development and marketing decisions. Glossier's inclusive approach and emphasis on minimalistic, natural beauty have resonated with consumers, leading to a loyal and engaged customer base.
- Allbirds: is a sustainable footwear brand that gained popularity by combining comfort, style, and eco-friendly materials. They introduced merino wool sneakers and focused on transparency and sustainability in their production processes. Allbirds' commitment to sustainability and innovation has allowed them to stand out in the competitive footwear market.
- Harry's: is another D2C shaving brand that disrupted the market by offering high-quality razors and grooming products at a lower price point than traditional brands. They also emphasized a simplified and enjoyable shopping experience, providing customers with personalized shaving plans and delivering products directly to their doorsteps.

These examples illustrate how brands have used innovation to challenge established industries and offer unique value propositions to consumers. By leveraging technology, adopting new business models, and prioritizing customer experience, these brands have successfully disrupted traditional retail and built strong customer relationships.

Innovation is related to disruption

Innovation and disruption are closely connected, as innovation often leads to disruptive changes in industries and markets. Here's how they are interconnected. Innovation is the catalyst for disruption. When organizations develop and introduce new ideas, products, technologies, or business models, they can disrupt existing markets and industries. Disruptive innovations often provide significant improvements or completely new alternatives to established products or services, challenging the status quo and creating a significant impact. Disruptive changes occur when innovative ideas or advancements fundamentally alter the way industries operate. These disruptions often create new markets or redefine existing ones, causing traditional players to lose market share or even become obsolete. Innovations that bring about disruptive change can reshape entire industries, business models, and consumer behaviors. Innovation can be a source of competitive advantage for businesses. Organizations that continuously innovate and introduce novel solutions gain a competitive edge over their competitors. By disrupting established markets or creating new ones, they can attract customers, capture market share, and drive growth. Disruption can pose challenges for established players. When disruption occurs in an industry, organizations need to innovate to adapt and stay relevant. They must develop new strategies, business models, and technologies to respond to the changing landscape and compete effectively. Disruption often triggers a cycle of iterative innovation. As disruption occurs, organizations learn from the new market dynamics and consumer needs, prompting further innovation to refine and enhance their offerings. This iterative process helps organizations stay agile, adapt to disruptions, and maintain a competitive position.

Sustaining Innovation	Disruptive Innovation
Problem is well understood	Problem is not well understood
Innovation Improves performance lowers cost increment changes	New Market
Existing Market	Innovation is dramatic and game changing
Customer is believable	Customer doesn't know
Market is predictable	Market is unpredictable
Traditional methods are sufficient	Traditional business methods fail

Enter CapUnderstanding the differenece between sustaining innovation and Disruptive innovation

Innovation and disruption are interconnected in a continuous cycle. Innovation drives disruption by introducing new ideas and technologies, while disruption necessitates further innovation to adapt and thrive in the changing landscape. The organizations that embrace and harness innovation can position themselves to disrupt markets or effectively respond to disruptive changes, thereby shaping the future of industries and driving growth.

Old sources of advantage are not relevant anymore

Old sources of advantage, like manufacturing power, distribution strength, even mastery of information flow, don't matter anymore. There's no longer any barrier to potential entrants or substitutes — in a digital world, competition can come from anywhere. Customers have real-time information about pricing, product features and competitors; they hold all the advantages. And the key source of supply now is talent — and talent can get up and leave. The competitive barriers that Porter defined matter far less now. Digital undermines all of them. The only way to survive one of these disruptions is to invest in customer relationships.

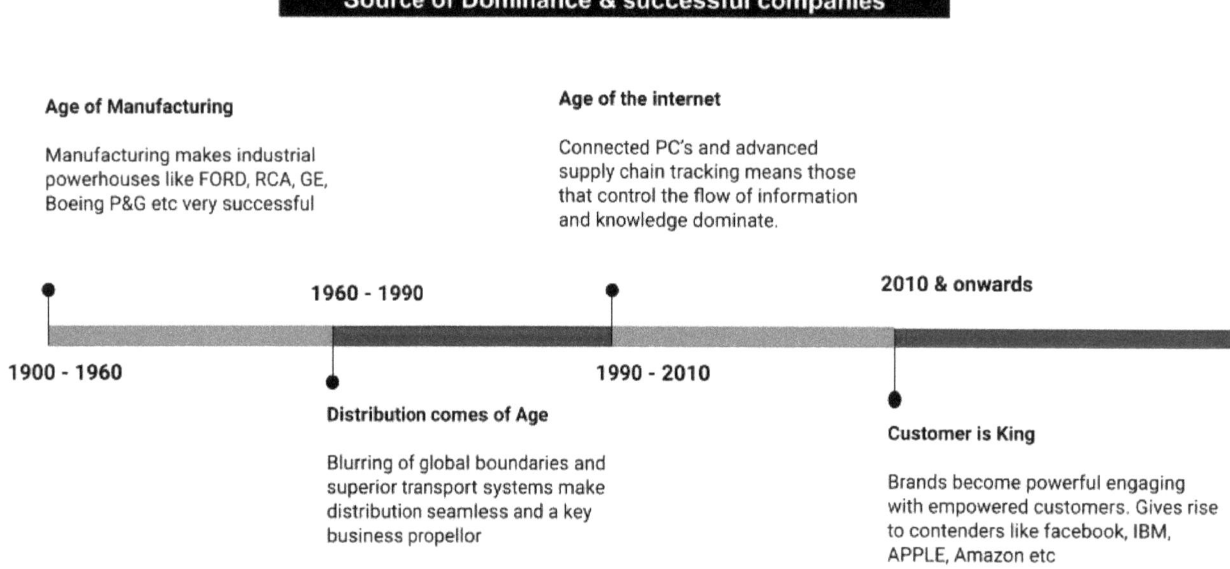

We are surronded as constant disruption either you ride it or face it. Its upto

We live in a universe of constant disruption. There is a paradigm shift in the way companies are thinking and this permeates the entire organization. Companies that successfully embrace this shift thrive in an era of perpetual disruption as they establish strong customer relationships built on trust, ultimately making strategic investments in their customer base.

> "*Disruption is not merely a singular event; rather, its a series of events and processes that play out over a period of time.*"

To survive in a disruptive environment you must understand and study the nuances of your and the incumbent's disruptive strategies. To do so you must identifying strengths, relative advantages, and evaluate future conditions:

1. Assess the strengths of the disruptor's business model: Analyze the key features and strategies that make the disrupter successful. Identify their unique selling points, competitive advantages, and innovative approaches. Understanding their strengths will help you anticipate their actions and devise effective countermeasures.
2. Recognize your own relative advantages: Evaluate your business's unique strengths and capabilities that differentiate you from the disrupter. This could include factors such as a loyal customer base, established brand reputation, proprietary technology, specialized expertise, or strong relationships with suppliers. By leveraging these advantages, you can fortify your position and adapt to the changing landscape.
3. Evaluate future conditions for co-option: Anticipate the disrupter's potential attempts to co-opt your current advantages in the future. Consider factors such as market trends, technological advancements, regulatory changes, and shifting consumer preferences. Assess how these factors may impact the disrupter's ability to leverage your strengths and what steps you can take to maintain a competitive edge.
4. Strengthen your core competencies: Focus on enhancing and expanding your core competencies. Identify areas where you excel and invest in continuous improvement. This could involve training employees, adopting new

technologies, fostering innovation, or developing strategic partnerships. By building upon your strengths, you can establish a robust foundation that is harder for disrupters to undermine.

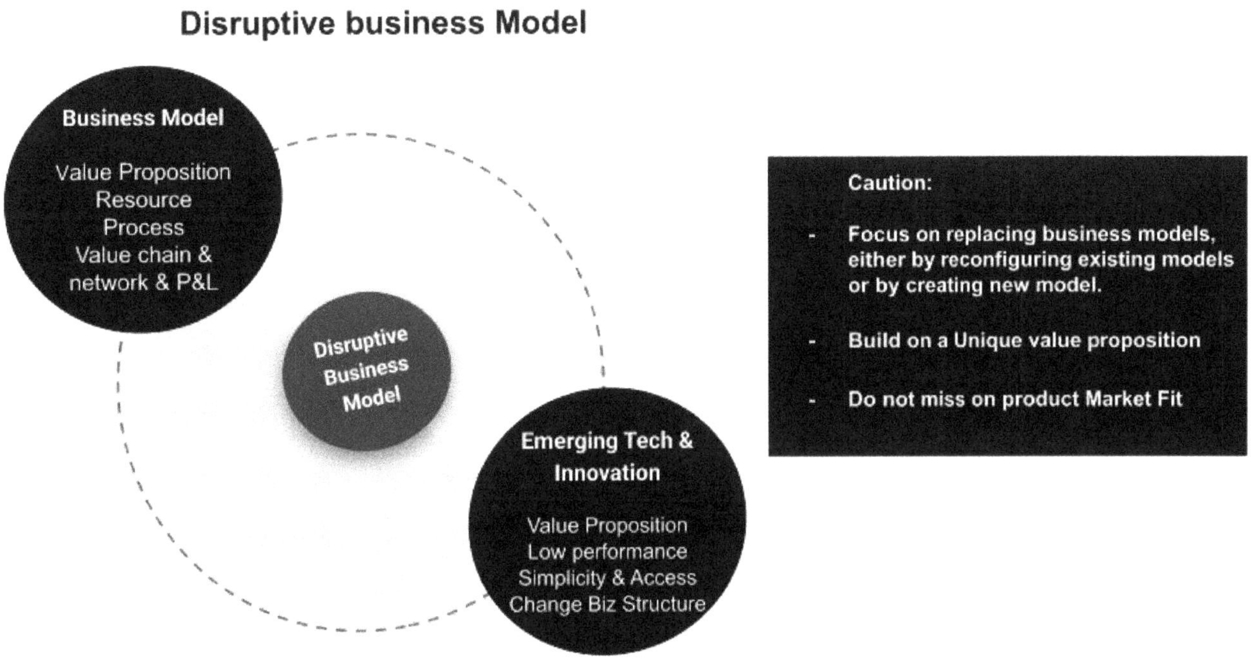

Disruptive business Model

Business Model
Value Proposition
Resource
Process
Value chain &
network & P&L

Disruptive
Business
Model

Emerging Tech & Innovation
Value Proposition
Low performance
Simplicity & Access
Change Biz Structure

Caution:

- **Focus on replacing business models, either by reconfiguring existing models or by creating new model.**
- **Build on a Unique value proposition**
- **Do not miss on product Market Fit**

A disruptive business model has to have a tech play and offer something valuable your. Something your competitors arent doing and cant replicate.

In order for a brand to succeed as a disruptor Maxwell Wessel & Clayton M. Christensen introduced a concept of an extendable core. The concept of an extendable core refers to the foundational capabilities and assets of an organization that can be flexibly adapted and expanded upon to pursue new opportunities and adapt to changing market conditions. It involves identifying and nurturing a core set of capabilities and resources that can serve as a solid foundation for growth and adaptation. The extendable core recognizes that businesses need to evolve and innovate to stay competitive in dynamic markets. Instead of relying solely on rigid and fixed strategies, organizations with an extendable core approach emphasize flexibility and agility. They develop a core set of capabilities, such as expertise, technologies, processes, or intellectual property, which can be extended, modified, or combined to create new products, services, or market positions. By building an extendable core, companies can leverage their existing strengths and competencies while exploring new avenues for growth. This approach enables them to adapt to changes in customer preferences, technological advancements, or market disruptions without starting from scratch. The extendable core is characterized by the ability to absorb new knowledge, pivot when necessary, and integrate different elements to create innovative solutions.

In practice, developing an extendable core involves continuously assessing the market landscape, identifying emerging trends, and aligning internal capabilities with external opportunities. It requires fostering a culture of learning, experimentation, and collaboration within the organization to facilitate the exploration and exploitation of new possibilities. By cultivating an extendable core, companies can remain agile and resilient in the face of uncertainty. They are better equipped to respond to disruptive forces, enter new markets, and seize emerging opportunities, while leveraging their existing strengths to maintain a competitive edge. The extendable core allows the disrupter to maintain its performance advantage as it creeps upmarket in search of more customers and profit. In the next step we need to access It's important to have a deep understanding of the jobs that people want your company to fulfill, as well as recognizing the jobs that a disrupter could potentially do better with its extendable core, is crucial in gaining clarity about your relative advantage. By comprehending these aspects, you can assess which areas of your business are most susceptible to disruption and, equally important, identify the parts that you can defend. When we talk about "jobs," we refer to the needs, desires, and problems that customers are seeking to address. Customers "hire" products or services to help them accomplish these jobs. To maintain a competitive edge, it is essential to understand the specific jobs that your customers are hiring your company to do. This understanding allows you to tailor your offerings to precisely meet those needs, ensuring customer satisfaction and loyalty. However, disruption can occur when a new player enters the market with a novel approach. This disrupter may possess an extendable core, which refers to its ability to leverage its unique strengths and competencies in innovative ways. Recognizing the potential of a disrupter to address certain jobs better than your company can be an eye-opening realization.

To gain a clearer picture of your relative advantage, you should assess the barriers that a disrupter would need to overcome in order to undermine your position in the future. These barriers could include factors such as brand reputation, customer loyalty, proprietary technology or processes, regulatory compliance, established distribution networks, economies of scale, or strong relationships with suppliers. By evaluating these barriers, you can identify the areas where your current business is most vulnerable to disruption. This analysis allows you to proactively address potential weaknesses and take measures to strengthen your position. For example, you might invest in research and development to improve your products or services, enhance customer experiences, or explore partnerships that leverage your existing strengths. Simultaneously, this approach helps you identify which parts of your business you can defend effectively. It allows you to allocate resources strategically, focusing on areas where you have a relative advantage and are less likely to be outperformed by potential disrupters. By protecting and enhancing these aspects, you can solidify your market position and maintain a competitive edge. Gaining a deep understanding of the jobs people want your company to do for them, while acknowledging the potential of a disrupter's extendable core, provides valuable insights into your relative advantage. By assessing the barriers a disrupter would need to overcome, you can identify vulnerable areas of your business and take proactive steps to defend them. This approach allows you to fortify your position in the face of disruption and remain competitive in the market.

Disruptive innovations stem from technological or business model advantages that have the potential to scale as disruptive businesses move upmarket in search of more-demanding customers. These advantages are what enable the extendable core and differentiate disruption from mere price competition. To understand this concept better, let's break it down:

- Technological or Business Model Advantages: Disruptive innovations are driven by advancements in technology or the introduction of a new business model that offers significant improvements over existing solutions. These advantages could include breakthrough technologies, cost-effective production methods, innovative distribution channels, or new ways of meeting customer needs. These advantages provide the foundation for disruptive businesses to enter the market and challenge established players.
- Scaling as Disruptive Businesses Move Upmarket: Disruptive businesses typically enter the market by targeting niche or underserved customer segments. They initially focus on providing a solution that may be simpler, more affordable, or more convenient than what existing players offer. However, disruptive businesses don't stop there. They leverage their initial success to gradually move upmarket and capture more demanding customers.
- Extending the Core: As disruptive businesses move upmarket, they continue to enhance their products or services based on customer feedback and evolving market needs. This process of extending the core involves adding features, improving performance, and addressing additional customer requirements. By doing so, disruptive businesses make their offerings more attractive to mainstream customers who may have initially dismissed them.

Disruptive innovations go beyond simply competing on price. While cost efficiency is often a characteristic of disruptive businesses, it is not the sole factor that differentiates them. Instead, disruptive businesses use their technological or business model advantages to offer a unique value proposition that resonates with customers.

This could be superior performance, enhanced user experience, novel functionalities, or a combination of factors that make their offerings stand out. Disruptive innovations arise from technological or business model advantages that enable scalable growth as disruptive businesses target more-demanding customers. These advantages allow businesses to continuously extend their core offerings, adding value and differentiation beyond price competition. By understanding and leveraging these factors, disruptive businesses can challenge and ultimately disrupt established players in the market.

To verify if you are truly a disruptor and can topple the incumbent you can map yourself on 2x2.

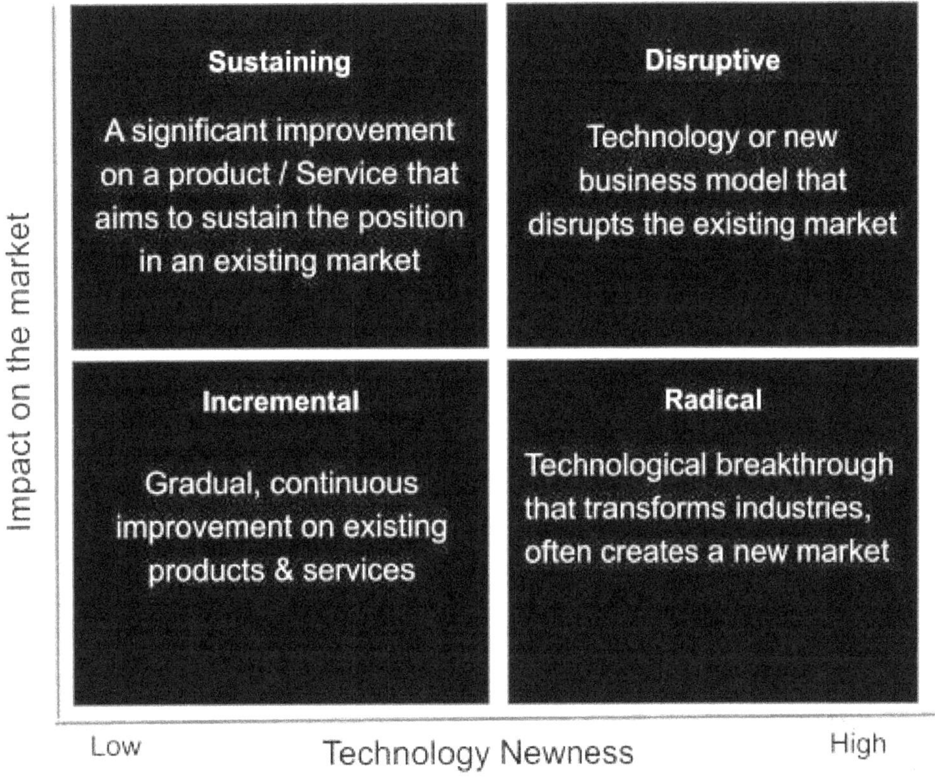

Exercise - Map your brands level of disruption in a 2x2

- Foster a culture of agility and adaptability: Develop an organizational mindset that embraces change and thrives in a disruptive environment. Encourage employees to stay informed about industry trends, promote cross-functional collaboration, and prioritize innovation. By fostering agility and adaptability, you can respond swiftly to market shifts and proactively address challenges posed by disrupters.
- Build strong customer relationships: Focus on delivering exceptional customer experiences and nurturing long-lasting relationships. Understand your customers' needs and preferences, and tailor your offerings accordingly. By providing superior value and maintaining strong customer loyalty, you can create a barrier against disrupters attempting to lure away your clientele.
- Continuously scan the competitive landscape: Regularly monitor the market and keep a close eye on the activities and strategies of disrupters. Stay informed about emerging technologies, startups, and potential industry disrupters. By staying ahead of the curve and being proactive in your approach, you can better anticipate and counteract disruptive forces.
- Foster a culture of innovation: Encourage a culture of innovation within your organization. Encourage employees to generate new ideas, experiment with different approaches, and embrace calculated risks. Establish mechanisms

for capturing and evaluating innovative concepts, and provide the necessary resources and support to bring promising ideas to fruition. By fostering a culture of innovation, you can drive continuous improvement and stay ahead of disruptive threats.

- Form strategic partnerships: Collaborate with other companies, startups, or industry players that complement your strengths and can help you navigate disruption. Seek partnerships that leverage combined capabilities and create mutual value. Strategic alliances can provide access to new markets, technologies, resources, and expertise, strengthening your competitive position in the face of disruption.
- Stay customer-centric: Ultimately, prioritize your customers' needs and preferences above all else. Regularly engage with them to gather feedback, understand their evolving expectations, and identify potential areas for improvement. By maintaining a customer-centric approach, you can adapt quickly to changing demands and ensure long-term relevance in the face of disruption.

CHAPTER TEN

Distribution & Revenue Generation Models

Distribution and revenue generation models can vary significantly across different business types and models. Here's an overview of these models in the context of B2B (Business-to-Business), B2C (Business-to-Consumer), C2B (Consumer-to-Business), C2C (Consumer-to-Consumer), drop shipping, and marketplaces:

1. B2B (Business-to-Business) B2B businesses sell products or services to other businesses. Distribution often involves direct sales, negotiated contracts, and long-term relationships. B2B revenue is primarily generated through bulk sales, subscriptions, licensing, and service contracts.
2. B2C (Business-to-Consumer) B2C businesses sell products or services directly to individual consumers. Distribution can involve physical stores, e-commerce websites, or third-party retailers. B2C revenue comes from individual product sales, subscriptions, one-time purchases, and advertising.
3. C2B (Consumer-to-Business) C2B is less common, where individual consumers offer products or services to businesses. This may include freelancers, influencers, or crowdsourced contributions. C2B revenue can be generated through direct payments, sponsored content, affiliate marketing, or consulting services.
4. C2C (Consumer-to-Consumer)C2C involves consumers selling products or services to other consumers, often through online marketplaces or classified ads. C2C revenue typically comes from transaction fees, listing fees, or subscription models for premium features.
5. Drop Shipping: Drop shipping is a retail fulfillment method where the seller doesn't keep products in stock but instead transfers customer orders to a manufacturer or wholesaler who ships the products directly to the customer. Drop shippers earn revenue by marking up the products' prices, and their profit is the difference between the wholesale and retail prices.
6. Marketplaces: Marketplaces connect buyers and sellers, allowing a wide range of products and services to be offered by various vendors. Marketplaces generate revenue through a combination of methods, including listing fees, transaction fees, subscription fees for sellers, and often advertising or sponsored listings.

The choice of distribution and revenue generation models depends on the type of business, target audience, and industry. Some businesses may even use a combination of these models to diversify their revenue streams and expand their market reach. Successful businesses tailor their approach to meet the specific needs and preferences of their customers and partners.

CHAPTER ELEVEN

Evolving Strategy & Tactics

In the ever-evolving realm of D2C (Direct-to-Consumer) commerce, the purchase journey has transformed into a non-linear adventure. It can kick off with an Instagram ad, a TikTok influencer's recommendation, or even a compelling tweet. Traditional business models that once stood the test of time now face the challenge of scaling in today's complex and constantly shifting e-commerce landscape.

Today's economic climate grants consumers an unprecedented abundance of choices, and they're ready to exercise their newfound freedom. In 2023, more than 70% of consumers made purchases from competitors rather than their preferred brands. As economic pressures continue, consumers are becoming more discerning and vigilant, always on the lookout for better deals. However, their criteria extend beyond price considerations. A significant portion of global consumers—50%, to be exact—express concerns about environmental, social, and governance (ESG) issues. While many aspects of the supply chain, such as freight, distribution, and fulfillment, may be beyond the control of businesses, consumers increasingly prefer to support ethical companies with sustainable practices. Therefore, it comes as no surprise that approximately 46% of consumers switch brands due to product shortages—opting for competitors who can meet their product needs.

In a world where over 60% of the global population is already using social media, consumers can swiftly discover new brands and products. They not only seek convenience but also immediate gratification, and the ability to access everything with just a click of a button has become the norm. Yet, the charm of in-store shopping persists, as many customers cherish the personalized touch it offers. For businesses operating on a global scale, elevating the customer experience ranks as a top priority, alongside increasing revenue. Today's customers demand a shopping experience that is personal, instantaneous, and responsive, regardless of where they are in the world.

Expect the Unexpected,The one thing remains constant: change. Over the past couple of years, countless businesses have showcased remarkable resilience in the face of unforeseen challenges, contributing to over $27 trillion USD in retail sales worldwide. However, it's essential to acknowledge that 64% of global businesses are still on the path to recovery from the adverse effects of the pandemic. Economic hurdles stemming from the pandemic were further compounded in 2022 when the Russia-Ukraine conflict led to sanctions that disrupted or even halted trade activities. This fiscal instability has triggered the highest inflation rate seen in the last four decades. During the early months of the pandemic, online shopping experienced a staggering 77% year-over-year surge, effectively accelerating the innovation and adoption of digital commerce by roughly five years. The landscape of D2C commerce is ever-changing, and businesses that can adapt and embrace this change are poised to thrive in this dynamic environment.

CHAPTER TWELVE

MOBILE FIRST D2C STRATEGY

The mobile-first direct-to-consumer (D2C) business model is revolutionizing the retail industry. By cutting out middlemen and selling directly to customers through mobile apps and websites, D2C brands have more control over the customer experience, pricing, and branding. A mobile-first approach means optimizing your marketing, customer acquisition, and product design for smartphones. Here are the key elements of a successful mobile-first D2C strategy:

Design a stellar mobile app. Your app should offer an easy and seamless purchasing experience with features like one-click checkout and order tracking. Ensure a flawless user interface that works well on multiple device types.

- Optimize your website for mobile. Even if you have an app, the majority of traffic to your website will come from smartphones. Ensure images are compressed, pages load quickly, and forms are simple to fill out on mobile screens.
- Use push notifications and SMS. These channels allow you to reach customers in the moments they are most receptive. Use them to deliver timely promotions, order updates, and product recommendations.
- Invest in influencer marketing. Partner with social media influencers in your niche who have large mobile-based followings. They can promote your brand and products to their engaged audiences.
- Collect customer data. With customer permission, gather data on shopping behaviors, preferences and product reviews to gain valuable insights that help you improve and personalize the mobile customer experience.

A mobile-first D2C strategy requires rethinking every aspect of your business to make smartphones and apps the central focus. But if executed properly, it can help you build a loyal customer base, gain valuable insights and establish a stronger brand identity.

The Consumer Buying Process

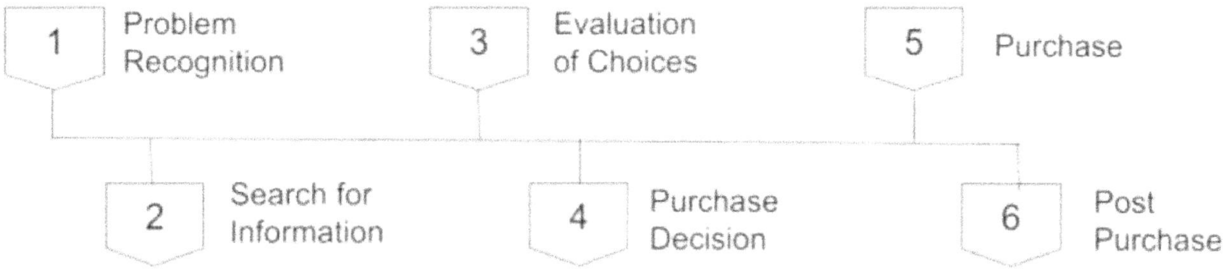

Stages of the digital consumer

An Emotional View of Consumers Consumers make purchasing decisions based on emotions just as much as rational thought. Joy, fear, hope and love motivate consumers to buy certain products and services. Sexuality and sensuality play a role for some purchases while escapism and a search for magic also drive demand. When marketers appeal to emotions, they can form strong connections with consumers. An advertisement showing a mother and daughter bonding over their skincare products may trigger feelings of nostalgia, family and happiness. This emotional appeal can create a lasting impression that influences future purchasing decisions. However, relying too heavily on emotions can backfire if the brand promise is not delivered. Consumers who feel deceived or manipulated may abandon the brand entirely. Therefore, marketers must balance emotional appeals with quality products and transparent messaging.

From a passive view, consumers driven by emotions can seem irrational and impulsive, buying whatever is promoted most heavily. But emotions are an innate part of the human experience that shape values and desires. When harnessed respectfully, emotions can help brands form meaningful relationships with their audiences.

An economic view sees consumers as rational beings who identify the product that maximizes value or utility. While this perspective holds true for some purchases, it does not account for the role of emotions, esthetics and symbolism that drive demand for many goods.

Consumers behave as both emotional and rational information processors, receptive to promotions at times yet also taking an active role in researching products that fit their needs and self-image. A balanced and multifaceted understanding of the consumer mind is crucial for marketing strategies that can resonate and succeed.

CHAPTER THIRTEEN

COMPETING IN THE DIGITAL AGE

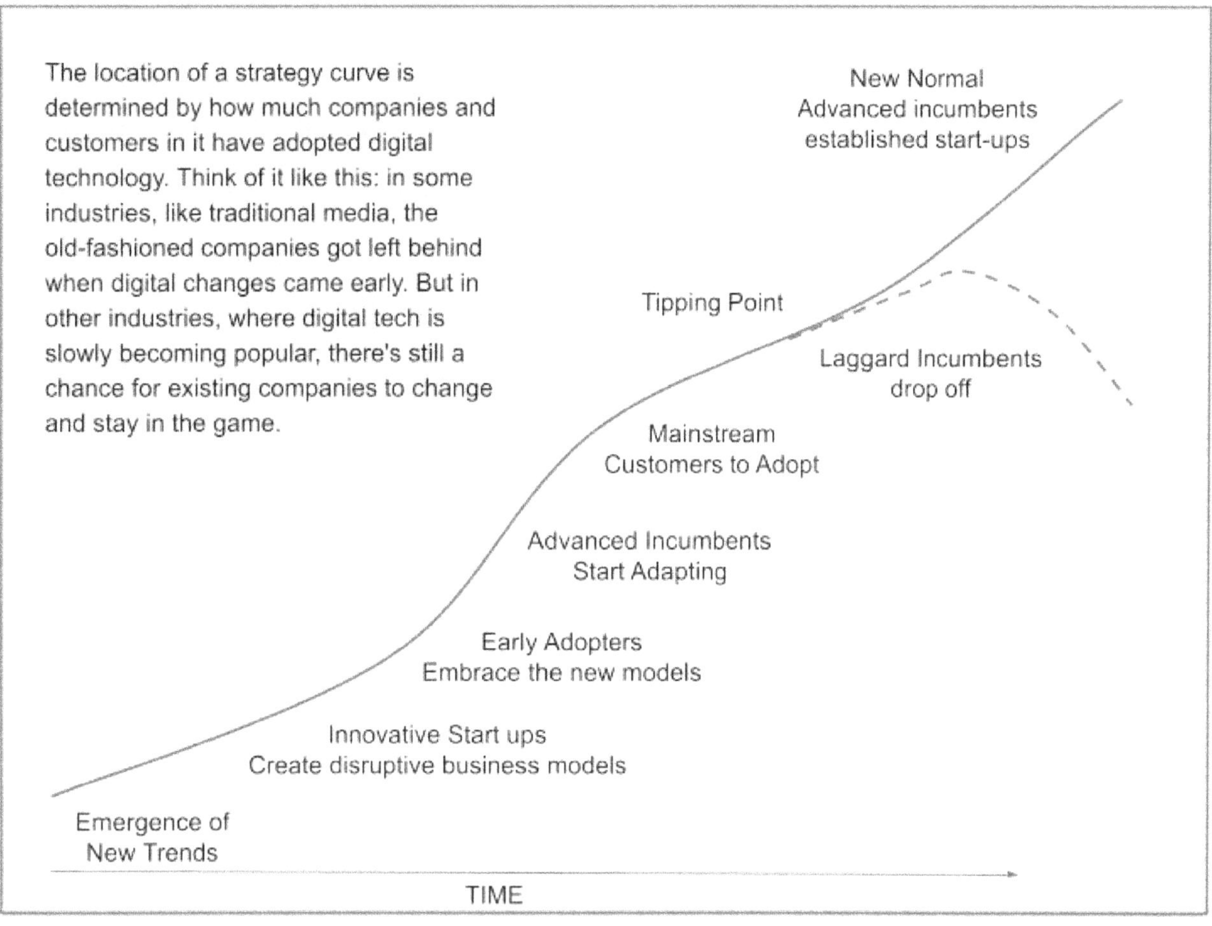

Digitial adoption is key the key to suceess in the digital 1st era

For direct-to-consumer brands to succeed, differentiation and experience are key. Competing against established brands with larger marketing budgets and retail shelf space is difficult. However, D2C brands have some distinct advantages that allow them to stand out from the crowd if leveraged properly. The first strategy D2C brands must follow is to focus on a niche. By targeting a specific customer segment that larger brands may overlook, D2C brands can carve out a unique positioning in the market. They can speak more authentically to that niche audience and provide precisely what those customers desire. For example, an athleisure brand may choose to focus exclusively on workout apparel for women over 40 rather than the mass market.

Secondly, D2C brands must provide an elevated customer experience. Since they sell directly to consumers, these brands own the entire relationship with their customers. They can capture valuable data, gain insights, and use those to constantly improve and personalize the experience. This can include a streamlined website, on-trend product designs, fast shipping, easy returns, and helpful customer service. The experience itself becomes a form of differentiation.

Third, D2C brands should leverage social media to build a sense of community and foster word-of-mouth marketing. Customers want to feel part of something bigger and align with brands that share their values. By engaging authentically with customers on social platforms, D2C brands can build this community and cultivate brand advocates who help spread the word.

By zeroing in on a niche audience, providing an exceptional direct-to-consumer experience, and leveraging social media, D2C brands can differentiate themselves from larger competitors and forge their own path to success. Focusing on these strategies will allow them to stand out from the competition and grow a loyal customer base.

Competitor analysis is the process of evaluating your direct competitors, products and marketing strategies. This is an evaluation that can define the difference between a survival business and a growth business. A quick way of doing this is to map out your positioning map comparing brands through quality and price. This will tell you exactly where you stand in the market and your distance from the incumbent.

Competitor Map Analysis

High Price
Brand D
Brand E
Brand A
Brand F
Low Quality
High Quality
Brand B
Brand C
Low Price

Exercise - Plot your brand honestly on the competitor map

New Pressures on Price & Margin

In the digital age, brands face a new competitive landscape characterized by remarkable transparency. Digital technologies empower consumers to effortlessly compare prices, service quality, and product performance with just a few clicks or swipes. This ease of comparison has the potential to commoditize products and services, as consumers increasingly seek comparable features and streamlined interactions. For example, banks have simplified their products for mobile phone purchasing, inadvertently converging their offerings with competitors pursuing a similar mobile-friendly approach.

Furthermore, third-party intermediaries have entered the scene, disrupting traditional relationships between companies and their customers. The proliferation of price-comparison websites, aggregating data across multiple vendors, has made it incredibly simple for consumers to compare prices and service offerings. In India, this trend is evident as even chain retailers, traditionally dominant in fast-moving consumer goods, have witnessed declining revenues due to consumers flocking to discounters after conducting price comparisons, even for staples like milk and bread.

These dynamics exert a downward pressure on returns across consumer-facing industries, and the disruptive forces are now extending their reach to B2B businesses. The digital age's impact on how brands compete is reshaping the competitive landscape, emphasizing the importance of providing value and quality while adapting to the evolving demands of an informed and empowered consumer base.

In the digital environment, brands find themselves competing in a transformed landscape where barriers to entry and traditional sources of product differentiation are being eroded. Unexpected competitors are emerging from the most unlikely places. For instance, web-based service providers in sectors like telecommunications and insurance can now access markets without the need for extensive distribution networks of physical offices and local agents. They're able to effectively compete by harnessing the power of data, analyzing risks, and understanding customer incomes and preferences.

Simultaneously, the digital realm has introduced new challenges and opportunities. Establishing a brand presence online can be costly, and consumer attention tends to gravitate towards a select few dominant brands. This shift is reshaping the competitive landscape across various industries. Companies like Singapore Post are investing in e-commerce businesses, leveraging their logistics and warehousing expertise. Japanese e-commerce giant Rakuten is using its expansive network to offer financial services, expanding their reach into diverse sectors. Tech titans such as Google and Twitter are eagerly pushing boundaries through innovative products like Google Wallet and Twitter's foray into the retail space.

Notably, the rise of digital competition often brings smaller, nimbler companies into the mix. While these challengers may not achieve the scale of industry incumbents, they can still disrupt established players significantly. In the retail industry, for example, entrepreneurial ventures are targeting specific product subcategories and aggressively undercutting prices, even on smaller volumes. This pressure forces larger companies to adapt and respond, highlighting the evolving nature of competition in the digital age.

Plug and play business models brands engage in fierce competition as they navigate a landscape that is continually evolving. The transformative power of this digital environment is redefining traditional business models. As transaction costs decrease due to digital forces, the conventional value chains are breaking down. Think of these third-party products and services as digital Lego blocks, ready to be seamlessly integrated into the gaps that emerge.

Take Amazon, for example; it has become a prime example of a company that offers a multitude of services. From logistics to online retail "storefronts" and IT services, it has crafted a dynamic ecosystem. Many businesses find it more efficient to incorporate these readily available offerings into their value chains rather than building them from the ground up to compete. This plug-and-play approach saves both time and resources.

In the travel industry, we witness a similar phenomenon. New portals are emerging, bringing together entire travel experiences, including flights, hotels, and car rentals. They achieve this by connecting stand-alone offerings from third parties, sometimes sourced from small companies or even individuals. These components are assembled on-the-fly with dynamic pricing based on real-time supply and demand. As more niche providers gain access to these new platforms, competition within the industry is reaching unprecedented levels, providing consumers with a broader range of options and services. The digital landscape is revolutionizing business operations, encouraging innovation, and intensifying competition across various sectors.

Today brands are competing on a global stage without the confines of borders. The relentless advance of digital technologies has ushered in an era where customers demand a seamless and unified experience. This places mounting pressure on global companies to standardize their offerings. In the realm of B2C, for instance, a significant number of US consumers have grown accustomed to e-shopping in the United Kingdom for the latest fashion trends. As a result, they now expect payment systems that effortlessly transcend borders, global distribution networks that ensure timely deliveries, and a consistent customer experience, regardless of their location.

In B2B markets spanning industries from banking to telecommunications, corporate buyers are exerting their influence on suppliers. They insist on services that are not only standardized across international borders but also capable of seamless integration with other offerings. These services should easily plug into the global business processes of the purchasing companies. An illustrative example is a global bank that has aligned its offerings with the borderless strategies of its major clients. It achieved this by creating a single website accessible across 20 countries, effectively replacing what was once an assortment of separate national or product touch points.

its important tpo bare in mind competing in the digital environment is an ongoing journey, marked by constant adaptation and innovation. Take the music industry, for example, where the traditional model of selling tapes and CDs evolved into the era of MP3s, only to be disrupted by the emergence of subscription models like Spotify. This transformation not only changed how music is consumed but also redefined revenue streams for artists and the industry as a whole.

In the transportation industry, digitization has ushered in a revolution. Mobile apps, in-car sensors, and cloud-stored data have given rise to nonownership models, exemplified by services like Zipcar. Instead of owning a vehicle, consumers pay to use them by the hour or day, offering greater flexibility and cost-effectiveness. Google's ongoing experiments with autonomous vehicles introduce even more radical possibilities, potentially reshaping the value proposition of the entire automotive sector. Auto manufacturers must adapt to meet the growing demand for automated, safer features as the digital transformation continues.

This digital shift has far-reaching implications, extending its transformative effects to related industries such as trucking and insurance. Automation is poised to lower transportation costs through innovations like driverless convoys, and the rise of "crash-less" cars will rewrite the risk profiles of drivers, impacting the insurance landscape. In the digital era, businesses need to anticipate and adapt to these seismic changes to remain competitive and relevant in an ever-evolving landscape.

CHAPTER FOURTEEN

DECISION MAKING AND ASSOCIATED TRADE OFFS

Lead customers or follow them ? In the dynamic digital environment, brands face an ever-evolving landscape where competition is fierce and the transformative effects on businesses are profound. To thrive in this digital era, brands must make crucial decisions regarding whether to lead their customers or follow them. Leading in the digital realm involves proactively shaping customer experiences and market trends. Brands that opt for leadership harness the power of innovation and technology to set new industry standards. They leverage data analytics to understand customer behavior and preferences, then create unique and compelling digital experiences. This proactive stance empowers them to anticipate and meet emerging needs and desires. One example of an Indian brand leading in the digital space is **BharatPe**. They transformed the payments and financial services sector by introducing a single QR code for all payment apps, simplifying transactions for businesses and customers.

On the other hand, following the customer involves a more reactive approach. Brands that follow observe and adapt to the changing preferences and behaviors of their audience. They are quick to embrace emerging digital trends and technologies based on customer feedback and market shifts. While this approach may seem less pioneering, it allows brands to stay relevant and responsive. A prime example of an Indian brand following its customers is Zoho Corporation, which consistently evolves its suite of business software products based on customer input and changing business needs. However, there is a third path, a balance between leading and following, where brands actively engage with their customers to co-create value. This approach involves a deep understanding of the customer journey, collaborative innovation, and the integration of customer feedback into product and service development. An Indian brand exemplifying this approach is **Myntra**. They collaborate with customers through personalized shopping experiences, virtual try-ons, and customer feedback to continually refine their e-commerce platform.

In the digital age, successful brands strategically decide whether to lead, follow, or collaborate with their customers to navigate the ever-changing landscape. Regardless of the path they choose, brands that leverage the transformative potential of the digital environment are better positioned to thrive and create lasting impacts on their businesses and industries.

Collaborate or compete with attackers: brands face a critical choice - whether to collaborate or compete with emerging digital disruptors. This decision-making process has a transformative effect on businesses, reshaping their strategies, operations, and market positioning.

Collaborate or Compete with Attackers: Brands have to decide whether to collaborate with new entrants or fiercely compete against them. Collaboration often involves forming strategic partnerships with tech startups or innovative companies to leverage their expertise and reach. This can result in mutual growth and innovation. On the other hand, some brands choose to compete head-on, either by developing in-house digital solutions or by acquiring disruptive startups. The decision hinges on the brand's goals, market position, and its ability to adapt to digital trends.

The Transformative Effect on Businesses: The decision to collaborate or compete with digital disruptors can have a profound impact on businesses. Collaboration can lead to accelerated innovation, expanded market access, and improved customer experiences. It can position established brands as forward-thinking and customer-centric. On the flip side, competition can drive internal innovation and help brands defend their market share. However, it may require significant investments in technology and talent. Regardless of the path chosen, businesses must be agile, responsive, and open to continuous transformation in the digital age.

1. Tata Consultancy Services (TCS): TCS has opted to collaborate with digital disruptors by establishing innovation labs and partnerships with startups. They focus on co-innovation and have embraced digital transformation in their services. TCS has remained a global IT services leader by staying ahead of digital trends, delivering cutting-edge solutions, and enhancing its competitive edge.
2. Flipkart: Initially a disruptor, Flipkart has both collaborated and competed. They've partnered with global e-commerce giant Walmart while competing with Amazon in the Indian market. Flipkart's collaboration with Walmart provided substantial financial backing, while fierce competition with Amazon has led to innovative customer-centric features and enhanced logistics capabilities.
3. Myntra: an e-commerce fashion platform, has chosen to collaborate by acquiring innovative fashion startups and partnering with top brands to strengthen their offerings. This collaborative approach has helped Myntra diversify its product range and deliver a personalized and tech-driven shopping experience to customers.

Indian brands are navigating a complex decision-making process to stay relevant and competitive. Their choices, whether to collaborate or compete, are shaping their transformative journeys in the ever-evolving digital ecosystem.

A question in the minds of all stake holders in a VUCA world is to scale or descale digital initiatives?brands compete in a dynamic landscape characterized by rapid technological advancements and changing consumer behaviors. This transformation has profound effects on businesses, shaping the decision-making process regarding whether to scale or descale digital initiatives. Presents brands with the opportunity to reach a global audience, engage customers through personalized experiences, and gather valuable data for strategic insights. To thrive, businesses must continually adapt their digital strategies to remain competitive. The decision-making process between scaling or descaling digital initiatives hinges on several factors. Its importat for Brands to gauge the market demand for their products or services in the digital sphere. If demand is high and growth potential significant, scaling digital initiatives is often the prudent choice. Conversely, if market conditions are unfavorable, descaling may be necessary to cut costs and refocus efforts.

Assessing available resources, including budget, technology, and talent, is vital. Brands should determine whether they have the capacity to scale without overextending or, conversely, whether they need to reallocate resources by descaling to optimize efficiency. Also Analyzing the competitive landscape helps brands understand how well their digital initiatives stack up against rivals. Scaling may be crucial to outpace competitors, while descaling can provide agility in adjusting to changing market dynamics. Brands should continually gather and analyze customer feedback to gauge the effectiveness of their digital initiatives. If customers express dissatisfaction or changing preferences, adjustments may be necessary, which could involve scaling certain aspects and descaling others. to succeed its imperative to keep pace with evolving digital technologies is essential. Brands must decide whether to scale their tech investments to remain innovative or descale older technologies that are no longer effective.

- Digital Transformation 1 : Flipkart is a leading e-commerce platform that scaled its digital initiatives to offer a wide range of products, introduce features like product recommendations, and improve user experiences. Their strategic acquisition by Walmart further exemplified the potential for digital scaling.
- Digital Transformation 2 : Zoho Corporation, a software-as-a-service company, has scaled its digital initiatives by offering a comprehensive suite of cloud-based applications for businesses. They've continually expanded their portfolio, catering to a global customer base.
- Digital Transformation 3 : MakeMyTrip, a travel booking platform, has significantly scaled its digital initiatives to provide a one-stop solution for travelers. They've introduced innovative features, including hotel and flight bookings, and mobile app-based services, catering to the evolving preferences of consumers.

These Indian brands exemplify the transformative power of digital initiatives and how strategic decisions regarding scaling or descaling can drive their competitiveness and relevance in the digital age. The ability to adapt and make informed decisions in this ever-evolving landscape is paramount for sustained success. Competing in the digital environment has transformative effects on businesses, shaping how they approach decision-making processes regarding the ownership of their digital agenda. This digital transformation necessitates senior management's time and attention as customer behavior and competitive landscapes evolve rapidly.

"The decision-making process often involves assessing whether to delegate or own the digital agenda."

One illustrative example is a global company that sought to digitize its processes to compete with a new entrant. In this case, the R&D function responsible for product design lacked the knowledge needed to create digital-ready offerings. Simultaneously, a business unit under pricing pressure relied heavily on functional specialists to redesign the back office. Ultimately, the CEO intervened, reorganizing the digitization effort around the client's decision journeys.

Amid the complexity of digitization, some companies introduce a new role: the Chief Digital Officer (CDO) or its equivalent. The CDO brings a digital mindset and focuses on orchestrating the digital agenda, offering a dedicated cross-functional approach. However, relying solely on CDOs to drive the digital agenda can carry risks. Some CDOs may lack the strategic breadth and depth of a CEO, potentially narrowing their focus to areas like marketing or social media. Others, serving as divisional heads, may struggle to garner support from functional units, impeding execution. Alternatively, CEOs can opt to personally "own" and direct the digital agenda from the top down. This approach is especially necessary when digitization is a top strategic priority, requires significant organizational resources, or involves navigating political challenges within business units or functions. Advancing the digital agenda is a critical endeavor for brands in the modern business landscape. The transformative effects of this agenda are profound, impacting how businesses operate and interact with their customers. The decision-making process regarding whether to delegate or own the digital agenda can significantly influence a brand's success in this digital era.

- Apple: Ownership Approach: Apple's co-founder, Steve Jobs, was renowned for his hands-on approach to the digital agenda. He was deeply involved in product design, user experience, and innovation. His leadership and vision shaped Apple's digital products, including the iPhone and iPad, and established the company as a global tech giant.
- Amazon: Ownership Approach: Amazon's CEO, Jeff Bezos, played a pivotal role in owning the digital agenda. His vision and focus on digital innovations, such as Amazon Web Services (AWS) and the Kindle, transformed Amazon from an online bookstore into a global e-commerce and cloud computing powerhouse.
- Tesla: Ownership Approach: Elon Musk, the CEO of Tesla, is known for personally driving the digital agenda of the company. He's been deeply involved in the development of electric vehicles and autonomous driving technology. Tesla's success in the electric car industry is a result of Musk's direct ownership of the digital innovation process.

Delegating the Digital Agenda:

- Procter & Gamble (P&G): Delegation Approach : P&G has delegated its digital agenda by appointing Chief Digital Officers to lead digital transformation. This approach allows for specialized focus and expertise in the digital realm while keeping the core business functions separate.
- General Electric (GE): Delegation Approach : GE has historically appointed Chief Digital Officers to oversee its digital initiatives, such as the Industrial Internet and IoT solutions. This delegation strategy allows GE to harness digital capabilities while maintaining focus on its industrial core.

- Coca-Cola:Delegation Approach : Coca-Cola has chosen to delegate its digital agenda by appointing a Chief Digital Marketing Officer to lead its digital marketing and e-commerce efforts. This allows for focused expertise in engaging consumers through digital channels.

Both owning and delegating the digital mandate have their merits and challenges. Owning it provides a clear top-down vision but requires the CEO's full commitment. Delegating it allows for specialization but may risk fragmented efforts. The choice ultimately depends on the organization's size, the importance of digitization to its strategy, and the leadership's willingness and ability to drive the digital agenda effectively.

CHAPTER FIFTEEN

UNDERSTAND YOUR CUSTOMER

Knowing your ecommerce customer and how to engage them is crucial to your online business success. There are several key aspects to consider. Understand their demographics. Who are your main customers in terms of age, gender, location and other demographic factors? This data will help you tailor your marketing and product offerings appropriately. For example, if most of your customers are female, focus your marketing imagery on women and product descriptions that appeal to women. Ecommerce businesses have the opportunity to reach a vast customer base. However, understanding customer demographics and identifying key target markets is crucial for a successful online store. Customer demographics refer to the statistical data about your customers, such as age, gender, income level, location, and more. Analyzing this data allows ecommerce businesses to identify their most valuable target markets and tailor their products, services, and marketing strategies accordingly. Some important customer demographic factors for ecommerce businesses include

- Age - Different age groups have different preferences, budgets, and shopping habits. Understanding the age distribution of your customers helps you optimize for their needs.
- Gender - Some products appeal more to one gender over the other. Knowing the gender split of your customers helps you refine your offerings and marketing.
- Location - Location data reveals which regions are most interested in your products. You can then optimize shipping, inventory, and marketing for those areas.
- Income - Income levels affect what products customers can afford and how much they are willing to spend. High-income customers may prefer higher-end products.

By understanding these key demographics, ecommerce businesses can focus on the most valuable target markets for their products or services. You can optimize pricing, product features, marketing messages, and more specifically for those high-potential customer segments. Over time, as your customer data grows, you'll gain even deeper insights into your most loyal customers to sustain long-term growth. Analyzing customer demographics and identifying the right target markets is a fundamental first step for any ecommerce business. The more you understand about your ideal customers, the better you can meet their needs and build a successful online store. You should go a couple of steps further and gather insights into their interests. What interests and hobbies do your customers have? What problems are they trying to solve by purchasing from you? Understanding their key interests beyond just your products helps you create more relevant and personalized content that resonates with them.

- Identify their pain points. What specific challenges or frustrations do your customers face that your products or services can solve? Focus your marketing messaging around alleviating those pain points to show customers how you can improve their lives.
- Listen to their feedback. Actively seek feedback from your customers through online reviews, surveys and social media. Then respond to that feedback to show them you care and are willing to improve based on their input. Incorporate their suggestions where feasible to enhance the customer experience.

- Test engagement strategies. Experiment with different online engagement strategies like email newsletters, social media posts, loyalty programs and live chat to determine which ones resonate most with your particular customers. Measure the results and optimize accordingly over time.
- Direct-to-consumer brands have revolutionized the retail industry through their ability to connect directly with customers and build strong brand loyalty. To succeed, D2C brands must implement effective engagement strategies across all touchpoints to develop meaningful relationships with customers. Here are some key brand engagement strategies for D2C companies:

Once you have deep insights and understanding of your consumer you can now personalise your interaction. Personalisation is at the core of D2C brand engagement. Customers expect their experience to be tailored to their preferences and needs. D2C brands can personalize recommendations, product offerings, communications, and promotions based on customer data. D2C brands can foster a sense of community among their customers through online forums, social media groups, and in-person events. This allows customers to interact with each other, form relationships, and gain value beyond the product itself. A strong brand community can become a powerful marketing channel.

- Customer service. Providing outstanding customer service and support helps build trust and loyalty. D2C brands have more control over the customer experience and can offer services like 1-on-1 concierge support, fast response times, and personalized solutions.
- Content marketing. High-quality, relevant content is an effective engagement tactic, especially when distributed across owned channels like email newsletters and the company website. Content can educate and inform customers while strengthening the brand's authority and expertise.
- Surveys and feedback. Regularly soliciting customer feedback through surveys, reviews, and focus groups gives D2C brands valuable insights into how to improve products and the overall experience. It also shows customers that their opinions matter.

D2C brands have a huge opportunity to engage and delight customers through personalization, community, customer service excellence, compelling content, and feedback loops. A strategic and holistic approach to brand engagement across all touchpoints is key to success. The next stage to understanding the consumer behavior is to understand what influences their decesion making. Direct-to-consumer/eCommerce brands rely heavily on data and insights from customers to inform product development and marketing strategies. A robust customer framework can help you organize the wealth of data you collect in a systematic way to make the right decisions for your customers. Here are key elements of an effective D2C customer framework:

- Customer personas: Create detailed profiles of your core customer segments based on demographics, behaviors, motivations, and goals. Personas bring your customers to life and ensure your decisions align with their needs.
- Customer journey mapping: Map out the steps a customer takes from awareness to purchase and ongoing engagement. Identify pain points, opportunities for improvement, and ways to enhance the experience at each stage.
- Customer insights: Gather data through surveys, focus groups, social listening, and analytics to gain a deep understanding of what customers value, what frustrates them, and how you can improve. Let these insights guide your product and marketing decisions.
- Voice of the customer: Establish processes to regularly collect and analyze customer feedback to keep the customer perspective front and center. Use tools like net promoter score (NPS) surveys and customer reviews.
- Customer metrics: Track key performance indicators (KPIs) that measure your impact on customers, like customer satisfaction, retention rates, and lifetime value. Monitor these metrics over time to evaluate progress.

By developing a robust framework grounded in customer insights, personas, journeys and metrics, you can make strategic decisions that will truly resonate with your customers and drive growth for your D2C brand. Keep listening to your customers, analyzing the data and adapting your framework as needed to stay aligned with their evolving needs. Personalize the experience by leverage the customer data you have gathered to create more tailored and relevant experiences for individuals. Send personalized emails, show product recommendations based on purchase history and recognize returning customers by name. All of this demonstrates you value them as individuals. And by understanding who your customers are and how to best engage them through digital channels, you can create stronger emotional connections that lead to increased loyalty, referrals and lifetime value. So get to know your online buyers, listen to their voices and continually test new engagement strategies to improve the relationship over time.

CHAPTER SIXTEEN

OKR's Vs KPI's

OKRs (Objectives and Key Results) and KPIs (Key Performance Indicators) are crucial performance measurement frameworks in business and strategic planning, each serving distinct yet complementary purposes. OKRs provide a top-down approach, aligning organizational objectives with measurable and time-bound key results, fostering clarity and focus. This framework encourages agility and innovation by setting ambitious goals and promoting a culture of continuous improvement. On the other hand, KPIs offer a bottom-up perspective, allowing organizations to track specific metrics that directly reflect performance against strategic objectives. Together, OKRs and KPIs create a comprehensive system for evaluating and enhancing business performance. While OKRs provide a directional guide, KPIs offer a granular view, ensuring that day-to-day activities contribute to the broader strategic vision. Combining these frameworks empowers businesses to set ambitious goals, measure progress, and adapt strategies in a dynamic and data-driven manner.but they serve different purposes and have distinct characteristics.

OKRs (Objectives and Key Results):

- Purpose: OKRs are primarily used for setting and measuring goals and objectives. They help organizations define ambitious, high-level objectives and track progress towards achieving those objectives.
- Structure: OKRs consist of two components: objectives and key results. Objectives are clear and ambitious goals that an organization or team aims to achieve. Key results are specific, measurable milestones that demonstrate progress toward the objectives.
- Scope: OKRs are often set at the company, team, or individual level and are intended to align and focus everyone's efforts on common objectives. They are forward-looking and aspirational.
- Timeframe: OKRs typically operate on a quarterly basis, although they can be set for different timeframes. They are meant to be challenging and push teams to achieve significant progress within a defined period.

KPIs (Key Performance Indicators):

- Purpose: KPIs are used for ongoing performance measurement and management. They provide a snapshot of how well an organization or a specific process is performing against established benchmarks or targets.
- Structure: KPIs are specific, quantifiable metrics that are used to track and assess the performance of various aspects of a business, such as sales, customer satisfaction, website traffic, or operational efficiency.
- Scope: KPIs can cover a wide range of operational, financial, and performance-related areas within an organization. They are often used for continuous monitoring and reporting.
- Timeframe: KPIs are typically used on an ongoing basis and can be monitored daily, weekly, monthly, or annually. They are designed to provide regular insights into performance.

KPIs Vs. OKRs: What's the Difference

	Key Performance Indicators	Objectives & Key results
What	Numbers that track the operation of your business	Action oriented goals & measures
Foundation	Based on past results or future goals	Mission based, aspirational & directional
Direction	Monitors the steady state & benchmarks	Audacious and bold, tied to mission
Triggers	Actions are prompted when numbers are off track	Actions are taken as issues
Duration	Measured on an ongoing basis	Time bound, often quarterly
Lifespan	Maintain quarter to quarter, year to year	Change from quarter, year to year

Exercise Draw clear line to differentiate OKR's vs KPI's

EXAMPLE OF KPIs and OKRs

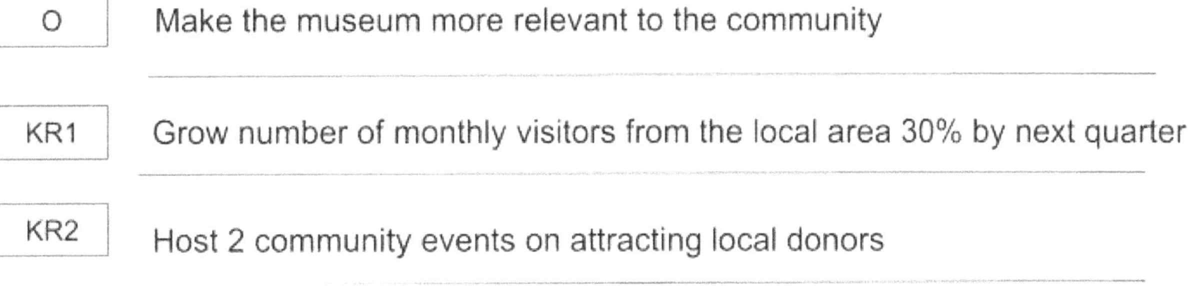

Exercise take a scenario and write down a clear set of actions to achieve the objective

Mapping out OKRs (Objectives and Key Results) and KPIs (Key Performance Indicators) is crucial for e-commerce brands for several reasons: OKRs enable e-commerce brands to set clear, high-level objectives that align with their strategic goals. By mapping OKRs, teams throughout the organization understand what they need to achieve to support the brand's mission and vision. OKRs force e-commerce brands to prioritize their objectives, ensuring that resources, time, and effort are directed toward the most critical and impactful goals. This prevents teams from spreading themselves too thin. KPIs provide specific, quantifiable metrics to measure progress and performance. They offer a way to track how well the e-commerce brand is doing in areas like sales, customer satisfaction, conversion rates, and more. Assigning specific KPIs to individuals or teams encourages accountability. Team members are responsible for achieving the key results associated with the objectives, fostering a sense of ownership and commitment. KPIs support ongoing performance monitoring. E-commerce brands can regularly assess their progress, identify areas that require improvement, and adjust strategies and tactics accordingly.

E-commerce is a dynamic and rapidly evolving industry. OKRs and KPIs help brands adapt to changing market conditions and customer preferences. When KPIs show a decline in a particular area, it signals the need for adjustments and innovation. KPIs provide data that informs decision-making. E-commerce brands can make informed choices based on real-time performance insights, rather than relying on intuition or assumptions. Clear and well-defined OKRs and KPIs enhance communication within the organization. Teams can easily understand the objectives, key results, and the metrics used to track progress. Achieving key results and meeting KPI targets can boost team morale. Recognizing and celebrating milestones and successes can motivate teams to excel. Brands that effectively map out and execute their OKRs and KPIs have a competitive edge. They can react swiftly to market changes, capitalize on opportunities, and deliver a superior customer experience. In the highly competitive e-commerce landscape, mapping out OKRs and KPIs is not just a good practice but a necessity. It provides the framework for strategic planning, performance management, and adaptability that e-commerce brands need to thrive and grow.

Key Differences:

- Focus: OKRs are more focused on setting and achieving strategic objectives, while KPIs are centered on ongoing performance measurement and management.
- Structure: OKRs consist of objectives and key results, while KPIs are specific metrics that measure performance in various areas.
- Timeframe: OKRs are often set for shorter periods and are more ambitious, while KPIs are used for continuous, ongoing performance tracking.
- Scope: OKRs are typically aligned with high-level goals and are designed to drive strategic alignment, while KPIs cover a broader range of operational and performance areas.
- OKRs are goal-setting frameworks that help organizations set and achieve strategic objectives, while KPIs are specific metrics used for ongoing performance measurement and management. Both are valuable tools in strategy and performance management, serving complementary roles in an organization.

CHAPTER SEVENTEEN

WHY DO YOU KEEP YOUR CONSUMERS ENGAGED

11 of the most prominent D2C Indian startups witnessed an average year-on-year revenue surge of more than 200%, according to Inc42 Plus. While the opportunity for business growth for D2C / ecommerce brands is abundant, there are challenges as well. Newer players are arriving in the market, along with traditional brands going direct-to-consumer. This means consumers have more choices, and capturing their attention is only the first step toward steady growth. Acquiring new customers is important, but so is retaining and nurturing your existing customer base. Customer engagement is key to converting customers into loyal brand advocates. In addition to acquiring customers, focus on these engagement strategies:

- Provide value. Think of ways to continuously add value for your customers through useful content, helpful tips, or exclusive offers. Look for opportunities to solve their problems or make their lives easier.
- Communicate proactively. Reach out to customers periodically through email, text, or social media to share news, promotions, and product updates. Ask for feedback to improve their experience. Timely, relevant communication shows customers you value the relationship.
- Make it personal. Use customers' names in your communications and tailor your messages to their preferences and purchase history. Showing you know and remember individual customers goes a long way.
- Reward loyalty. Implement a loyalty program with rewards, discounts, or other perks for repeat customers. Even small gestures can encourage customers to continue choosing your brand.

Customer engagement is crucial to business growth and success. Engaged customers bring in more revenue, purchase more products, and spread positive word of mouth. While customer engagement may seem like an obvious business priority, its impact is often undervalued. Here are some reasons why you should focus on customer engagement:

- Increases revenue. Research shows that highly engaged customers generate 23% more revenue than average customers. As customers develop a deeper connection with your brand, they tend to buy more products and services.
- Improves customer retention. Engaged customers remain loyal to your brand for a longer period. They are less likely to switch to competitors. This reduces customer acquisition costs and improves overall profit margins.
- Boosts word of mouth marketing. Satisfied and engaged customers become your brand's advocates, referring new customers through positive recommendations. This organic marketing is more effective at attracting new customers than paid advertising.
- Enhances product feedback. Engaged customers are willing to provide feedback to help improve your products and services. This input can help identify new opportunities and drive innovation.

To reap these benefits, focus on actively engaging customers through all phases of the buyer journey. Listen to customers, provide personalized experiences, gather feedback, and resolve issues promptly. The more you can foster a sense of partnership with customers, the more engaged they will become - translating into tangible business growth. Consumer engagement should be a top priority for any business that wants to grow and thrive. The impact goes beyond higher revenues - it also strengthens customer relationships that form the foundation for long-term success. Given that incentives and loyalty programmes are among the most successful methods for interacting with customers, these statistics shouldn't come as a surprise to you. After signing up for yours, a consumer will start to think of you as one of their top options, which will make it simpler for you to promote their interaction with and affiliation with your company.

Create a customer loyalty programme that quickly onboards customers if you want to encourage them to interact with your brand. Your engagement metrics will increase if you make sure to advertise it effectively. You've probably seen how Starbucks does it, or if you want to look closer to home, Chaayos. They increase consumer loyalty and encourage a cycle of recurrent purchases by providing incentives for each purchase and each store visit, respectively. Nudge Guest (And Window) Shoppers To Sign Up.Entice Guests (And Windows) Browsers To Register. Why is it that ecommerce giants such as Amazon, Flipkart and Myntra monitor customer activity and behavior around their websites? It has to do with the level of service you can offer to purchasers who have made accounts with your business - making all the hard work worthwhile.

In the domain of strategic thinking and customer relations, the four bonds of loyalty — trust, identification, commitment, and intimacy — form the foundation for understanding and cultivating enduring connections with customers. Trust is the cornerstone, as customers must believe in the reliability and integrity of a brand or product. Identification involves customers seeing themselves reflected in the values and ethos of the offering, creating a sense of belonging. Commitment is crucial for long-term loyalty, requiring both parties to invest in the relationship. Lastly, intimacy goes beyond transactional interactions, fostering a deep understanding of customers' needs and preferences. Together, these bonds create a symbiotic relationship where customers feel not just satisfied, but emotionally connected to a brand. Acknowledging and nurturing these bonds is instrumental in deciphering customer motives, enabling businesses to tailor strategies that resonate on a personal level, engendering sustained loyalty and advocacy.

To roll out an effective aand successful loyalty program its imperative to understand and leverag the four bonds of loyalty—emotional, social, structural, and financial—is essential for authors and strategists aiming to connect with their audience and comprehend customer motives. Emotional bonds are rooted in the customer's feelings and experiences, creating a deep connection that goes beyond transactional interactions. Social bonds arise from shared values, interests, and a sense of belonging, tapping into the communal aspects of loyalty. Structural bonds are formed through convenience, reliability, and habit, reflecting the customer's dependence on a consistent and efficient experience. Financial bonds involve economic incentives, such as discounts or exclusive offers, reinforcing loyalty through tangible benefits. By recognizing and nurturing these bonds, authors and strategists can craft narratives and campaigns that resonate on multiple levels, fostering a robust and enduring connection with their audience based on a nuanced understanding of customer motivations.

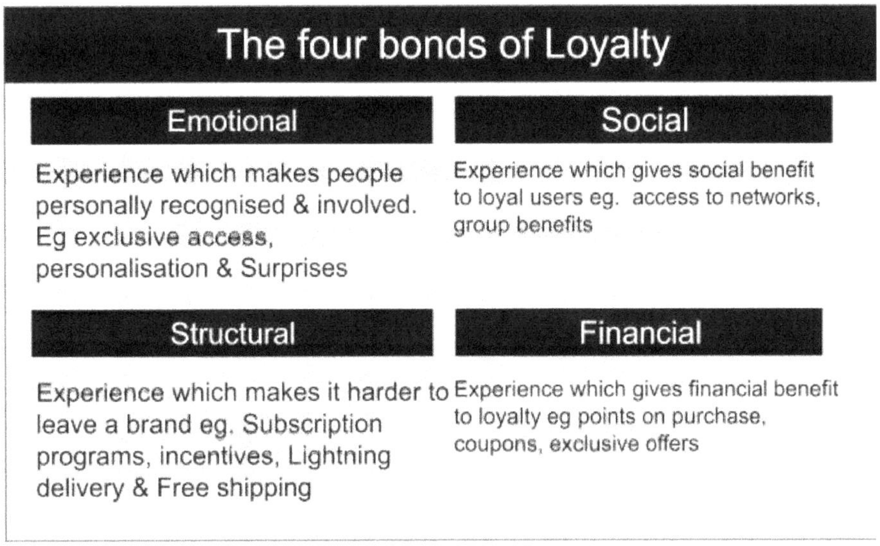

The four bonds of Loyalty

Emotional

Experience which makes people personally recognised & involved. Eg exclusive access, personalisation & Surprises

Social

Experience which gives social benefit to loyal users eg. access to networks, group benefits

Structural

Experience which makes it harder to leave a brand eg. Subscription programs, incentives, Lightning delivery & Free shipping

Financial

Experience which gives financial benefit to loyalty eg points on purchase, coupons, exclusive offers

To make a loaylty program work you need all 4 pillars to be equally relevant

CHAPTER EIGHTEEN

STANDING OUT IN A SEA OF COMPETITION

As the barriers to entry for launching an online store become lower and lower, competition in the direct-to-consumer space is only set to intensify. Almost every consumer category has seen a rise in the number of available vendors and this trend shows no signs of slowing. So how can new D2C brands differentiate themselves and build loyal customer relationships in such a crowded marketplace? The answer lies in focusing on your brand and the customer experience you provide. Building a strong brand revolves around consistency. Consistently delivering on your brand promise, providing a quality product or service, and engaging customers in a way that aligns with your brand values. Customers form attachments to brands that meet and exceed their expectations each time. For D2C brands, engaging customers on a regular basis through email newsletters, social media, and loyalty programs is critical. These frequent brand touchpoints increase brand recall and top-of-mind awareness over time. Customers who interact with your brand messaging more often are more likely to think of your brand when making a purchase in your category. Regular communication also provides opportunities to drive repeat purchases. Whether highlighting new product launches, offering discounts to loyal customers, or providing recommendations based on past purchases, brands that stay front of mind for customers have more chances to convert them into repeat buyers.

As competition rises, your brand and customer relationships will become the ultimate differentiators for any D2C business. Focus on consistency, frequent communication, and personalized engagement to build a loyal customer base that advocates for your brand and keeps coming back. Nurturing those relationships now will set your brand up for long-term growth and success in an increasingly crowded market.

Increase Lifetime Value And Reduce Churn: Customer engagement is crucial for business growth in today's competitive landscape. With the ever-rising cost of customer acquisition, spending all your marketing budget on attracting new customers is not a sustainable growth strategy. An effective customer engagement strategy helps you retain and deepen relationships with existing customers, ultimately improving lifetime value and reducing churn.

Here are some benefits of a strong customer engagement strategy: Increased loyalty and repeat purchases. By staying in touch with customers in between purchases, you can remind them of your value proposition and make them aware of new products and services. This leads to higher customer loyalty and repeat purchases.

- Positive word-of-mouth. Engaged customers are more likely to recommend your business to family and friends. Their endorsements carry more weight and credibility, helping you acquire new customers through word-of-mouth marketing.
- Insights for product improvements. Engaging with customers regularly provides valuable insights into what they like and dislike about your offerings. You can use this feedback to make timely improvements that customers will appreciate.
- Opportunities for upselling and cross-selling. By nurturing relationships with customers over time, you find opportunities to upsell them complementary products and cross-sell them adjacent products. This expands revenue from existing customers.

An effective customer engagement strategy goes a long way in improving customer lifetime value, reducing churn, and fueling sustainable business growth. So invest in the right tools and channels to stay connected with your customers, and reap the rewards of higher customer loyalty, advocacy, and revenue.

CHAPTER NINETEEN

CUSTOMER BEHAVIOUR & DECISION MAKING

Consumer behavior is the study of when, why, how and where people do or do not buy a product. It basically depends on the psychology of the consumer. It attempts to understand the buyer decision making process both individually & in groups. Its the study of individual consumers' demographics & behavioral aspects to understand their want and decision making pattern. There are several reason why consumer behavior is important to study.

- First, it helps researchers better understand how consumers make their buying decisions. This knowledge can be used to develop strategies for increasing profits by targeting the most likely consumers of a given product or service.
- Second, it helps them understand how to best market products and services to different types of consumers.
- Finally, it helps them predict future changes in consumer tastes or preferences so that businesses can respond accordingly.

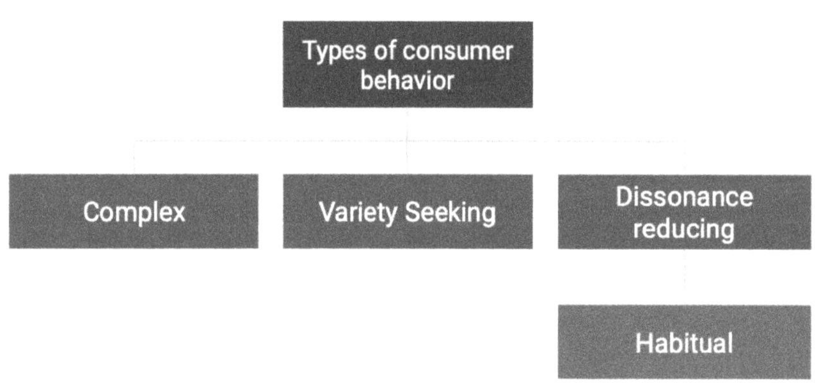

Consumer behavior types

Consumer behavior models provide insights into how individuals make purchasing decisions. Here are descriptions of four common models and examples of Indian brands that align with each:

1. Complex Buying Behavior: This model represents situations where consumers are highly involved in the purchase decision and invest significant time and effort in evaluating options. They consider multiple factors, such as features, quality, price, and brand reputation. Complex buying behavior is often associated with high-value or

infrequent purchases. Example: When consumers are buying a new smartphone, they engage in complex buying behavior. Brands like Apple and Samsung in India cater to this by offering a wide range of features, quality assurance, and marketing their brand reputation.

2. Variety-Seeking Buying Behavior: In this model, consumers are looking for change or novelty. They may switch brands or products to experience something different. This behavior is common for low-involvement and everyday products, such as snacks or personal care items. Example: In the Indian market, consumers exhibit variety-seeking buying behavior when choosing snacks. Brands like Kurkure, Lay's, and Bingo introduce new flavors and limited-edition options to cater to consumers seeking variety.
3. Dissonance-Reducing Buying Behavior: This model comes into play when consumers experience post-purchase dissonance or regret. They seek information and reassurance to confirm that they made the right choice. Dissonance-reducing buying behavior is typical for significant purchases with perceived risks. Example: Buying a car in India often involves dissonance-reducing buying behavior. Brands like Maruti Suzuki and Hyundai address this by offering warranties, after-sales service, and positive customer reviews to reassure buyers.
4. Habitual Buying Behavior: In this model, consumers make frequent and low-involvement purchases with little consideration. They have brand loyalty and stick to familiar products out of habit. This behavior is typical for everyday items like toiletries. Example: When purchasing toothpaste, many Indian consumers exhibit habitual buying behavior. Brands like Colgate and Pepsodent have built strong brand loyalty, making customers consistently choose their products. Understanding these consumer behavior models helps Indian brands tailor their marketing and product strategies to meet the specific needs and preferences of their target audiences. Diving deeper gives us insights into consumer behavior rational and these can be bucketed into two types.
5. Rational choice theory – This theory assumes that consumers are rational beings who make decisions based on their preferences and resources available to them. It also assumes that consumers can easily make comparisons between brands and products, so they can select their favorite brand or product based on price and quality.
6. Social Influence Theory – This theory says that consumers are influenced by others around them when making purchasing decisions. These influences can come from family members, friends or peers who have similar tastes as theirs. For example, if someone buys a new car, then everyone else will want one too because they want to be like that person!

Product & Patronage Motives	
Product & Patronage MotivesProduct Motives Primary Secondary	**Patronage Motives** Price Quality Location Services Variety Personality of the owner
Emotional & Rational Motives	
Emotional Motives Love of others Social acceptance motive Vanity Motive Recreational motive Emulate motive Comfort & convenience motive	Rational Motives Monetary gain Efficiency in operation Dependability
Inherent & Learned motives	
Inherent motives are those which come from physiological & basic needs such as hunger, thirst, sleep etc. If these motives are not satisfied then consumer feels dissatisfied and feels mental tension. Learned motives are those which are learned or acquired by a person from environment and education like social status, acceptance, fear, security etc.	
Physiological & Social buying Motives	
Physiological motives are those which are driven by learning, perception or attitude. Social buying motives are those which are influenced by the society in which the consumers live.	

Deep dive to understand purchase motives

Consumer behavior models may sound complicated, but they're not. They're a way to create a "buyer behavior story" that you can use to refine and improve your customer experience. As a whole, buyer behavior refers to an individual's buying habits based on influences from their background, education, personal beliefs, goals, needs, desires, and more. Businesses aim to understand buyer behavior through customer behavior analysis, which involves the qualitative and quantitative analysis of a target market. Even though this data can tell you your customer's favorite brand of socks, it doesn't mean much if it doesn't tell you why they purchased that brand of socks. That's where consumer behavior models come in. Consumer behavior models contextualize results from customer behavior analysis studies and help you get to the "why" of purchasing decisions.

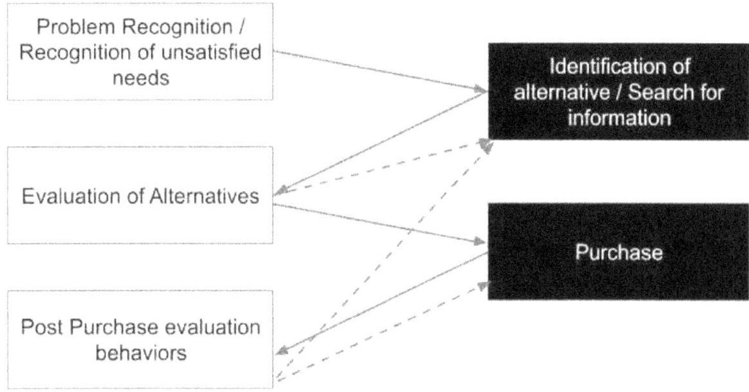

Exercie put yourself in the consumers shoes and workout what motivates a consumer to purchase.

Customer behavior models are invaluable tools for both strategy and marketing experts as they offer a deep and data-driven understanding of a business's unique customer base. By analyzing patterns, preferences, and interactions, these models unveil insights into the decision-making processes of customers. This knowledge empowers businesses to tailor their marketing strategies, ensuring they resonate with the specific needs and desires of their audience. Consequently, companies can more effectively attract and engage customers, offering personalized experiences that enhance customer satisfaction and loyalty. Understanding customer behavior through models allows for the creation of targeted campaigns, improved product development, and the optimization of overall customer experience, ultimately leading to increased retention rates and long-term business success. These models are classified either into traditional or contemporary.

TRADITIONAL CONSUMER BEHAVIOR MODELS	CONTEMPORARY CONSUMER BEHAVIOR MODELS
Learning Model	Engel-Kollat-Blackwell (EKB) Model
Psychoanalytical Model	Black Box Model
Sociological Model	Hawkins Stern Model
Economic Model	Howard Sheth Model
	Nicosia Model
	Webster and Wind Model

Within consumer behavior models you have the old school and the new age.

Traditional behavior models were developed by economists hoping to understand what customers purchase based on their wants and needs. Traditional models include the following:

Learning Model

1. Psychoanalytical Model

2. Sociological Model
3. Economic Model

Learning Model of Consumer Behavior

Buyers are driven to satisfy basic needs required for survival like food and needs from life experience like fear of guilt

The Learning Model of customer behavior theorizes that buyer behavior responds to the desire to satisfy basic needs required for survival, like food, and learned needs that arise from lived experiences, like fear or guilt. This model takes influence from psychologist Abraham Maslow's Hierarchy of Needs

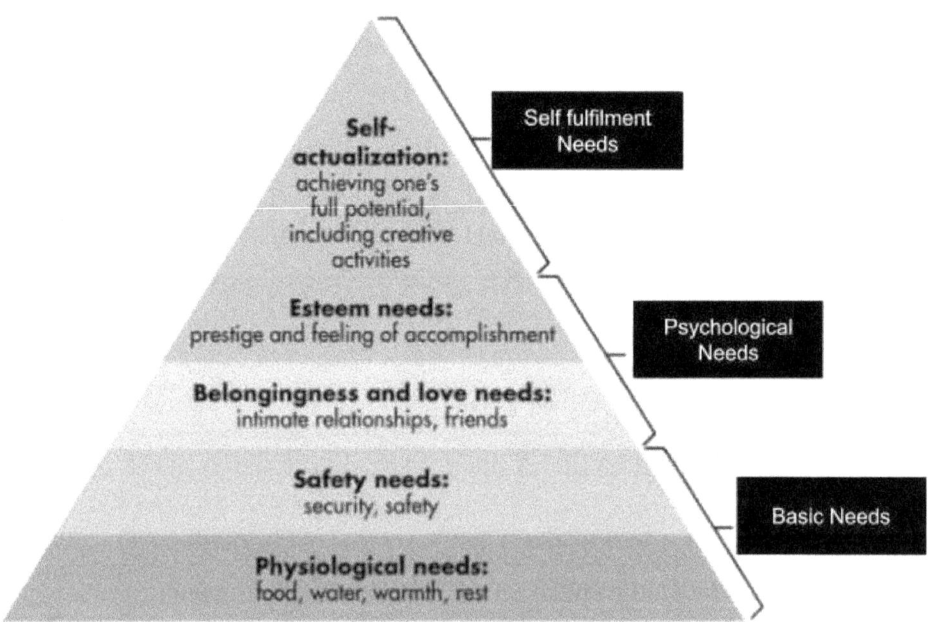

Maslow's Hierarchy

The bottom level of this hierarchy represents basic needs, and ascending sections describe learned needs, or secondary desires, that allow consumers to feel as though they've reached self-fulfillment. The Learning Model says that consumers first make purchases to satisfy their basic needs and then move on to meet learned needs. For example, a hungry customer would fulfill their need for food before a learned need to wear trendy clothing. If you're a multipurpose business that sells products that meet all levels of customer needs, this model applies to you. For example, Target is a United States-based department store that sells hundreds of products. Super Targets are larger versions of the chain that also sell groceries. When a customer visits a Super Target, they first see products that satisfy their basic needs — the grocery section. They're probably also seeing produce first, as these items are seen as the most nutritious and necessary for survival. After produce, customers move on to other aisles that satisfy learned needs, like purchasing their favorite cookies, clothing items, or beauty accessories. You can think of it like this: If you're a business with a significant amount of in-store options, improve the customer experience and speak to their buyer behavior by first leading them to the products that will satisfy their innate needs. Without doing this, they may navigate through your store anxious about meeting those needs and spend less time browsing other products and making additional purchases. Once they feel comfortable, they'll move on to satisfy the desires that bring them joy rather than help them survive.

Psychological Model of consumer Behavior

Individual consumers have deep rooted motives, both conscious and unconscious, that drive them to make a purchase.

Sigmund Freud is the father of psychoanalysis. The psychoanalytical model draws from his theories and says that individual consumers have deep-rooted motives, both conscious and unconscious, that drive them to make a purchase. These motives can be hidden fears, suppressed desires, or personal longings. Thus, customers make purchases depending on how stimuli from your business, like an advertisement on Instagram, appeal to their desires. It's important to note that, since these desires can be unconscious, customers don't always know why it appeals to them; they just know it feels right to have it. This model is unique in terms of application, but it's relevant to businesses that sell an image that accompanies their products or services. For example, say you sell glasses. We all long to fit in and feel like we're valued and seen as capable, smart people. Glasses are sometimes a symbol of intelligence, so you'd want to appeal to this desire when crafting a customer experience. You may instruct marketing to create ad campaigns that display pictures of people wearing your glasses in educational settings or doing things that society labels as 'smart.'

3. Sociological Model of consumer behavior

Sociological Model of consumer Behavior

Purchases are influenced by an individual's place within different social groups, family & friends

The Sociological Model of consumer behavior says that purchases are influenced by an individual's place within different societal groups: family, friends, and workgroups, as well as less-defined groups like Millennials or people who like yoga. An individual will essentially purchase items based on what is appropriate or typical of the groups they're in. For instance, C-Suite executives are expected to be professional and formal. People who hold these jobs will make purchases that speak to and uphold this group's rules, like formal business wear. This model can apply to most businesses, especially those that create products and services relevant to specific groups. To use the Sociological Model, you'd want to create experiences that speak to how these groups usually act. One example is brands that sell exercise equipment. You sell to and appeal to consumers that are part of a societal group that likes to work out. To delight these customers, you'd want to sell to their desires, like equipment that improves performance or an insulated water bottle that stays cold and leaves them satisfied during their breaks. By doing this, you're speaking to the consumer in that specific group and showing them that your product will help them retain their position in that group. Check out an ad from Nike. They're selling this shoe to the undefined group of people who like to run, claiming that it will improve their speed and help them fit in with the group.

Economic Model of consumer Behavior

Consumer try to meet their needs while spending as few resources as possible.

The economic model of consumer behavior is the most straightforward of the traditional models. This model argues that consumers try to meet their needs while spending as few resources (e.g. money) as possible. That means that businesses and manufacturers can predict sales based on their customers' income and their products' price. If companies offer the lowest-priced product, they may feel that they're guaranteed a consistent level of profit. While the economic model is the easiest to understand, it's also the most limited. A buyer may have other reasons for purchasing a product aside from price and personal resources. One such example would be prescription medicine in the U.S. healthcare industry. While the price of a prescription drug may exceed the buyer's resources, the buyer would still have to find a way to purchase it and meet their needs. They might open a credit card or take out a personal loan to pay for the medicine. Thus personal income and price don't affect the purchasing decision here; instead, need does.

Contemporary Models

Contemporary models of consumer behavior focus on rational and deliberate decision-making processes rather than emotions or unconscious desires. The contemporary models include:

1. Engel-Kollat-Blackwell (EKB) Model
2. Black Box Model
3. Hawkins Stern Model
4. Howard Sheth Model
5. Nicosia Model
6. Webster and Wind Model

1. Engel-Kollat-Blackwell (EKB) Model of Consumer Behavior

Engel Kollat Blackwell (EKB) Model

There are 5 stages

Stage 1 - Awareness

Stage 2 - Information Processing

Stage 3 - Evaluation

Stage 4 - Purchasing Decision

Stage 5 - Outcome Analysis

The Engel-Kollat-Blackwell model of consumer behavior outlines a five-stage decision process that consumers go through before purchasing a product or service.

- Awareness: During this stage, consumers view advertisements from a business and become aware of their need, desire, or interest, to purchase what they've just discovered.
- Information Processing: After discovering a product or service, a consumer begins to think about how the product or service relates to their past experiences or needs and whether it will fulfill any current needs.
- Evaluation: At this point, consumers will research the product they've discovered and research options from competitors to see if there is a better option or if the original product is the best fit.
- Purchasing Decision: A consumer will follow through with a purchase for the product that has beat out competitors to provide value. A consumer may also stop the process if they change their mind.
- Outcome Analysis: After making a purchase, a customer will use what they've bought and assess whether their experience is positive or negative. After a trial period, they'll keep a product and maybe decide to become repeat customers or express dissatisfaction and return to stage three.

EKB says that consumers make decisions based on influencing factors that they assess through rational insight. This model applies to businesses that have many competitors with similar products or services. If your product market is highly saturated and competitive, the goal is to outshine your competitors by meeting customers at every stage of their journey. Increase visibility for your business during the awareness stage through Search Engine Optimization. Show them how your product or service will benefit them and give them the resources they need to weigh you against your competitors, like customer reviews and testimonials, free trials, discounts for bulk purchases. Lastly, and provide excellent after-sales support to show them that you care about their business even if they make a return.

Stimulus Response Model of consumer Behavior

Stimuli - Eg. marketing messages & external factors

Black Box - Internal influences & decision making process)

Purchase Decision -

The Black Box model, sometimes called the Stimulus-Response model, says that customers are individual thinkers that process internal and external stimuli to make purchase decisions. The graphic below illustrates the decision process.

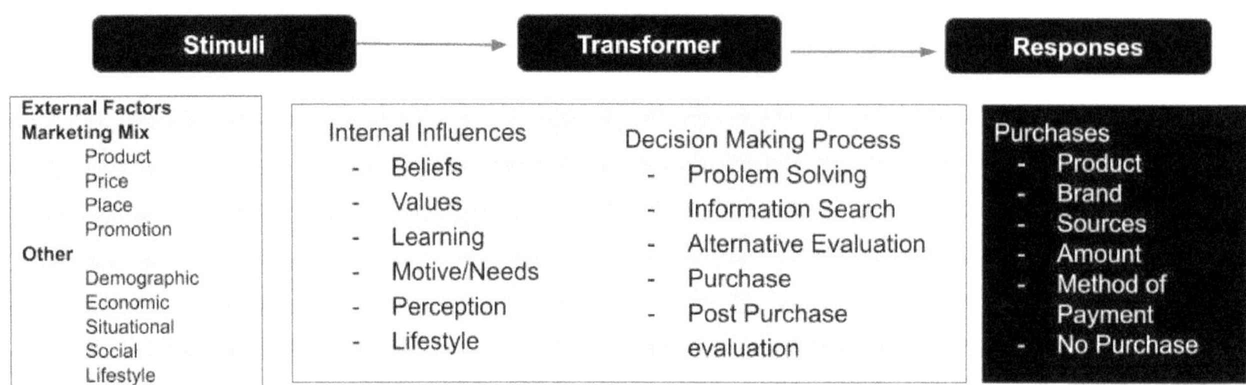

It may look complex, but it's a fairly straightforward path. A consumer comes into contact with external stimuli from your business' marketing mix and other external stimuli, and they process it in their mind (black box). They relate the external stimuli to their pre-existing knowledge, like personal beliefs and desires, to make a decision. In short, this model says that consumers are problem solvers who make decisions after judging how your product will satisfy their existing beliefs and needs. Since consumers only follow through with a purchase after understanding how a product relates to their experiences, this model can benefit businesses selling products that go along with a lifestyle.

Case in point: cars. Different brands sell their cars to specific types of buyers. Jeeps and Subarus are for those that engage in outdoor activities and need a sturdy, reliable vehicle. At the same time, Mercedez Benz and Lexus' are marketed to those who want luxurious driving experiences. Even though the machinery is relatively similar, these brands speak to the pre-existing life values that customers have, and they promise that purchasing their vehicle will uphold their values.

3. Hawkins Stern Impulse Buying Model

Hawkins Stern Impulse Buying Model

Within this model there are 4 purchase types:

Type 1 : Escape Purchase
Type 2 : Reminder purchase
Type 3 : Suggested Purchase
Type 4 : Planned Purchase

The Impulse Buying theory is an alternative to the Learning Model and EKB, as it claims that purchases aren't always a result of rational thought.

When we think of impulse buying, we typically imagine picking up a candy bar or a pack of gum right before checking out. These are certainly impulse purchases, but Hawkins Stern categorizes them into four different types:

- Escape Purchase: Sometimes called pure impulse, this involves purchasing an item that isn't a routine item or on a shopping list. Consumers are drawn to these items through appealing visuals.
- Reminder Purchase: A consumer makes a reminder impulse purchase when they come across a product through in-store setups, promotional offers, or a simple reminder that a product exists, like a strategically placed ice cream scoop in the freezer aisle of a grocery store.
- Suggested Purchase: Suggested impulse purchases occur when a consumer is made aware of a product after a recommendation or suggestion from an in-store salesperson or online algorithms. For example, seeing an ad that says, "Other people who bought this shoe you're about to buy also purchase these socks." The consumer didn't know the socks existed, didn't plan to buy them, but now the suggestion has told them that they need them.
- Planned Purchase: Although planned is the opposite of impulse, these purchases occur when a consumer knows they want a particular product but will only buy it if there is a deal involved. An unexpected price drop could lead a customer to make a planned impulse purchase.

The Hawkins Stern Model applies to most businesses, as there are no limits to what a customer with this purchasing behavior will buy. Create a tailored customer experience by putting care into product displays, creating AI algorithms for online shopping, or placing items on sale to appeal to your shoppers who are planned purchase impulse buyers.

Howard Sheth Model of buying Behavior

Type 1 : Extensive problem solving (awareness of brand options)

Type 2 : Limited problem solving (engaging in brand comparisons)

Type 3 : Habitual response behaviors (Continually choosing a brand)

The Howard Sheth model of consumer behavior posits that the buyer's journey is a highly rational and methodical decision-making process.

In this model, customers put on a "problem-solving" hat every step of the way — with different variables influencing the course of the journey. According to this model, there are three successive levels of decision-making:

- Extensive Problem-Solving: In this stage, customers know nothing about the product they're seeking or the brands that are available to them. They're in active problem-solving mode to find a suitable product.
- Limited Problem-Solving: Now that customers have more information, they slow down and begin comparing their choices.
- Habitual Response Behavior: Customers are fully aware of all the choices they have and know which brands they prefer. Thus, every time they make a purchase, they know where to go.

We've all gone through some version of these stages. Let's look at an anecdotal example. When I first started buying glasses online, I had no idea which retailers I should use or whether the glasses sold online would be the same quality as the opticians' offerings. I searched online to find a high-quality online glasses retailer (extensive problem-solving). I found a few choices and started comparing them from both a pricing and quality standpoint (limited problem-solving). I eventually chose one, and that's the retailer I've used ever since (habitual response behavior). But these stages aren't that simple. According to the Howard Sheth model, I was under the sway of several stimuli during this process:

- Inputs: This refers to the marketing messages and imagery a consumer receives while they're going through the decision-making process. "Inputs" also refers to any perceptions and attitudes that come from the consumer's social environment, such as their friends, family, and culture.
- Perceptual and Learning Constructs: This may sound complicated, but this stimulus is simply the customer's psychological makeup and psychographic information. Perceptual and learning constructs may include needs, preferences, and goals.
- Outputs: After inputs and perceptual and learning constructs are mixed together, you get the output. The output is the customer's resulting action under the influence of marketing messages, social stimuli, and internal psychological attributes. It can result in the customer paying more attention to a certain brand over another.
- External Variables: This is anything that's not directly related to the decision-making process, such as weather or religion, that still may sway the customer's decision.

Nicosia Model of buying Behavior

Step 1 - The business characteristics and the consumers characteristics

Step 2 - Search & evaluation

Step 3 - Purchase decision

Step 4 - Feedback

The Nicosia Model places emphasis on the business first and the consumer second. It argues that the company's marketing messages determine whether customers will buy. Simple, right?

While it's an attractive model because it places all the power on businesses, it's unwise to ignore the customer's internal factors that lead to a purchase decision. In other words, while you may offer the wittiest and most effective marketing copy ever, a customer's internal attributes may have more sway in some instances over others.

The model is comprised of four "fields":

1. The business' characteristics and the customer's characteristics. What does your marketing messaging look like? And what's your customer's perception of that messaging? Are they predisposed to be receptive to your message? The latter is shaped by the customer's personality traits and experiences.
2. Search and evaluation. Similar to the Howard Sheth model's "limited problem-solving" stage, the customer begins to compare different brands here based on the company's messaging.
3. Purchase decision. The purchase decision will occur after the company convinces the customer to choose them as their retailer or provider.
4. Feedback. During the feedback field, the company will determine whether it should continue using the same messaging, and the customer will decide whether they will continue to be receptive to future messages.

6. Webster and Wind Model of Organizational Buying Behavior

Webster & Wind Model of organisational buying Behavior

The are 4 variables

Variable 1 - Environmental Variables

Variable 2 - Organisation Variables

Variable 3 - Buying Center Variables

Variable 4 - individual Variables

The Webster and Wind Model is a B2B buying behavior model that argues there are four major variables that affect whether an organization makes a purchase decision. Those are:

Environmental Variables: Environmental variables refer to any external factors that could sway a purchase decision. Customer demands, supplier relationships, and competitive pressure are a few examples. Broader variables apply, too, such as technology, politics, and culture.

- Organizational Variables: Organizational variables refer to internal factors that could sway a purchase decision, such as the organization's goals and evaluation criteria.
- Buying Center Variables: Who makes the final purchase decision? Who has the authority to sign the contract, and who influences the buying process? Buying center variables take all of this into account.
- Individual Variables: These variables refer to the demographic and psychographic information of the individual prospect at the business. What's their education and level of experience? What are their goals and desires?

After taking all of those variables into account, organizations are then able to chart a predictable buyer's journey for their target customers. If you take the time to create buyer personas, you'll discover how your customers plan, or don't, to purchase your products and services. If they say a deal entices them, pay close attention to the Hawkins Stern Impulse Buying Model. If they report strong ties to their social groups, refer to the Sociological Model. Your brand is built to solve your customers pain points and its our customers who will inform your strategy and help you create tailored experiences that speak to their buyer behavior and leave them feeling satisfied after every purchase. Pay very close attention to your customers they will inform your strategy

CHAPTER TWENTY

MARKET SEGMENTATION

Segmentation is the process of identifying subsets of buyers within a market that share a similar needs and demonstrate similar buyer behavior. It divides a market into groups of customers with similar needs, behaviors or demographics. Segmentation allows companies to focus their marketing efforts on specific groups, rather than trying to reach all consumers. Segmentation can be achieved through many different methods including: demographic analysis, geographic analysis, psychographic segmentation (personality traits), psychographic segmentation (attitudes), behavioral segmentation (purchasing trends) and more!

Objectives of market Segmentation

- To understand the needs, wants, desires and buying habits of customers.
- To formulate marketing programs for each consumer group according to their nature.
- To develop new products according to the consumer's changing needs.
- To expand market & market share.
- To provide satisfaction to consumers.
- To make the marketing strategies and policies consumer oriented.

Successful market segmentation is a critical aspect of effective marketing and involves dividing a broad target market into smaller, more manageable segments that share similar characteristics and needs. To achieve successful market segmentation, several key criteria should be met:

1. Measurability: Segments should be quantifiable, meaning that you can measure the size, purchasing power, and other relevant characteristics of each segment. This allows you to assess the potential of each segment and allocate resources accordingly.
2. Accessibility: You must be able to reach and access the identified segments through marketing channels that are suitable and cost-effective. If a segment is not accessible, it's challenging to market to them effectively.
3. Substantiality: Segments should be of sufficient size to justify creating and implementing marketing strategies. Very small or niche segments dont warrant dedicated marketing efforts.
4. Homogeneity: Within each segment, individuals or entities should share similar characteristics and needs. The segment should be internally homogeneous while being distinct from other segments. This ensures that marketing messages are relevant to the segment's members.
5. Distinctiveness: Segments should be different from one another. If segments are too similar, it may not be cost-effective or practical to create separate marketing strategies for each.
6. Actionability: You should be able to develop and implement marketing strategies that effectively cater to the unique needs and preferences of each segment. If you can't take actionable steps to appeal to a segment, segmentation may not be useful.

7. Sustainability: Segmentation criteria should remain relatively stable over time. Changing demographics or behaviors may impact the sustainability of a segment. It's important to consider the long-term viability of your segmentation strategy.
8. Profitability: The segments should be financially viable. The revenue generated from each segment should exceed the costs associated with marketing and serving that segment.
9. Alignment with Business Goals: Market segments should align with your overall business goals and objectives. Segmentation should support growth and pofitability.
10. Research and Analysis: Market segmentation should be based on thorough research and data analysis. This may involve market research, surveys, data collection, and the use of analytics tools to identify and validate segments

Establish overall strategy	The brand's segmentation strategy is to use a niche-marketing approach. The brand is targeting a particular audience because they are in need of a product that can help them overcome their frustrations with traditional choices. This niche-marketing approach should be consistent with brand mission and objectives because it allows them to create an engaging experience for their target audience.
Decide the basis For segmentation	segmenting is understanding your own market characteristics—what makes up people who buy from you? What do they like? What don't they like? Once you know what makes up your customers, you can use that information to create more effective marketing campaigns.
Select segmentation variables	There are many different types of segments, including demographic and psychographic. Demographic segments include age, gender, and location; psychographic segments include personality traits, values, and beliefs.
Profile the segments	After segmenting the market, marketers have to analyze his customers in those segments. They must find out what type of customers are there in that market. It is important to know who are your target audience because if you don't know who your target audience is then how you can sell anything to them?
Evaluate segment attractiveness	Market segmentation evaluation is the process of determining whether a brand should target a specific segment of customers. This can be done by evaluating the profitability of each segment, as well as its demand potential, revenue earned from each segment, and expenditures incurred on it.
Select segment	When it comes to marketing, there are many different ways to think about segmentation. Some marketers may choose to focus on one segment at a time, while others may consider multiple segments at once.Ultimately, the best approach is to consider all the segments that you have identified and try to identify the most profitable one. This approach is called target marketing.

Market segmentation process

Successful market segmentation provides businesses with a deeper understanding of their customers, allowing them to tailor marketing strategies and offerings to meet specific needs. When done correctly, it can lead to increased customer satisfaction, higher sales, and more efficient resource allocation.

Sustainability	Segment must be large enough to warrant a special marketing mix.
Identifying measurability	Segments must be identifiable and their size must measurable
Accessability	Members of targeted segments must be reachable across multiple channels.
Responsiveness	Unless segment responds to a marketing mix differently, no separate treatment is needed.
Homogenity	Customers in one particular segment should be similar in terms of their behaviour
Profitability	There should be sufficient demand for your products and services in the segment selected which perform and give you a profitable ROI

Criteria for successful segmentation

Delving deeper into market segmentation is crucial to arrive at the right audience for several significant reasons:

1. Enhanced Relevance: Deeper segmentation enables businesses to craft marketing messages, products, and services that resonate more closely with the specific needs, preferences, and behaviors of a particular audience. This heightened relevance increases the likelihood of attracting and retaining customers.
2. Efficient Resource Allocation: By pinpointing a well-defined audience, businesses can allocate their resources more efficiently. They can focus their marketing efforts and budgets on the segments most likely to yield the highest returns, rather than spreading resources thinly across a broad market.
3. Competitive Advantage: Deeper segmentation often uncovers niche or underserved markets. By catering to these segments, businesses can gain a competitive advantage by becoming the go-to choice for a specific audience. This can lead to increased market share & loyalty.
4. Improved Product Development: A deep understanding of a segment's needs and preferences can guide product or service development. This results in offerings that align closely with what the audience desires, increasing the likelihood of successful product launches.
5. Personalized Marketing: Deeper segmentation allows for personalized marketing efforts, which are increasingly valued by consumers. Tailored messages and experiences foster a stronger emotional connection with the brand and improve conversion rates.
6. Reduced Wastage: Marketing to a broad, undifferentiated audience can lead to wastage of resources and missed opportunities. Deeper segmentation minimizes these inefficiencies by targeting the audience most likely to convert.
7. Better Customer Experience: Understanding a segment's unique characteristics enables businesses to provide a more satisfying customer experience. This includes personalized support, recommendations, and solutions that address the specific challenges or desires.
8. Effective Communication: Deeper segmentation aids in crafting more effective communication strategies. Messages can be tailored to address the specific pain points, aspirations, and language that resonate with the chosen audience.

9. Market Expansion: By mastering one segment, businesses can use that success as a foundation for expanding into adjacent segments. This strategic approach often provides a smoother pathway to growth.
10. Adaptation to Changing Markets: In dynamic markets, deeper segmentation allows businesses to stay agile and adapt quickly. They can identify shifting trends, emerging segments, and evolving customer needs and respond proactively.
11. Delving deeper into market segmentation helps businesses identify and connect with the most receptive and profitable audience. It not only improves marketing efficiency but also enhances customer satisfaction, product development, and overall competitiveness. Tailoring strategies to address the unique characteristics of specific segments can lead to long-term success and sustainable growth.

Market segmentation is the process of dividing a broad target market into smaller, more manageable segments based on shared characteristics, needs, and preferences. There are several types of market segmentation that businesses can use to refine their marketing strategies and better target their audiences. Here are some common types of market segmentation:

1. **Demographic Segmentation:** This segmentation divides the market based on demographic factors such as age, gender, income, education, occupation, marital status, and family size. *Example:* A clothing brand targeting young adults with trendy apparel based on age and fashion preferences.
2. **Geographic Segmentation:** It categorizes the market based on geographic factors, including location, region, climate, population density, and urban or rural areas. *Example:* A beverage company offering different products for warm and cold regions.
3. **Psychographic Segmentation:** Psychographic segmentation focuses on consumers' lifestyles, values, interests, attitudes, and personality traits. *Example:* A fitness brand targeting health-conscious individuals who value an active lifestyle.
4. **Behavioral Segmentation:** This segmentation divides the market based on consumer behaviors, including purchasing habits, product usage, brand loyalty, and response to marketing efforts. *Example:* An e-commerce platform offering personalized recommendations based on past purchase behavior.
5. **Benefit Segmentation:** Benefit segmentation classifies the market based on the specific benefits or solutions that consumers seek from a product or service. *Example:* A skincare brand offering products for different skin types (e.g., oily, dry, sensitive) based on the benefit desired.
6. **Occasion Segmentation:** Occasion segmentation looks at when and why consumers use a product or service. It helps tailor marketing efforts for specific events or occasions. *Example*: A chocolate brand promoting gift packaging for special occasions like Valentine's Day.
7. **Usage Rate Segmentation:** This segmentation categorizes consumers based on their usage frequency and volume of a product or service. It distinguishes between light, moderate, and heavy users. Example: A coffee brand offering loyalty rewards for frequent customers.
8. **Loyalty Status Segmentation:** Loyalty status segmentation categorizes customers based on their loyalty to a brand. It identifies loyal customers, occasional users, and non-loyal customers. Example: A hotel chain providing exclusive perks to loyal guests.
9. **Generational Segmentation:** This segmentation focuses on generational differences, such as Baby Boomers, Generation X, Millennials, and Generation Z, to tailor marketing to specific age groups. *Example:* A tech brand customizing its messaging for Gen Z's tech-savvy preferences.
10. **Cultural and Ethnic Segmentation:** cultural backgrounds, languages, customs, and traditions to target specific cultural or ethnic groups. *Example:* A food brand offering culturally relevant products for different ethnic communities.

The choice of segmentation type depends on the product, industry, and the specific goals and needs of the business. Effective segmentation allows businesses to create tailored marketing strategies.

CHAPTER TWENTY-ONE

Understand & Define your Target Audience

Target marketing is the process of identifying a group of customers at whom entire marketing efforts are directed. In target marketing, marketers identify some parts of the market, select one or more of them and develop suitable products and other elements (price, place, promotion) for each target market selected. Marketers use target marketing to direct their marketing efforts toward specific groups of buyers, who may be more likely to buy a particular product or service than others in their industry. Targeting allows companies to focus their resources on areas that will yield the best results for their business.

Target marketing differs from mass marketing in that it focuses on specific groups rather than the entire market. It also differs from niche marketing in the sense that target marketers do not target only one small segment of the market; rather, they may choose several different segments to target.

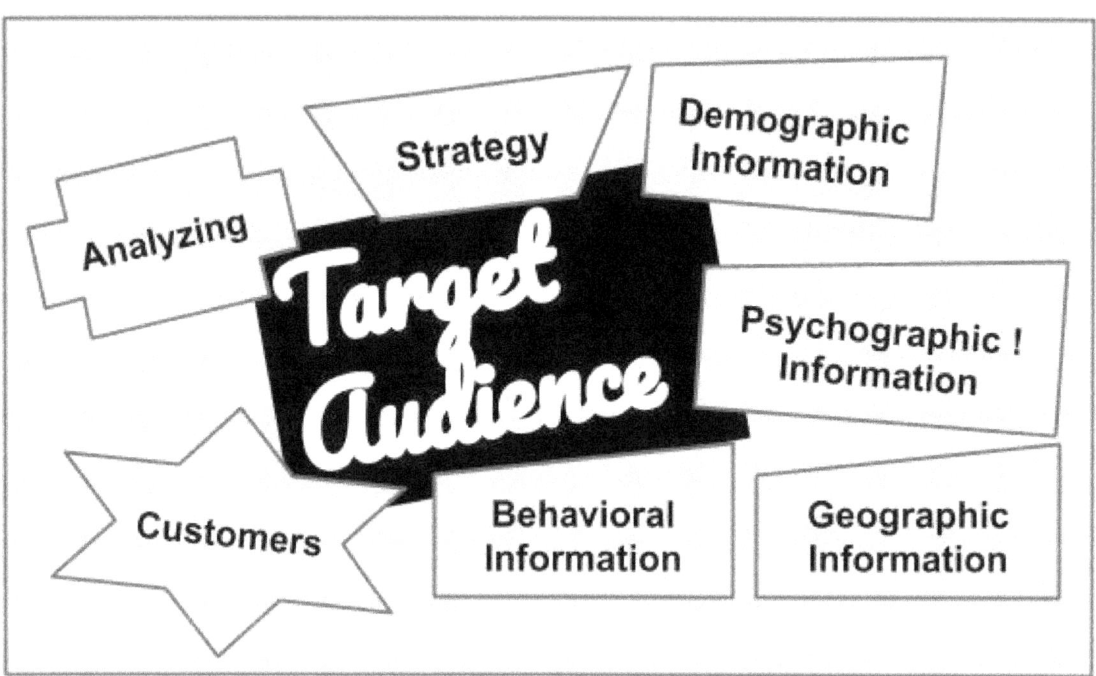

Exercise - Determine your product market fit

Selecting the right Target Market

In the total market approach, one market mix is created and directed at the entire market for a particular product. This can be advantageous because it allows for maximum exposure of a product to consumers. However, it may also result in over-saturation of the market, which can lead to decreased brand awareness.

In the concentration approach, one marketing segment is targeted through a single market mix. In this case, there are multiple segments within a total market but only one segment is targeted as the primary target market. This approach can be advantageous because it allows for focus on one segment with its needs and wants in mind rather than trying to appeal to everyone simultaneously. However, it may result in less exposure than direct marketing efforts towards multiple segments would provide.

In multi-segment approaches, two or more distinct groups within a total market are targeted through different marketing mixes or strategies suited specifically to each group's needs and wants. For example: P7 G (Toyota) targets two different groups within their total market: young adults who want an affordable vehicle that they can use while commuting back and forth from work; and families with children who need something safe and reliable that can transport them all comfortably at once without breaking down too often (which is especially important when kids are involved).

Advantages of Target Marketing

Target marketing is a strategy that helps firms to identify and reach out to specific groups of customers. It enables the firm to tap marketing opportunities better, and also offer suitable products or services to each target market. There are various advantages of target marketing such as:

1. It enables the firm to tap marketing opportunities better.
2. A firm can offer suitable product/service to each target mkt, thus they can serve better and also could develop loyal customers.
3. It can expand the market share for companies.
4. Possible to build up a company's brand image in the relevant target market.
5. Target marketing is suitable in cases of services rather than products because services are intangible goods therefore cannot be sold directly but need some kind of promotion before being purchased by consumers.

CHAPTER TWENTY-TWO

BRAND BUILDING AND ITS NUANCES

> “*"You need to change the orientation of a company so that people think of brands as assets. Then you must manage your portfolio of brand assets." - David Aaker*”

Companies need a brand guide for strategic and marketing reasons to ensure consistent and cohesive communication across all touchpoints. A brand guide serves as a comprehensive document that outlines the essential elements of a brand, including its visual identity, tone of voice, messaging, and overall personality. By providing clear guidelines on logo usage, color schemes, typography, and other design elements, a brand guide ensures that every piece of communication reflects the company's identity accurately. This consistency not only enhances brand recognition but also builds trust among consumers, as a uniform brand experience creates a sense of reliability and professionalism. From a marketing perspective, a well-defined brand guide aids in crafting targeted and effective campaigns, fostering a strong, recognizable brand presence in the competitive market. Overall, a brand guide serves as a strategic tool, aligning internal and external messaging to reinforce the brand's values and differentiate it in the minds of consumers.

A brand guide is a rulebook that describes a brand's typology, colours, logos, images, etc. This guide helps brands represent themselves, both to the general public and their target audience. All content pieces, whether they are blog posts, social media posts, corporate presentations, or business cards can be better written and designed following the guidelines mentioned in the brand guide. The brand guide is to clearly define your brand image by following the best practices in design while maintaining consistency across all media channels such as social media and websites. You can also use it as an inspiration tool for your creative team or clients.

Make your brand a force to recon with

When creating your own brand guide for your business or organization, you will want to consider the following:

1. What is your vision for your brand? What do you want it to look like?
2. Do you have a clear idea of who your target audience is?
3. Do you know what makes your company different from other companies in its industry?
4. How do you want people to perceive you? The way they think about you matters!A brand guide should contain information about:

The first part of any brand guide must focus on the brand's purpose and how it came into being. This section describes the brand timeline, the founder's mission, vision, and how the founder intends to add value to businesses through the brand story. This brand story is also an opportunity to showcase the brand's unique personality, what the brand stands for. For example, a playful brand can write its brand story in a fun, cheerful manner. In order to keep readers engaged and interested in your company or product, make sure you include an interesting story about how your company was founded and what motivated your founders to create it. You can also include information about any challenges that were encountered during the early stages of creating your product or service, so that your audience understands how far you've come since those early days. Make sure that your brand story doesn't just focus on what happened at one time in history; instead, it should be timeless—something that will resonate with future generations as well as current ones!

When you're creating a logo, it's important to make sure it's unique and memorable. This is where the brand logo comes in. A brand logo is a name, symbol, drawing, etc., that helps people recognize it and showcases the brand's unique identity. There are two types of brand logos: primary brand logos and secondary brand logos.

1. Primary Brand Logo: The primary brand logo is the most used brand logo that will be the main representation of the brand and will be used most frequently as a part of the brand's communication techniques.
2. Secondary Brand Logo: While the primary brand logo will be the main representation of the brand, the importance of the secondary brand logo cannot be ignored. The secondary brand logo is chosen when the primary brand logo cannot be used in a specific place, like on a document representing the brand. For example, the primary brand logo may be too big, and hence, the brand may use the secondary

Your brand logo is the most valuable asset you have. It is the visual representation of your brand and should be treated as such. Having a strong brand logo means that your company's image is consistent, which creates a more reputable image for you and your business. Having a consistent image across all channels will also make it easier for customers to understand what your company does and how they can interact with you. This will help them feel more connected to your brand and potentially give them reasons to choose you over other businesses in similar industries. It is important to note that there are some aspects of branding that are not controlled by your own company, like things like colour schemes, font choices and other branding elements like imagery or images used within the brand logo itself. These things should be dictated by whoever created these elements when designing them (if they aren't already).

The colour palette refers to the range of colours that the brand wishes to use in all platforms it uses to represent itself, like official documents and social media platforms. The palette is designed to make sure that the brand's identity is consistent across all platforms. In addition, it helps ensure that colours are used in a harmonious way to create a cohesive whole. A brand's colour palette should be created with a purpose in mind: the goal being to achieve visual harmony within the brand's identity. The palette should also be flexible enough so that changes can be made if necessary or wanted by future owners of the brand. So, for example, Zomato uses the colours red and white to represent itself on social media platforms, and these colours stay consistent.

There is no one-size-fits-all solution for brand typography. Brand typography refers to the visual meaning of a brand, which changes according to the font and colours selected in the brand's typography. While determining how the brand's typography should be like, the blank space, font size, and color contrast are all critical things to consider. The choice of font is an important decision because fonts can influence how people perceive a brand. Fonts can also make or break an entire design—and that's why it's so important to choose wisely. Here are some important things you need to know about choosing fonts:

1. Size matters: If you want your font size to be small enough so that only one word is visible at a time (like when reading on a mobile phone), then you need a miniscule amount of space between each letter in order for it not to look too crowded together.
2. Don't get carried away with fancy fonts: You don't have to use fancy fonts just because they're trendy or cool; there's no need for flashy typefaces unless your message needs them

There are a number of factors that go into determining the tone of your brand's voice. The first is the target audience for whom you want to speak. To determine this, you should consider their age, their location, and everything else about them that might affect how they approach your product or service.Next, think about what type of messaging would resonate with your audience. For example, if your target audience is young adults who live in California and have an affinity for artsy things, then perhaps you should consider using a more relaxed tone rather than one that is authoritative or serious. Finally, ask yourself whether a specific form of messaging would resonate with them before deciding on the tone of voice for your brand! Its crucial to understand brand imagery, it refers to a brand's aesthetic that evokes certain feelings in the target audience's minds. It focuses on ensuring that the right message is conveyed to the brand's audience and they have strong emotions like hope, optimism, reliability, etc., whenever they come across or engage with the brand. Some attributes related to brand image may include minimalism, straightforwardness, boldness, etc. A well-executed brand portfolio/communication/products will help a company depict their ideology for brand imagery. This helps the company's audience relate to the brand better because it depicts its values through its products and services. Another example is that of a fashion designer who specializes in bold designs. Their designs depict brand imagery as bold colors, bold designs, and much more. This way, a brand's portfolio/ communication/products depict their ideology for brand imagery. This helps the brand's audience relate to the brand better.

Models of brand building

Brand building is crucial because it creates a strong, recognizable, and trusted brand identity, which in turn drives customer loyalty, competitive advantage, and long-term business success. It differentiates a business from its competitors and conveys its values and promises to customers. It influences their perceptions, loyalty, and purchase decisions, ultimately driving business success. Two influential brand building models are Jean-Noel Kapferer's Brand Prism and the Brand Ladder Model:

Brand Prism by Jean-Noel Kapferer: Brand Prism is a six-sided model that examines a brand from six different angles: physique (product), personality, culture, relationship, reflection, and self-image. It delves into the emotional and psychological aspects of a brand. Example: Luxury brand Rolex is known for its physical attributes (precision watches) and is associated with the personality traits of success and achievement. It reflects a culture of excellence and creates a relationship with wearers who seek prestige. This, in turn, shapes their self-image.

Brand Ladder Model: The Brand Ladder is a model that outlines the progression of a consumer's relationship with a brand. It starts from a basic product understanding at the bottom rung and progresses to higher levels of brand loyalty and advocacy. Example: Consider a coffee brand like Nescafé. At the bottom of the ladder, consumers see it as a coffee product. As they move up, they may form associations with quality and reliability, leading to brand preference and eventually brand loyalty.

Key Differences: Brand Prism explores the emotional and psychological dimensions of a brand, while the Brand Ladder focuses on the consumer's evolving relationship with the brand. Brand Prism considers the brand's personality and the consumer's self-image, delving into brand identity and perception. The Brand Ladder primarily focuses on the consumer's journey and the levels of loyalty and advocacy they reach. Both models offer valuable insights into brand building, but they approach it from different angles. Brand Prism delves deeper into brand identity and psychology, while the Brand Ladder maps the consumer's journey towards brand loyalty.

Jean-Noel Kapferer's Brand Prism, often referred to as the brand prism model, is a comprehensive framework for brand building. It explores the various facets of a brand and its relationship with consumers. The process involves six dimensions or facets:

1. Physique: This dimension represents the tangible attributes of the brand. It includes the product itself, its design, features, and packaging. Brands focus on creating a unique and appealing physical appearance.
2. Personality: Brands, like individuals, have personalities. This dimension defines the brand's character and traits. Is the brand playful, sophisticated, rugged, or trustworthy? Defining a personality helps create a distinct identity.
3. Culture: Brands often align with cultural values and norms. Understanding and associating with a particular culture helps the brand connect with consumers who share those values. It can be a national, regional, or subcultural identity.
4. Relationship: This dimension emphasizes the brand's interaction with customers. Brands aim to build strong, lasting relationships with consumers. It includes factors like customer service, loyalty programs, and engagement.
5. Reflection: Reflection represents how the brand is perceived and what it reflects about consumers who use it. It answers questions like, "What does using this brand say about me?" The brand reflects the self-image of its users.
6. Self-Image: This dimension examines the ideal self image that the brand's target customers aspire to have. Brands can help consumers bridge the gap between their current self-image and the self-image they desire.

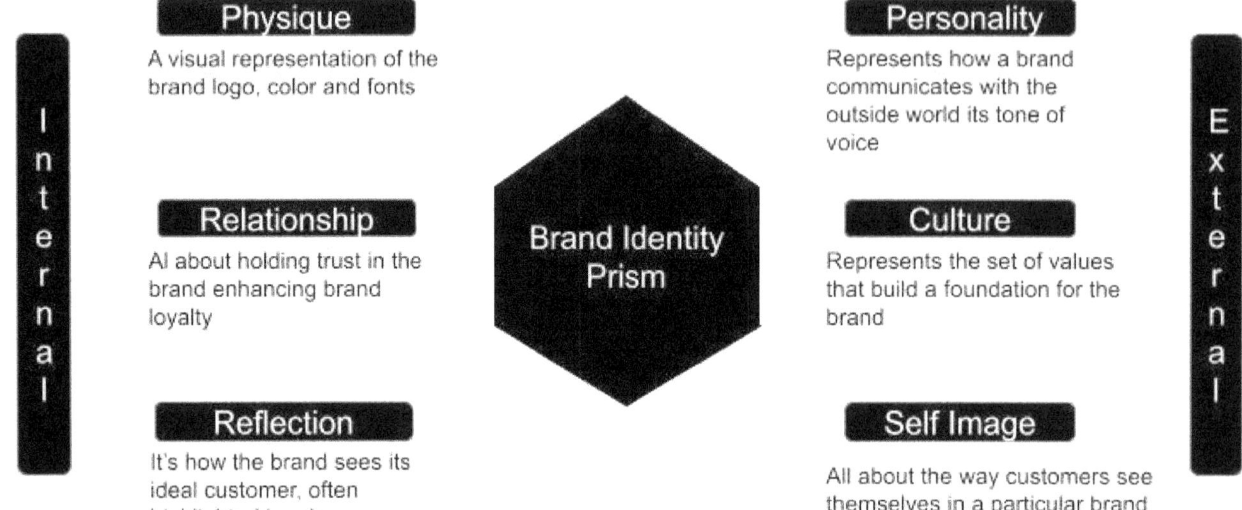

Brand prism model of bran building

This model helps brands build differentiators by allowing them to understand and define these six dimensions. By carefully crafting each facet, brands can create a unique identity that stands out in the market. It also helps brands communicate their product-market fit by aligning their brand attributes with the values and aspirations of their target audience. Example - Myntra (E-commerce Brand): a popular Indian e-commerce brand, has effectively utilized the Brand Prism model.

1. Physique: Myntra focuses on a user-friendly website and app interface, ensuring a seamless shopping experience. They also offer a wide range of products and brands, appealing to a broad audience.
2. Personality: The brand's personality is dynamic and trendy. It caters to fashion-conscious consumers, positioning itself as a hub for the latest fashion trends.
3. Culture: Myntra aligns with the culture of fast-paced, ever-changing fashion trends, especially among the youth in India.
4. Relationship: Myntra invests in strong customer relationships through personalized recommendations, loyalty programs, and prompt customer support.
5. Reflection: Myntra reflects the self-image of its customers as fashionable, trendy, and up-to-date with the latest fashion trends.
6. Self-Image: Myntra helps customers bridge the gap between their current self-image and their desired image by offering a vast selection of fashion products.

The Brand Prism model has enabled Myntra to create a unique brand identity in the competitive e-commerce space, effectively communicating its product-market fit to a fashion-conscious audience.

The Brand Ladder Model of Brand Building: is a concept of how brands and products evolve over time. The idea was developed by Professor Kevin Keller at the University of Maryland. Brand Laddering is a framework that helps marketers understand how consumers make decisions about brands and products. It also helps marketers understand what needs to be considered in the design process. Brand Laddering evolved from the concept of Laddering described above. Professor Kevin Keller defines Brand Laddering as "Brand Laddering involves progression from attributes to benefits to more abstract values or motivations. Laddering involves repeatedly asking what the implication of an attribute or benefit is for the customer." He also suggests that there is a means-end chain which takes the following structure: Attribute (descriptive features) lead to benefits (meaning attached to attributes) which leads to values (enduring personal goals and motivations).

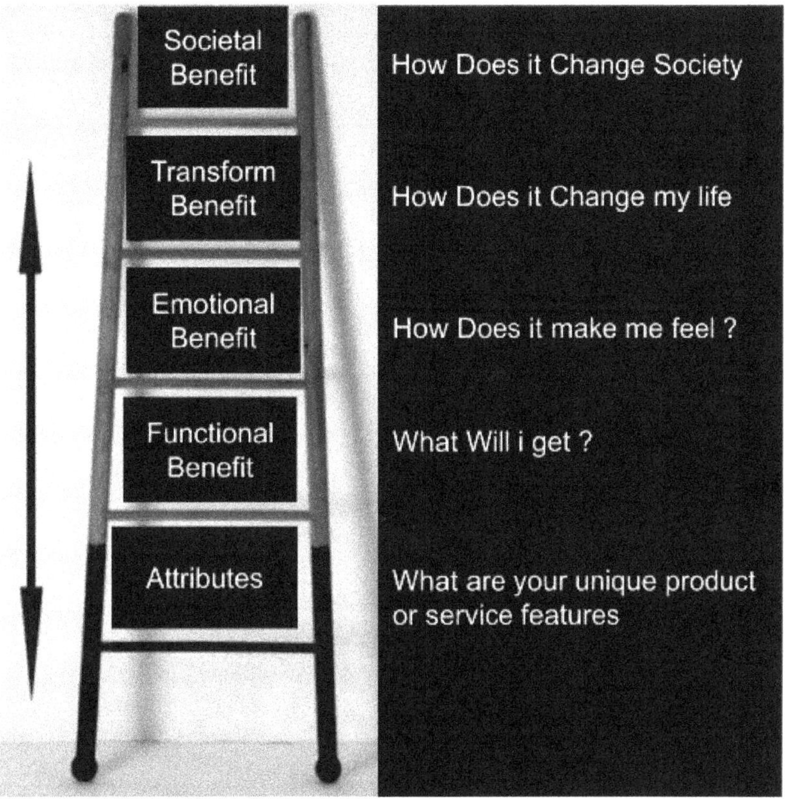

Brand Ladder Model of Brand building

Steps to define the brand ladder:

1. Step 1: Target Consumer. Use research to understand the relevant needs, values, attitudes, and behaviors that define them. Make sure you can easily empathize with this consumer as a person.
2. Step 2: Define your product/service attributes. Consider all of your offerings. Focus on those that truly stand out and provide your brand with a competitive advantage.
3. Step 3: Identify the tangible benefits that your product/service attributes deliver. Review each item listed and ask yourself "what functional benefit or advantage does this attribute provide?"
4. Step 4: transformation Ask yourself "what value do I get from that?" Narrow your list to the most compelling Consumer Benefits and highlight the ones that can truly transform your life.
5. Step 5 Now you are on the top most step. Review your Consumer Benefits from a more emotional perspective. Go deep, and ask yourself "how does this brand make me feel?" Narrow to what your brand can own.

Brand Laddering is a strategy that brands use to create a hierarchy of products, based on their perceived value and desirability. The fundamental objective of brand laddering is to create icons. Brand Laddering off late is the most sought after strategy in the Indian marketing space. Let us see a couple of examples.

1. Initially Maggi Noodles built its brand on its product qualities like 'easy to cook', 'two-minute noodles' and taste. Later the brand shifted its promotion to health platform and positioned itself as 'taste bhi, health bhi', which moves the brand from attributes to benefit positioning.
2. Johnson & Johnson is now synonymous with mother – child relationship.

3. Raymond has moved from the basic functionality of apparels to an abstract meaning of 'A complete man' and 'Feels like heaven'.
4. Nike personifies authentic athleticism.
5. Harley Davidson is synonymous with masculinity, free spirit and rebelliousness

The laddering technique is a marketing strategy that uses the association of a product with several attributes, each of which is linked to one point on the ladder. It requires a good amount of preparation for its success. Unless the brand succeeds in building its association with the functional attributes, the laddering WILL NOT come off successfully. Consumers have to climb the steps of the ladder from one stage to the other with ease. If a brand tries to ladder up without establishing its functional expertise, consumers will find it hard to believe in the brand's claim and all the work will fail. The brand should first establish it's Points of Parity (POP) in its category at par with its competitors and establish itself in terms of performance. Only then it will succeed in its laddering technique. The outcome Is a strong brand image. Below are a few definations of a brand image to help you understand the process better

"*"A unique set of associations within the minds of target customers which represent what the brand currently stands for and implies the current promise to customers" – Martin Roll*

"The uncontrolled outtake of a brand in a customer's mind based on experiences, impressions and/or assumptions" – OVO

"The current view of the customers about a brand ... a unique bundle of associations within the minds of target customers" – Management Study Guide

"A set of features and ideas that customers connect in their minds with a particular product or brand" – Cambridge Dictionary

"The perception of a brand in the minds of persons" – American Marketing Association

"The impression in the consumers' mind of a brand's total personality (real and imaginary qualities and shortcomings)" – BusinessDictionary

"A set of associations relating to things like product attributes, benefits or price, that are organized in meaningful ways." – David Aaker, per The Branding Journal

"Perceptions about a brand reflected as associations in the minds of consumers." – Kevin Lane Keller, per The Branding Journal"

CHAPTER TWENTY-THREE

TRACK YOU CUSTOMER LIFE CYCLE

The AAARRR framework, also known as the Pirate Metrics, is a model used to analyze and optimize various stages of the customer lifecycle in the context of digital marketing and business growth. It consists of the following stages:

1. Acquisition: This is the stage where you attract visitors or potential customers to your brand or platform. It involves various marketing channels, such as social media, content marketing, SEO, paid advertising, and referrals.
2. Activation: After acquiring visitors, the goal is to activate them by encouraging specific actions. Activation might include signing up for a newsletter, creating an account, or taking a free trial of a product or service.
3. Retention: Once users are activated, the focus shifts to retaining them. Retention strategies aim to keep customers engaged and coming back for more. This could involve providing valuable content, excellent customer support, or loyalty programs.
4. Revenue: Revenue generation involves turning engaged users into paying customers. It's the stage where you monetize your customer base through sales, subscriptions, or other revenue-generating actions.
5. Referral: Satisfied customers can become advocates for your brand. Encouraging referrals and word-of-mouth marketing can be a powerful way to acquire new customers through your existing customer base.

Now, let's consider an example of a brand that has effectively utilized the AAARRR framework:

The AARRR framework, also known as the Pirate Metrics, consists of five stages: Acquisition, Activation, Retention, Revenue, and Referral. It's a popular framework for analyzing and optimizing the customer lifecycle. Let's look at an example of an Indian e-commerce brand that successfully built its brand using the AARRR framework: Flipkart.

1. Acquisition: Flipkart focused on acquiring users through various channels, including digital marketing, social media advertising, and partnerships. They ran targeted campaigns, offering discounts and promotions to attract new customers. The Flipkart app was promoted heavily, encouraging users to download and install it for a more seamless shopping experience.
2. Activation: Once users signed up, Flipkart ensured a smooth onboarding process, making it easy for users to navigate the platform. They implemented personalized recommendations based on user preferences and browsing history to enhance the user experience. Activation also involved incentivizing the first purchase with exclusive discounts and offers.
3. Retention: Flipkart invested in building a robust customer support system to address queries and concerns promptly, fostering a sense of trust and reliability. They introduced loyalty programs, such as Flipkart Plus, offering benefits like free and faster shipping, early access to sales, and exclusive rewards to encourage repeat purchases. Regular communication through email newsletters and push notifications kept users engaged and informed about ongoing promotions.

4. Revenue: Flipkart implemented a variety of revenue-generating strategies, including a diverse product range, exclusive partnerships with brands, and the introduction of private labels. The platform frequently hosted sales events like "Big Billion Days," offering massive discounts to drive sales and boost revenue. They optimized the user interface to facilitate upselling and cross-selling, encouraging users to add more items to their carts.
5. Referral: Flipkart leveraged referral programs, encouraging existing users to refer friends and family by offering incentives such as discounts or loyalty points for successful referrals. Social media played a crucial role in word-of-mouth marketing, with users sharing their positive experiences and product recommendations.

By strategically implementing each stage of the AARRR framework, Flipkart successfully built a strong e-commerce brand in India. Their focus on customer acquisition, activation, retention, revenue generation, and referral programs contributed to their growth and market dominance in the Indian e-commerce landscape.

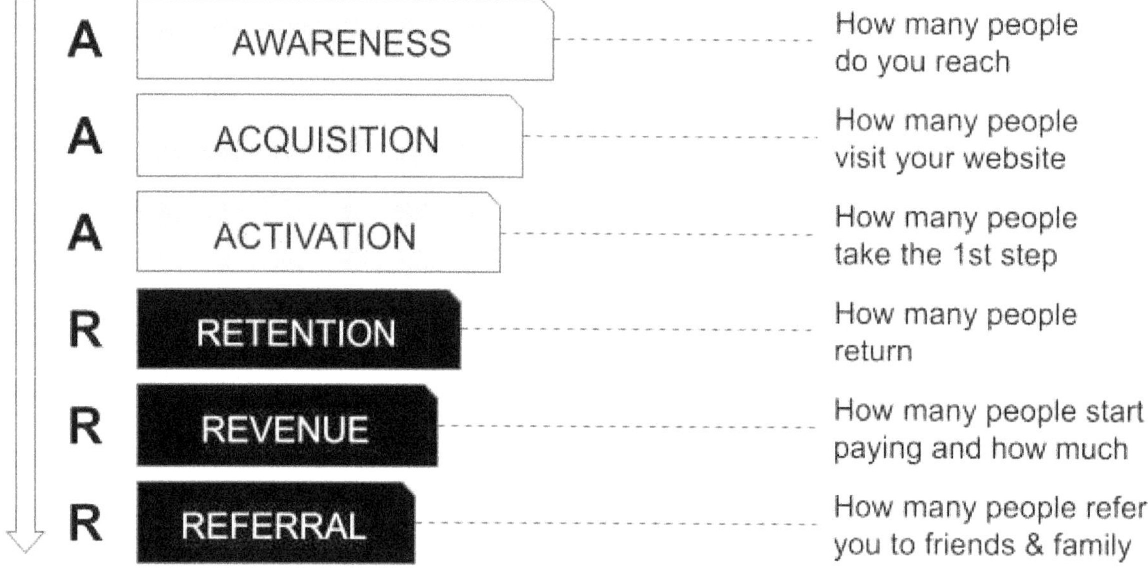

Exercise Map out your weekly, monthly, quarterly and yearly customer lifecycle

By effectively implementing the AAARRR framework, Dropbox transformed from a startup to a multi-billion-dollar cloud storage service with millions of users. Their strategy covered all aspects of the customer lifecycle, from acquisition and activation to retention, revenue generation, and referrals, making them a prime example of successful brand building using this model.

CHAPTER TWENTY-FOUR

LEAD CONVERSION JOURNEY / FUNNEL

I also want to explore the topic of acquisition in the sense of getting eyeballs to your website. Many businesses, especially those that just start out, struggle with getting traffic to their website or app. I strongly recommend utilizing The Bullseye Framework as introduced by Gabriel Weinberg, founder of DuckDuckGo and author of Traction, at this stage.

The Bullseye Framework proposes that you look at all 19 channels that can possibly drive traffic to your website or product, but after brainstorming every channel, focus on one channel and test its success for your business in a small scale version. If you see success, scale that channel. If not, move on to testing another channel. It's basically an acquisition channel testing version of the MVP process. Weinberg states that for every business at different stages of growth one singular channel will be the main traffic driver. So find that channel and tweak every part of your communication until you see explosive (or something like it) growth. If every traction channel fails, there's likely something wrong with your product/market fit. Three fundamental questions you want to be asking yourself about your acquisition:

1. What channel is driving the most traffic ?
2. What channel is driving the most valuable traffic, in other words, performs best (%) in terms of customer conversion?
3. What channel has the lowest customer acquisition cost ($), i.e. cost per customer converted?

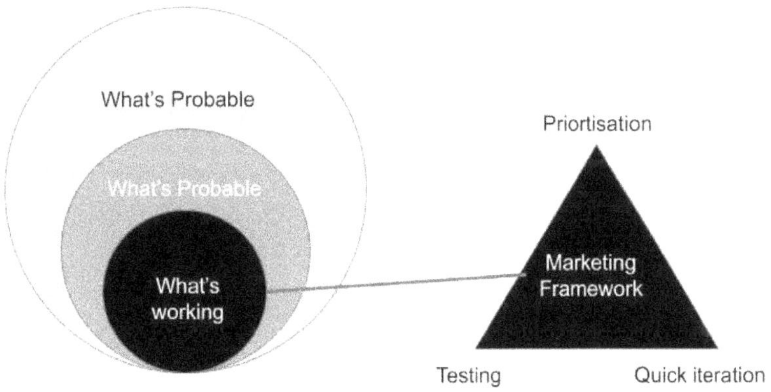

Which marketing channels to priortise ?

Activation is about the first experience your customer has with your product on. It's crucial to get your user to the "Aha Moment", which is the first time the user realizes the real value in your product. Its important the consumer realised this as quickly as possible so that he/she keeps coming back.

Activation can be split into two different parts:

1. The Purchase Journey - The steps a customer takes from finding a product to making a purchase
2. The Customer Experience (UX) - How happy customers feel after making their purchase

Many businesses fail to create an AHA moment for their users, because they underestimate how much energy it takes for consumers to understand what you are offering. In order to achieve the Aha moment, we must create a positive first experience for users. This means that we should always make sure our website or app is easy to use and intuitive. This way users will be able to find what they need without any problems and they will become familiar with your brand. The better you get to know your customer, the more valuable your product becomes. That's why it's important to test your designs and functionality with real people before launching them on the market. This way you can fine-tune everything until you reach perfection!

Retention — What's your repeat purchase rate and how to improve it?Customer retention is the most important metrics to look at when evaluating a company's marketing efforts and the success rate of their entire product range. Retention measure how many and how often do consumers come back to purchase/use your product. For an e-commerce business that means someone not only buys from you once but multiple times. For an app, that means that users keep coming back and opening / using the app. For a SaaS business, that means that people who are subscribed to your software keep using it (often) and stay subscribed. Retention is also important for new users as well as those who have been using your product for years — but it's often overlooked because it doesn't seem as obvious a metric as acquisition or conversion rates (which are easy to measure). But there are some things you can do to encourage customer retention without spending money on marketing or advertising. Make sure customers have everything they need to use your product: Your software should be ready to use out of the box so users don't have to spend time figuring out how everything works together before they can start getting value from it.

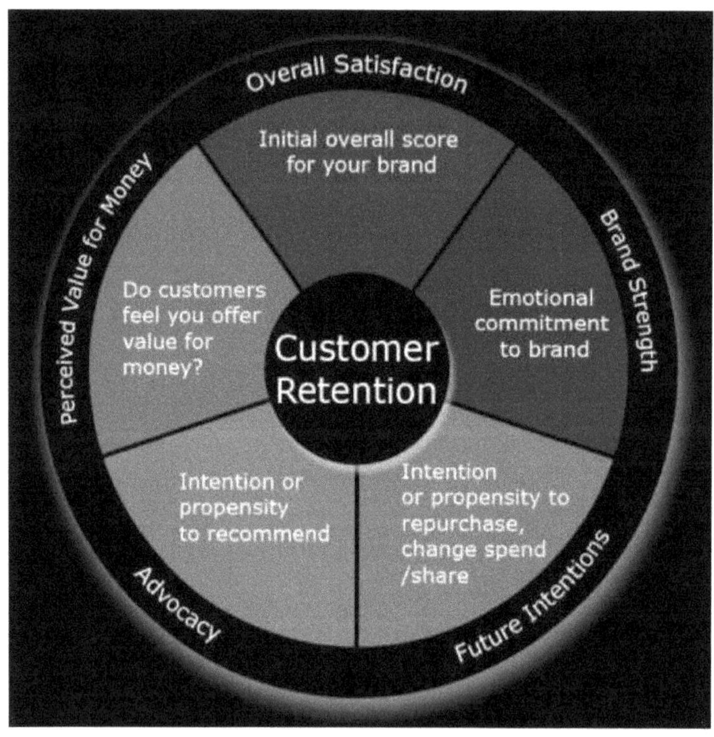

Your churn rate will tell you if you have achieved a good product/market fit. If a lot of people are dropping off your product after they start using it then clearly something might be wrong with either your product or your messaging. It's also important to know how much money you are losing from each customer and what the average lifetime value is for those customers. This can help you figure out which of your customers need new features, and what features are most valuable to them. If your churn rate is high, then it could be because:

1. Your product isn't meeting the needs of customers – this may mean that you have an incomplete product, which means that it isn't solving any problems for users or providing value. You could try adding more features or improving on existing ones until you get a better understanding of what your customers want from your product.
2. Your messaging isn't clear enough – maybe users aren't getting what they want from using the app or finding information on it confusing. Try adding more detail to the copywriting or structuring the app in a way that makes sense to users

Referral — "Turn your customers into your advocates?" The most cost effective way to drive growth is through referral. The best way to drive referrals is by having a systematic process in place that incentivizes, generates and manages them on a consistent basis. To really drive referrals you need to have a systematic process in place that incentivizes and generates them on a consistent basis. The most effective referral programs are those that reward your most valuable customers with special offers or discounts, as well as provide incentives for helping you grow your business. Dropbox figured that out early on and their referral program was one of the main drivers of their growth. Hotmail essentially built its own referral program without the user even consciously knowing by including "Get a free e-mail account with Hotmail" in every email that was sent from a Hotmail address. An important metrics you want to keep a close eye on for referrals is the Net Promoter Score (NPS), which measures how willing customers are to recommend your company's products or services. It lets you know how satisfied and loyal your customers are to the brand. The other metric is the customer satisfaction rate, or how many people who buy something from you say they were happy with their experience. This can be measured by asking customers for feedback on their experience as well as gathering data on how often they buy from you again in the future.

The Net Promoter Score (NPS) is a metric you want to keep a close eye on for referrals. It's an index that ranges from -100 to 100 and measures how willing customers are to recommend your company's products or services. It lets you know how satisfied and loyal your customers are to the brand.

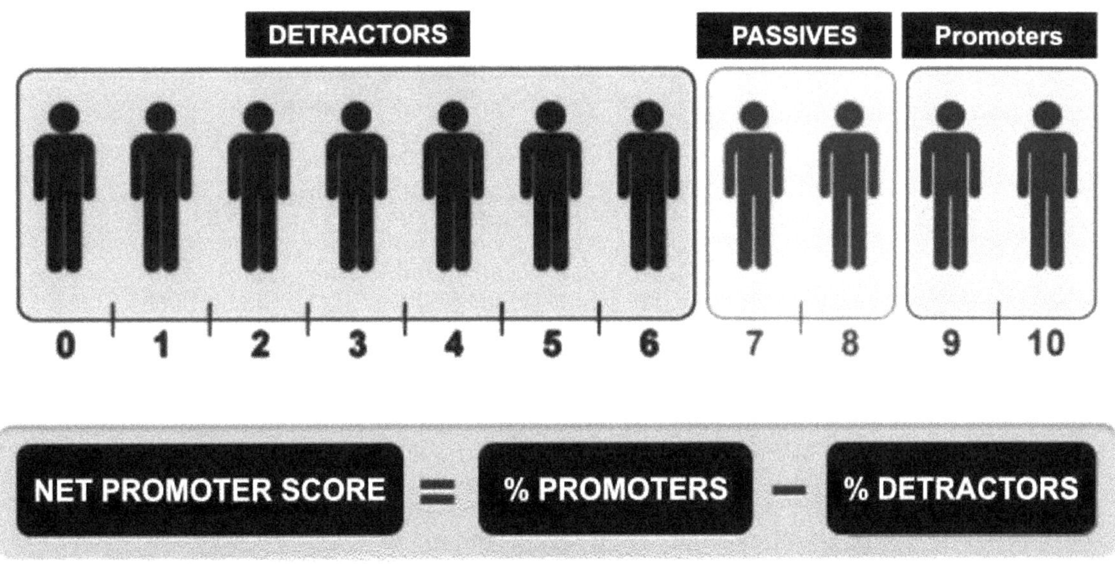

Net promoter score to track customers satisfaction

The NPS is calculated by asking respondents a series of questions about their relationship with a company, including:

1. How likely are you to recommend this company to a friend or colleague?
2. How likely are you to re-purchase from this business in the future?
3. How likely are you to tell other people about this business?

The answers to these questions form a score between -100 (unlikely) and 100 (likely), which can be broken down into three different categories:

- Promoters – These customers will definitely recommend your business and are extremely loyal to it. They are highly satisfied with your product or service and will tell others about it if asked.
- Passives – These customers won't necessarily encourage others to use your product or service, but they aren't likely to turn them away either! They may not be as happy with your product or service as Promoters but they still feel satisfied overall.

Another metric to pay attention to is the Viral Coefficient. The viral coefficient is the number of users a customer refers to you. A viral coefficient of two would mean that one customer on average refers two new customers to you. Your viral coefficient needs to be larger than one to have growth.

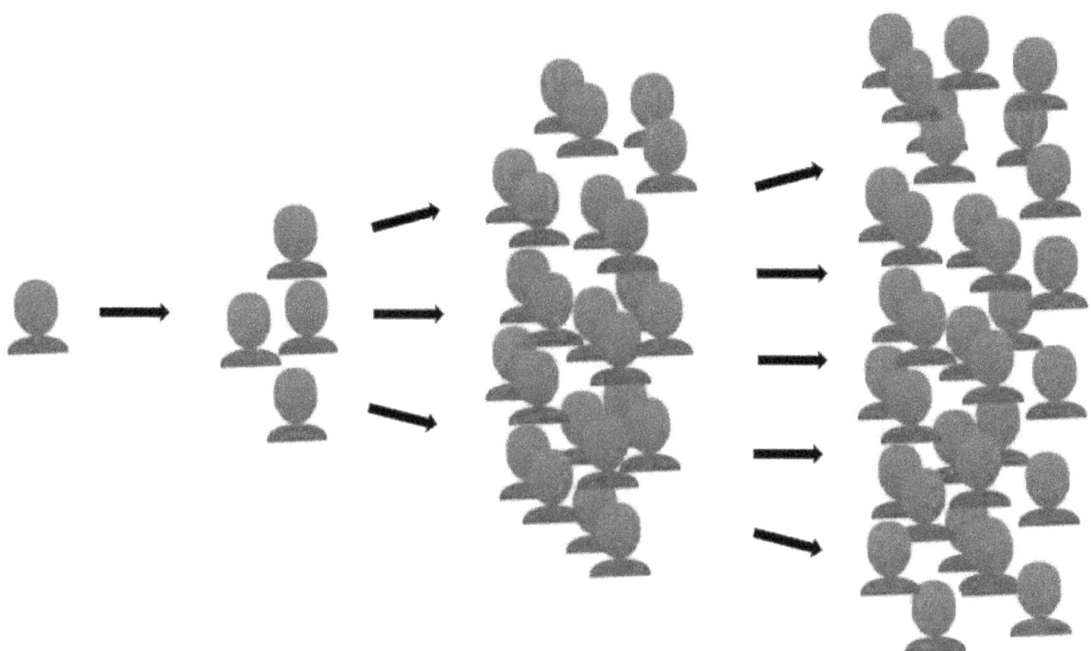

Virality - Are your customers happy enough to involve others?

CHAPTER TWENTY-FIVE

IMPROVE USER EXPERIENCE - HEART MODEL

The HEART framework is a methodology to improve the user experience (UX) . The framework helps a company evaluate any aspect of its user experience according to five user-centered metrics: Accessibility, Efficiency, Relevance, Accuracy and Trustworthiness. It was developed by Rodden developed HEART to help Google's UX design teams narrow their focus to only a few key user metrics and to quantify those metrics so they could evaluate them objectively.

HEART Model

	GOALS	SIGNALS	METRICS
HAPPINESS	Users find the platform easy to use, fun & helpful	Respond to surveys Leaving 5 star ratings Leaving user feedback	Net Promoter Score Customer satisfaction rating Number of 5 star reviews
ENGAGEMENT	Users enjoy the content and engage regularly	Spend more time on the platform	Average session length Average session frequency Number of conversions
ADOPTION	New users see the value in the product or the feature	Staying active Account signup Using a new feature	Download rate Registration Rate Feature adoption rate
RETENTION	Users come back to complete the journey	Staying active Renewing a subscription Making repeat purchases	Churn rate Subscription renewal rate
TASK SUCCESS	Users accomplish the goal with ease & quickly	Finding & viewing content quickly Completing tasks efficiently	Search exit rate Crash Rate

How do you fare in comparison to users?

The framework is based on the principles of usability engineering and is used for evaluating software products. It can be used for both web and desktop applications but not for mobile apps because there are no metrics for mobile apps yet. HEART stands for Human-centred Evaluation Of Software Technology which means that it focuses on how users will interact with your product. This way you can make sure your product serves them well and improves their experience while they use it. To use this framework, a team will identify goals, signals, and metrics for each of HEART's five categories, as the above visual shows. This Goals-Signals-Metrics framework also originated at Google, and it is very straightforward:

- Signals: Indicators that your team is making progress toward its goals. For Engagement, a sign might be "users are spending more time per session in our software."
- Metrics: Quantifiable data points indicating success or failure. For Retention, a useful metric might be "reduced churn."

There are many advantages to using HEART, such as: Valuable trends and business intelligence. Because this framework tracks and measures the same user experience from multiple angles—user happiness, retention, etc. it can help the company identify essential patterns such as how improving one metric might weaken another. The team might learn, for example, that when it focuses resources on increasing user adoption, it also lowers the product's happiness score. This information can help the team make adjustments in how it builds and markets its products.

A key reason Kerry Rodden created HEART was to help Google's UX designers focus on a handful of important areas of the user experience and tune out the rest. She saw that many designers and researchers were becoming overwhelmed with the massive amounts of raw usage data. By using this framework, a team can devote its attention and energy to just those areas of the user experience they believe will have the most significant strategic impact on the product and the company's bottom line. The data that UX and product teams will generate over time using the HEART framework can uncover valuable insights about which of these five elements most significantly and consistently lead to increased revenue. If the company sees over time that investing in boosting retention adds more to the bottom line than investing in engagement, the UX or product team will know where to places its resources on a new product if both engagement and retention rates are low. Apart from UX teams the HEART framework can also be a useful framework for product managers—specifically to help them weigh competing projects to determine which offer the most strategic value. Product teams can use HEART as a prioritization framework when they have more ideas or requests for features and enhancements than their cross-functional team can work on in a given timeframe. Not all five elements of HEART will be relevant to every feature, product, or website that a UX team wants to quantify. In some cases, the team will use only four or even three of the categories.

CHAPTER TWENTY-SIX

PERCEPTUAL MAPPING - MARKET RESEARCH

Perceptual mapping is a marketing research technique that helps businesses visualize how consumers perceive their products or brands in relation to those of their competitors. It is a valuable tool for understanding how customers make decisions about which products to buy, and for developing marketing strategies that will help a company's brand stand out from the competition. Perceptual maps are typically two-dimensional, with the axes representing two key attributes that customers use to evaluate products or brands. For example, a perceptual map for cars might have one axis representing price and the other axis representing fuel efficiency. The company's own brand would be plotted on the map, along with its competitors. By analyzing the position of its brand on the map, a company can see how it is perceived by customers relative to its competitors. This information can be used to identify opportunities to improve the company's brand image or to develop new products or services that better meet the needs of its target market. Perceptual mapping can be used to answer a variety of marketing questions, such as:

1. How do consumers perceive our brand compared to our competitors?
2. What are the key attributes that consumers use to evaluate our product or service?
3. Where are the gaps in the market where we can introduce new products or services?
4. How can we reposition our brand to better appeal to our target market?

Perceptual mapping is a valuable tool for any marketer who wants to understand how customers perceive their brand and to develop strategies that will help their brand succeed in the marketplace. Some of the benefits of using perceptual mapping:

1. It can help you understand how your customers perceive your brand and your competitors' brands.
2. It can help you identify gaps in the market where you can introduce new products or services.
3. It can help you position your brand in a way that appeals to your target market.
4. It can help you track changes in customer perception over time.
5. If you are looking for a way to improve your marketing strategy, perceptual mapping is a tool that you should consider using.

Here are some examples of how perceptual mapping can be used:

1. A company that sells luxury cars might use perceptual mapping to identify how its cars are perceived by customers relative to other luxury cars on the market. This information could be used to improve the company's marketing strategy or to develop new features for its cars.

2. A perceptual map for luxury cars might show that Mercedes-Benz is perceived as being more expensive and luxurious than BMW, while BMW is perceived as being more sporty and agile.
3. A perceptual map for coffee brands might show that Starbucks is perceived as being more expensive and high-quality than Folgers, while Folgers is perceived as being more affordable and convenient.
4. A company that sells budget-friendly cars might use perceptual mapping to identify how its cars are perceived by customers relative to other budget-friendly cars on the market. This information could be used to improve the company's marketing strategy or to develop new features for its cars.
5. A company that sells a variety of products might use perceptual mapping to identify how its products are perceived by customers relative to other products in the same market. This information could be used to improve the company's marketing strategy or to develop new products that better meet the needs of its target market.

Perceptual maps can be a valuable tool for marketers, but it is important to remember that they are just a snapshot of how consumers perceive a brand at a particular point in time. Consumer perceptions can change over time, so it is important to regularly update perceptual maps to ensure that they are still accurate.

Exercise: Perceptual Mapping for Target Market Understanding to gain insights into how our target market perceives our brand and competitors, and identify positioning opportunities.

1. Materials Needed: Whiteboard, markers, and a list of key competitors.
2. Instructions:

    - Introduction: Explain the purpose of the exercise: to visualize how our target market perceives our brand and competitors in relation to key attributes.
    - Attributes Selection: Identify key attributes or factors that are essential to your product or industry. These could be quality, price, convenience, reliability, etc. Write these attributes on the whiteboard.
    - Competitor Listing: List your brand and key competitors on the whiteboard. Place them along a horizontal axis (X-axis).
    - Scoring: Distribute a set of scorecards to participants. Each participant should rate each brand (including yours) on a scale for each attribute. For example, a scale from 1 (low) to 5 (high) for each attribute.
    - Data Collection:Ask participants to independently score each brand for each attribute.Collect and tabulate the scores for each brand.
    - Plotting the Map: Use the collected data to plot each brand's position on the perceptual map. Each brand will have coordinates on the map, showing their perceived strengths and weaknesses in relation to the chosen attributes.
    - Group Discussion: Lead a discussion based on the plotted map: What does the map reveal about how our target market perceives our brand and competitors? Are there any gaps or opportunities for differentiation? What can we learn about our competitive positioning?
    - Action Planning: brainstorm strategies to strengthen our brand's position in the target market. Identify areas to enhance strengths or address weaknesses.
    - Follow-up: Assign responsibilities for implementing the strategies discussed during the exercise. Set a timeline for periodic reviews to track changes in perception.

This exercise allows brand owners to visually understand how their brand is positioned in the minds of their target market compared to competitors. It provides actionable insights for improving brand positioning and competitive strategies.

CHAPTER TWENTY-SEVEN

Differentiation Strategy POP Vs POD

The first step in creating a brand's/product's positioning is to decide what the brand/product is trying to do. This means identifying the target audience, defining their needs and wants, understanding how they live their lives, and what they value in life. Once you have a clear understanding of your target audience and their needs and wants, you can create a brand/product positioning that matches your target audience. The best way to do this is by looking at other brands in the category for both points-of-parity (POP) and points-of-difference (POD).

	SNICKERS		KitKat
Points of Differentiation	• Positioned as a food that satiates hunger • Not too expensive • Targeted towards hetrosexual males • Many ingredients • Associated with athletics and intensive activities	• Promotes healthy lifestyle • Offers wide range of chocolate products • Priced higher than competitors	• Targets men & women of all ages • Low Prices • Nestle offers other confectionery products
Points of Parity	World renowned brands Advertising Platforms		Most Recalled chocolate brands Innovative product categories

In order to be successful, brands must have both sufficient POP and POD.

This is because consumers are willing to pay more for brands that have products or services that are considered equal, but also different from other brands in the marketplace. The reason for this is because consumers feel like they are getting something special and unique when purchasing a product. For example: if I want to buy a new car, I want it to be better than the other cars out there. If I were able to compare my car with another car while driving it around town, then I would know whether or not my car is truly better than all others on the market. On the other hand, consumers will not pay more for products/services that are considered similar in most categories of products/services. For example: if I wanted to buy a new computer, I would probably not pay more than $500 for one that was similar to an existing model (i.e., Apple Computers). In addition, if I were able to compare my computer with another one while using it on a daily basis at home or at work, then I would know whether or not my computer was truly better than all others on the market. The concept of point of parity is based on the idea that customers have a choice. If you are going to sell your product, you have to be able to make it competitive with your competitors. The key to competing successfully is in understanding what motivates your customers, how they perceive your product and how much they are willing to pay for it.

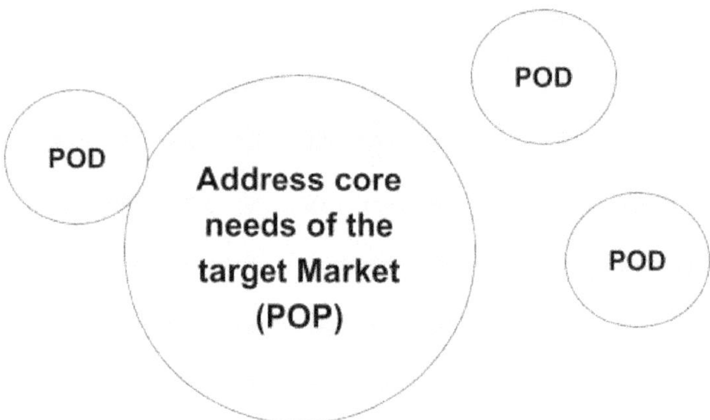

Establishing a relatable connection with your target audience is of paramount importance.

Points-of-parity (POPs) – POP associations that are not necessarily unique to the brand but may be shared by other brands i.e. where you can at least match the competitors claimed best. Point of parity is a business strategy that focuses on creating a point where your business is the same as your competitors to be a buying consideration for your customers. For example, if you sell a product that is the same as another company's products, then you have a point of parity. Points-of-difference (PODs) – POD attributes or benefits consumers strongly associate with a brand, positively evaluate and believe they could not find to the same extent with a competing brand i.e. points where you are claiming superiority or exclusiveness over other products in the category. Point of difference refers to the factors of products or services that establish differentiation. Differentiation is the way in which the goods or services of a company differ from its competitors. Indicators of the point of difference's success would be increased customer benefit and brand loyalty. However, an excessive degree of differentiation could cause the goods or services to lose their standard within a given industry, leading to a subsequent loss of consumers. Hence, a balance of differentiation and association is required, and a point of parity has to be adopted in order to allow a business to remain or further enhance its competitiveness. The point of equilibrium between differentiation and association is called the point of parity. It is defined as the point where all products are priced at their marginal cost. In other words, it is the level at which each product has a similar price to other products in its category or subcategory.

Significance of Points of Parity = Standing out from the competitors

As a marketing expert, it's vital to understand that Point of Parities (POPs) serve as your shield against competitors' strengths, while your Point of Differences (PODs) act as your unique advantages. To ensure your brand's success, it's crucial to first assess whether your brand might be lacking in POPs within your core positioning. Without well-defined and effectively communicated POPs, your PODs, no matter how exceptional they are, lose their significance within your category. In essence, without strong POPs, your brand's distinctiveness can't shine through, even if it leads the way in your industry. Sumarrysing Point of Difference (POD) vs. Point of Parity (POP)

1. Points of difference (PODs) are attributes or benefits strongly associated with a brand, which consumers positively evaluate and believe are not readily available with competing brands. Think of Coca-Cola's secret recipe

as a POD that sets it apart from other cola brands.

2. On the other hand, points of parity (POPs) are associations that are not unique to a brand but may be shared by other brands in the same category. An example would be the presence of caffeine in soft drinks, which is a POP shared by many brands.
3. While POPs may not be the sole reason to choose a brand, their absence can be a reason to avoid it. It's important to establish a strong POD, but equally important to match competitors on POPs to remain competitive.

"As a late entrant into the market, many brands look at making the competitor's POD into a POP for the category and thereby create a leadership position by introducing a new POD."

The three types of difference are:

1. **Brand performance associations:** These are associations that are created by a customer's experience with a brand, product or service.
2. **Brand imagery associations**: These are the mental images customers have of your brand and its offerings.
3. **Consumer insight associations:** This is what customers know about your brand and how it relates to their lives and their lives outside of work (e.g., family).

The last only comes into play when the others are at parity. Insight alone is a weak point of difference, easily copied. Putting these together, check their desirability, deliverability and eliminate contradictions. Desirable characteristics include being new, novel and different from competitors' products or services. They must be consistent with the brand's mission and values as well as its positioning strategy. They should also be consistent with what consumers expect from brands in the category based on their experience with similar brands in their category. In such cases Brand ambassadors are the most valuable form of brand connect because they have built a relationship with the target audience, which allows them to be more effective than other forms. Brand ambassadors have a deep understanding of your product and are able to explain it in an understandable way.A brand ambassador is someone who is passionate about your brand and wants to promote it to others. They can be influencers or social media personalities, or they could simply be customers who love the product and want others to know about it as well.The key to having a successful campaign with a brand ambassador is finding someone who is willing to promote your product on their own terms. If a brand ambassador has their own audience, they will be more likely to promote your product if they feel like it's something that's in line with their interests and passions.

The Significance of Points of Parity (POPs) in Marketing

Points of Parity (POPs) play a crucial role in marketing strategy, as they enable businesses to stand out from their competitors. Here's why they are so important, along with some examples:

1. **Differentiation and Competitive Advantage** When a business differentiates itself from competitors, it can potentially increase its revenue. Differentiation limits consumers' choices, leading them to choose a specific company's products or services. For instance, consider Apple's ecosystem of products, where seamless integration between devices sets it apart from competitors. This differentiation strategy makes it more competitive and boosts its income.
2. **Effects on Brand Loyalty** By narrowing consumers' choices through differentiation, businesses can cultivate brand loyalty. When consumers have fewer alternatives, they are more likely to develop strong relationships with a particular brand. Take Starbucks, for instance, which has created a unique coffee culture and customer experience that fosters brand loyalty and sets it apart in the coffee industry.

Balancing Differentiation and Standardization Excessive differentiation may lead to products losing their standard, while a lack of differentiation won't benefit businesses either. Striking a balance between point of difference and point of parity is critical for success. Businesses can look at the positive features of a competitor's product (POP) and enhance them to achieve differentiation (POD).For example, Samsung's Galaxy smartphones often match Apple's iPhone (POP), but they introduce innovative features (POD), like the S Pen, to distinguish themselves in the highly competitive smartphone market.Understanding and leveraging both POPs and PODs is essential for brand success. It's not just about being different from competitors but also meeting consumers' expectations within the frame of reference in which the brand operates. By finding the right balance, brands can create a compelling and unique value proposition that sets them apart and fosters brand loyalty. Run an exercise to understand the concept better:

1. The first question is, "Have we established a frame?"A frame of reference signals to consumers the goal they can expect to achieve by using a brand. A frame helps consumers make sense of your product's attributes and benefits; it provides a context for understanding what your product does. A well-formed frame should also be consistent with your brand's personality (e.g., fun, reliable) and positioning (e.g., premium).
2. The second question is, "Are we leveraging our points of parity?"Certain points of parity must be met if consumers are to perceive your product as a legitimate player within its frame of reference. Points of parity are those qualities that are shared by other brands in the same market; they're the things that give customers confidence in the idea that you're offering something that works just like everyone else's does. They're what make a difference for people who want something better than what they've got but don't know how to get it.
3. The third question is, "Are the points of difference compelling?"A distinguishing characteristic that consumers find both relevant and believable can become a strong, favourable, unique brand association capable of distinguishing.

Situation	What to emphasise
When the firm is a me too competitor	In this case being a weaker competitor, the goal is to piggy back on the success of the market leader by highlighting many points of parity
When the firm is a market leader	This is the reverse of the situation from the above. To maintain market leadership the brand needs to be viewed as superior. Thus highlighting the need to focus on relevant points of difference.
When the firm enters an established and mature market	In this case the likelihood of switching is relatively lower, so points of difference are required to break the habitual loyalty
When the firm is in a fast growing market	Fast growing markets have primary demand (1st time customers) Therefor points of parity positioning will be quite successful in capturing new customers.
When there is diversity of needs, even when looking at fairly narrow market segment	When there is a significant diversity of consumer needs a points of difference positioning should ensure that reasonable market share is generated
In a target market where the firm already offers multiple products	To reduce the risk of cannibalization of sales, the firm would need to have more emphasis on points of differentiation
In a relatively price sensitive market	The goal in this scenario would be to provide additional benefits, in order to reduce the importance of price in the decision. Therefore points of difference positioning emphasis would be required.

To quote Master Shifu once again "The true path to victory is to find your opponent's weakness and make him suffer for it. And to take his strength and use it against him until he finally falls or quits"

CHAPTER TWENTY-EIGHT

PRODUCT POSITIONING STRATEGY

Product positioning is the act of creating an image about the brand, product or service in the minds of the customers. It is a marketing technique that involves determining how to position a product in the market so that it differs from competitors' products, and what attributes are important for consumers to perceive about your product relative to its competition. Product positioning attempts to differentiate a product from its competitors by creating an image in the minds of consumers that makes them view your product as superior. The only product positioning that counts is what your customers' think. If a customer isn't thinking about it, your product doesn't occupy that position. "

Create a differentiation strategy. If you want to create a successful product, you need to know what it's going to be before you start. When creating a new product, it's easy to rush through the process without taking the time to consider how your finished product should be perceived by its customers. Without an ideal product positioning statement, you won't know where you want your product position to be at the end of development.

"*" Product positioning strategy is what gets your product position from point A to point Z "*"

If you don't know what you want your customer to believe about your product, how are you going to communicate with them? How are you going to create coherent marketing communications plans? Before you even begin the product development process, start with an ideal product positioning statement. Then you now know where you want your product position to be at the end of development.The positioning statement is the core of your marketing strategy, and it's what you use to guide your product development, messaging, and customer acquisition..

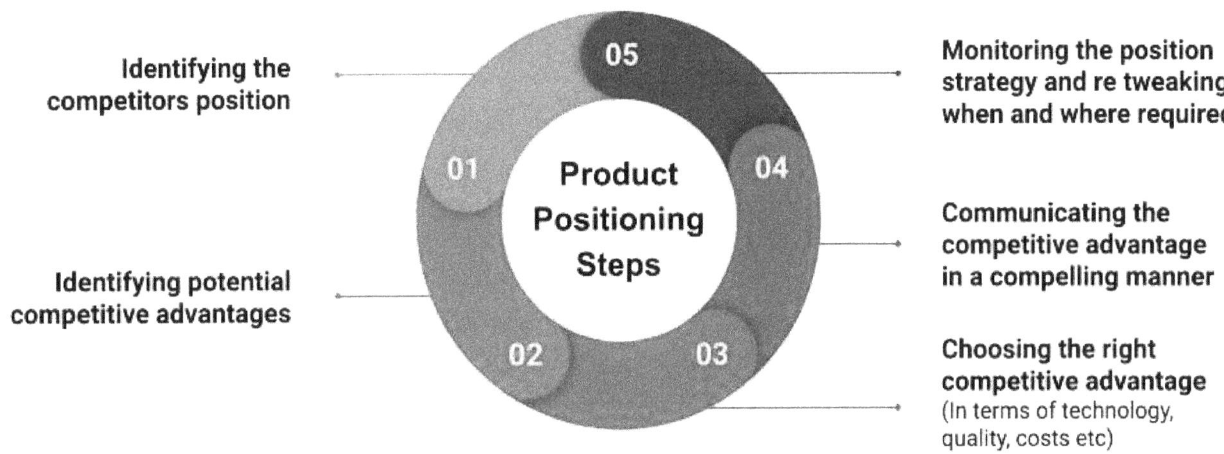

But before you begin with your product you must know what other competitors in your space are doing

Once you have all the relevant information break down the positioning statement into its component parts. In this case, you want to know if: The customer understands the difference between your product and the competition. If they don't understand what makes your product different from the competition, they won't be able to tell others why they should buy it. The customer understands the benefits of buying this product over other products on the market. If they don't understand how this product will make their lives easier or better than others in its category, then they won't be as likely to buy it as one of their first choices. Break down each part of this positioning statement to arrive at your position statement:

- "We make [product] easier for [customer type]."
- "We use [technology] to make [product] better."
- "You'll want this if you want [benefit]."

You need to reiterate and convey your positioning statement over and over again to your existing customer and convey "we are aware you like our stuff, but here's more of what you WILL love!". Now comes the tricky part of addressing a new customer. You have no information on them yet. Which makes it important to make a very compelling statement and convey to the customer that they need to hear you out "Why this product will be good for them specifically and why they should trust us as a brand." Thus creating a latch on effect.

Address multi needs with one product

Segmentation is a technique used to help a product stand out by focusing on multiple audiences with different needs, but with the same product. When you market a product to multiple segments, each segment will have its own unique needs that must be addressed in order to make the product successful These segments can be defined by geography (geographic segmentation), demographics (demographic segmentation), psychographics (psychographic segmentation), or behavioral characteristics (behavioral segmentation).

1. Differentiation: The uniqueness of a product can't be duplicated, making it ideal for a differentiation strategy.Companies that offer unique products often use this strategy to differentiate themselves from the competition. For example, the iPhone is known for its sleek design and ease of use. It is a unique product that cannot be easily copied by other companies. This allows Apple to maintain its position as a market leader.
2. Liverage video : Video content is a great way to show potential customers what makes your company different from the competition and why they should choose you over them. When you're on mobile, it's especially important to focus on the unique features of your business and how they can help your clients. If you want to create differentiation, leverage videos on mobile platforms by telling potential customers what makes your business unique and how your product or service can help them.
3. Comparative: Comparative positioning strategies work by placing products right next to other brands to highlight their competitive edge. This strategy is most effective when the product being compared is similar or identical to the one being promoted, but it can also be used with dissimilar products if they are meant for the same audience.

Incentivise consumers : Brands that don't want to compete on discounting incentivise customers at multiple touch points even if they don't purchase. The stand is because they have enough data to know customers are willing to pay more for products and services of higher quality, and the incentivisation via a rewards program is just one way to keep consumers engaged. Rewards points are a way to provide value without cutting prices. It's one way for brands to give customers something extra, and they appreciate it—in fact, a recent survey showed that consumers perceive rewards points as having a higher value because they have earned them by purchasing products. These are just a few of the many ways to position your brand. The best way to position your brand will depend on your specific target market and your unique selling proposition.

Here are some examples of how well-known brands use these techniques:

1. Comparative positioning: Nike often compares its shoes to those of its competitors, such as Adidas, in terms of comfort, durability, and performance.
2. Differentiation positioning: Apple positions itself as a premium brand that offers innovative products with a sleek design.
3. Segmentation positioning: Dove targets women with its beauty products by focusing on the message that all women are beautiful, regardless of their body type or skin color.

By using one or more of these techniques, you can help your brand stand out from the competition and appeal to your target market. Below are some additional tips for developing a successful brand positioning strategy:

Do your research: Before you can develop a successful brand positioning strategy, you need to understand your target market and what they are looking for in a product or service. Be clear and concise: Your brand positioning statement should be clear and concise. It should be easy for consumers to understand what your brand stands for. Be consistent: Your brand positioning statement should be consistent across all of your marketing materials. This will help to create a strong and memorable brand identity. Be flexible: Your brand positioning strategy may need to change over time as your business grows and evolves. Be prepared to adapt your strategy as needed. By following these tips, you can develop a successful brand positioning strategy that will help you to stand out from your competitors and attract new customers.

CHAPTER TWENTY-NINE

5 TYPES OF POSITIONING STRATEGIES

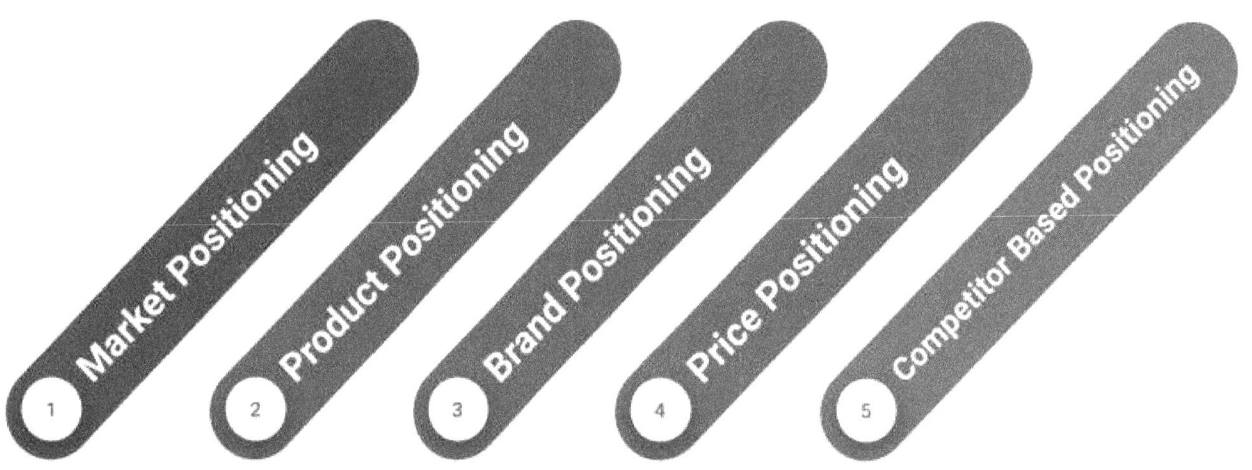

Market positioning strategy when aligned with the business strategy is lethal

Developing a market positioning strategy is a critical to a company's business strategy. The strategy will determine how prospective customers view your brand or product. Successful brands like Gucci, Rituals, rolls royce etc have made market positioning an integral part of their business strategy and have established themselves as a luxury status symbols delivering exquisite high quality product at high prices. Market positioning involves actively establishing brand identity. To develop an effective positioning strategy, you must have a clear idea of what you want to sell. If you have many competing products on your shelves, the strategy will help you determine which niche you should own. This can be accomplished by identifying your target audience and then comparing your product to others in order to gain an advantage over competitors. You want prospective customers to perceive that your brand has special value or benefits that cannot be found elsewhere.

1. Product Positioning
2. Brand Positioning
3. Price Positioning
4. Competitor-based Positioning
5. Developing your product positioning statement

To develop your product positioning statement, you need to answer the following questions:

1. Who is your target customer? What are their needs and wants? What are their pain points?
2. What does your product do? What are its features and benefits? How does it solve your target customer's problems?
3. How is your product different from the competition? What makes it unique? What value does it offer that other products don't?
4. Why should customers choose your product over the competition? What are the reasons why your product is the best choice for your target customer?

Once you have answered these questions, you can start to develop your product positioning statement. A good positioning statement is clear, concise, and persuasive. It should be able to quickly and easily communicate the value of your product to your target customer. Here is an example of a product positioning statement: *you can use this as an exercise for your product* For [target customer], [product name] is the [product category] that [solves problem or meets need] by [unique feature or benefit]. For example, a product positioning statement for a new smartphone might be: For busy professionals, the new iPhone 14 Pro is the smartphone that gets things done by offering the fastest processor, the best camera, and the longest battery life. A product positioning statement is a powerful tool that can help you to market and sell your product more effectively. By taking the time to develop a strong positioning statement, you can ensure that your product is seen as the best choice for your target customer. Here are some additional tips for developing a product positioning statement:

1. Keep it short and simple. The best positioning statements are no more than a few sentences long.
2. Be specific. Don't just say that your product is "the best." Explain why it's the best and how it benefits your target customer.
3. Be memorable. Your positioning statement should be memorable and easy to understand.
4. Be relevant. Your positioning statement should be relevant to your target customer's needs and wants.

By following these tips, you can develop a product positioning statement that will help you to market and sell your product more effectively.

CHAPTER THIRTY

PRODUCT MANAGEMENT STRATEGY

The Significance of Product SKUs in E-commerce - Product SKUs, also known as "product variants" or "product editions," serve as the foundational elements of a product listing on an e-commerce platform. The terminology used may vary depending on location and industry-specific norms. For instance, some retailers refer to them as "color options" when describing the different shades available to customers when purchasing a product. As a product manager and strategist, it is essential to approach product management from three distinct levels: core, attractive, and indifferent.

1. Core Level: At the core level, we focus on the fundamental benefits that a product offers to consumers. These are products with a substantial market size and high demand.
2. Attractive Level: The attractive level encompasses additional benefits added to differentiate the product and emphasize its Unique Selling Proposition (USP). These extra features or attributes make the product more appealing and distinctive.
3. Indifferent Level: Products at this level may lack differentiating features and are often perceived as commodities within the market. They may not possess unique qualities or benefits that set them apart.

As an e-commerce and product stake holder, understanding the role of product SKUs is crucial for effectively presenting and marketing products at both the core and attractive levels. Through well-crafted SKUs, product managers can emphasize the unique attributes that distinguish their products, making them more appealing to customers in a highly competitive marketplace. When defining your product management strategy for e-commerce, it is essential to consider the significance of product SKUs as they play a pivotal role in how products are perceived and chosen by consumers. Additionally, it's important to set a clear product management strategy that aligns with business goals, caters to a customer-centric approach, offers a competitive advantage, fosters innovation, guides targeted marketing efforts, shapes pricing strategies, manages inventory efficiently, and ensures a seamless product lifecycle management. This comprehensive strategy is fundamental for e-commerce brands to succeed in a dynamic and competitive online retail landscape. let's take the example of "Flipkart," one of India's leading e-commerce brands, to understand their product management strategy.

Flipkart's Product Management Strategy:

1. Customer-Centric Approach: Flipkart places a strong emphasis on understanding its customers' needs and preferences. They use data analytics to track user behavior and gather insights, enabling them to tailor product offerings to specific customer segments.
2. Market Expansion: Flipkart has consistently expanded its product range to meet evolving market demands. They have ventured into various categories, including electronics, fashion, home goods, and more, ensuring a diverse and extensive product catalog.

3. Exclusive Partnerships: Flipkart has forged exclusive partnerships with brands and sellers to offer unique products to its customers. This strategy helps them differentiate their product offerings from competitors.
4. Private Labels:Flipkart has introduced private label brands in categories such as electronics and fashion. These labels offer quality products at competitive prices, giving Flipkart more control over product quality and pricing.
5. User Experience Enhancement: The company focuses on enhancing the user experience through a user-friendly interface, personalized recommendations, and seamless checkouts. They continually iterate on their platform to improve the overall customer experience.
6. Pricing Strategy: Flipkart employs dynamic pricing strategies, including discounts, flash sales, and special promotions. They strategically price products to attract budget-conscious shoppers while maintaining profitability.
7. Inventory Management: Efficient inventory management ensures that Flipkart minimizes overstocking and understocking issues, leading to cost savings and the ability to meet customer demands promptly.
8. Data-Driven Decision-Making: Flipkart relies on data and analytics for decision-making. They use this data to optimize product listings, pricing, and inventory management, and to identify emerging market trends.
9. Continuous Innovation: Flipkart is known for its innovative approaches, such as launching the "Flipkart Plus" loyalty program and experimenting with augmented reality (AR) shopping experiences to stay ahead in the e-commerce game.
10. Scalability: The company's product management strategy is designed for scalability, allowing them to add new categories, products, and services to cater to a broader customer base.
11. Sustainable Practices: Flipkart has introduced eco-friendly packaging and promotes sustainable products to align with changing consumer preferences and environmental concerns.
12. Competitive Advantage: Flipkart differentiates itself through its customer service, reliable delivery network, and a wide range of payment options, providing a competitive edge in the e-commerce market.

Flipkart's product management strategy revolves around offering a wide array of products, enhancing the customer experience, and staying adaptable to market changes. It is a prime example of a successful e-commerce brand that has used a robust product management strategy to achieve and maintain its market leadership in India.

CHAPTER THIRTY-ONE

Customer Care - An Important Differentiator

This stat is sobering, but not surprising: "After one negative experience, 91% of customers will never do business with that company again," according to a research. And the stat isn't really sobering, especially in this day and age, when one bad customer experience can spread on social media like wildfire and wreak havoc for your brand. It's easy to see why this is a problem: while you may have built up a loyal base of customers who love everything about your brand, it's unlikely that they're willing to put themselves out there by singing your praises on social media if they've had a bad experience. What's more, those who don't have a strong opinion either way aren't likely to share their experiences with others unless they're overwhelmingly positive—which means that if even just one person has had a negative experience with your company in recent memory (or ever), it could take years for anyone else to try it out for themselves!

The world has changed. The customer journey is no longer linear, with predictable steps. Today's customers come to you from all over the place, and they expect a more personalised experience than ever before. AI and bots are two tools that can help you deliver that experience, but only if you know how to use them effectively. One of the most important aspects of your customer engagement model is knowing what context you need to pull in from your association with your customers. This will allow you to deliver a more personalised experience by delivering content that is relevant to their current situation and needs.

The expansion of direct-to-consumer (D2C) businesses has been one of the most significant trends over the last decade. This tactic enables businesses to sell their products directly to consumers rather than through retailers. Thanks to the internet and social media, connecting with customers directly without depending on brick and mortar businesses is now easier than ever. This trend will undoubtedly become more pronounced in the future years. As consumers get increasingly comfortable making purchases from brands, direct-to-consumer (D2C) businesses are becoming more sophisticated in their marketing and business practices. As a result of this trend, there are many things that need to be considered when starting a D2C business: how do you build trust with your customers? How do you encourage them to buy from you instead of another brand? How do you provide excellent customer service? And how can your business stand out from all of the other ones out there trying to sell similar products?

Hacks to scale D2C revenue through customer care.If you're a D2C business, you know the importance of good customer service. By managing your brand consistently and offering support across all channels, customer communication management enables you to more successfully address the problems that your users are experiencing. This is particularly important in an age when customers are increasingly turning to social media to voice their concerns. The result? A more positive brand image and improved customer retention rates. Customer communication management strengthens customer relationships by enhancing your overall communication strategy to increase customer acquisition and customer retention.

Committed customer care managers

As a business owner, you want to see your customers succeed. You want them to be happy with their purchase and experience the intended effects of your product or service. But how do you measure success? How do you know if your customers are satisfied? Are you sure that they are experiencing the effects you intended them to experience? How can you make sure that they don't need more support than what's already been provided? Customer success does not aim to increase sales. Instead, it focuses on helping customers experience your product's or service's intended effects. The growing significance of customer success led to the creation of the new position of customer service managers (CSM), who is in charge of enhancing the customer experience within their organizations. A CSM and a sales manager are frequently confused with one another. However, that is false. In an ideal world, a CSM would help clients transition from the sales stage into the support stage. Instead of serving as a customer support representative, a CSM's role is to build strong relationships with clients and provide timely value propositions. Integrated IVR Solutions - At an early stage dont waste your time and money here.

1. Chat Bot If you want to build a successful business, you need to start building relationships with your customers. And if you want to build relationships with your customers, you need to have customer service at the heart of your business. The majority of customers demand quick, dependable service with some level of customization. If you don't offer it, they'll defect to a rival that does. Relationships are built on initial interactions, which you can strengthen by offering chatbots on your website. A chatbot enables users to immediately begin "talking" with someone to get their questions answered. Even though the initial communications will be automated, you can and should contact chatbot users to learn how you can help them more. Eg's Wati, Tellephant etc
2. Frequently seek consumer feedback / NPS We know that your customers are the most important part of your business. We also know that you want to do everything possible to make sure they're happy. That's why it's so important to ask for their feedback, so you can make sure they feel heard and valued, and so you can fix any shortcomings in your product or service. Feedback helps you understand what customers think of your brand, which is incredibly valuable in terms of future growth and development. It also opens a conversation with them, which makes them feel more connected to your brand. Feedback makes customers feel heard and valued—and that's how we build relationships!. In order to make your customers feel invested in your business, it's critical that you not only collect customer feedback but also act on it. Eg's - Google forms, NPS score, Ratings etc.
3. Use CRM to scale your D2C business A CRM helps you make an impact on your audience and outperform the competition. If you want to be successful as a D2C brand, you need to engage your customers and make an impact. A CRM can help you do this by allowing you to analyze customer data so that conversations with them are based on their interests and preferences. This will help initiate the conversation at the appropriate time. But if you want to have contextual conversations with your customers as a D2C brand, then you need to understand them better. A CRM can help with this too! A customer relationship management (CRM) tool allows you to compile and manage all of your customer's information in one place so that different types of customers can be divided into segments based on their preferences, purchasing patterns, and other characteristics. With the aid of a CRM, you can more clearly understand which marketing channel delivers the best outcomes for your campaigns. To learn more about each customer, you can create 360-degree customer profiles so that total visibility into ongoing operations is provided by a CRM. It helps keep track of every customer interaction Eg: Clevertap, Webengage, Contlo etc
4. omni channel communication When it comes to customer service, omnichannel communication is the way to go. A recent study showed that businesses with effective omnichannel strategies retain 89% more clients on average than those with ineffective omnichannel strategies, which only retain 33%. Your customers will be reached wherever they are by using an omnichannel communication strategy that connects online and offline channels seamlessly. An omnichannel communication strategy also breaks down the silos between various customer touch points. Before thinking about the best ways to offer a consistent experience across the identified channels, it is crucial to ascertain the communication channels that your customers favor. Use a chatbot on your website, social media pages, and mobile application, for example. Last not the least the most important action is to measure your customer communication metrics to understand whats working and whats not.

CHAPTER THIRTY-TWO

CHOOSE THE RIGHT D2C PLATFORM TO SCALE

In a world where we have every product imaginable at our fingertips, consumers are looking for authenticity—they want to know that the products they buy come from real people who care about what they do. They want to feel like you're one of them, not just another company trying to make a buck off their backs. Direct-to-consumer e-commerce means the manufacturer/producer sells direct to consumers. In a more traditional retailer model, the manufacturer/producer sells to a wholesaler, wholesale distributor, retailer, and then to a consumer. Innovation brands have the best opportunity to build direct relationships with their customers through direct-to-consumer e-commerce (D2C). A D2C eCommerce platform eliminates the need for intermediaries. In addition to offering a great user experience, a great payment experience, and the utmost security, the best online store platforms are also feature-rich. eCommerce platforms are the backbone of an online retailer. They are software programs that allow companies to launch, host, and manage their online stores.

Benefits of D2C eCommerce Platform

1. Customers can buy your products in just a few clicks – With eCommerce, customers can browse through a wide array of products, search for an item, read product descriptions and place orders in minutes.
2. No more waiting in line – With eCommerce, you don't have to stand in line at a store or wait for someone to help you find what you need. Your customers can shop from home or work at any time of day or night and get exactly what they want within minutes.
3. Better experience for customers – When your platform is well-designed and well-developed, consumers will have an easy time using it, which will make their experience as enjoyable as possible. Pick a product that scores high in Ease of Use, or you might regret it later. It will be much more pleasant for you too when you don't have to spend your days guiding customers through a process that should be simple.
4. The world is a global village and your business can be too – with eCommerce!
5. 24/7 "Doors" are always open – eCommerce sites are designed to cater to customers from every corner of the world, operating in different time zones, so they never shut down. Without being limited to just a few geographical locations, your business is alive and running 24/7. You can automate your site to make your products and services available at any time. Using artificial intelligence (AI) processes such as chatbots, live chats, and virtual assistants, eCommerce can also offer automated customer support 24/7.

The world is digital, and there's no turning back and as a business owner, you have to embrace the digital world in order to stay relevant. One of the many advantages of eCommerce is convenience. Convenience has been proven to be one of the most important decision factors for consumers. With just a few clicks, your products can be delivered to your customer's home or office. It is important to remember that your customers demand convenience, so if you don't meet their needs, they're probably looking for better shops. There will always be a place for eCommerce to flourish in the digital world. It will make your data more secure. It's vital that you choose a platform that protects your clients' personal information, ensuring that they will continue to shop safely. By doing your homework now, you'll save yourself a lot of headaches later on.

Your eCommerce platform is the backbone of your online business and will have a major impact on its long-term growth and success, whether you're selling locally or expanding into new markets across the globe. It's also important to choose a B2B or D2C solution that addresses the unique needs of B2B and D2C businesses. We understand how important it is to find the right eCommerce platform for your business because we've been there ourselves. We know that once you find the right solution, it can help you improve your online sales and take them from being just another channel in your marketing plan to being an invaluable tool for growing your brand and increasing customer loyalty. Eg. Platforms - Sekel Tech, Dukaan, Shopify, Big Commerce, Woo Commerce, Pixpa, Squarespace, Volusion, Elementor, Magento,

Here are the top 6 factors to consider.

Scalability Are you looking to grow your business? If so, you need to choose an eCommerce platform that can handle it. No matter how much traffic your online store receives now, you need to prepare for the increased demand that will come as your business attracts new customers and scales. Make sure your eCommerce platform can handle high traffic before choosing one. You wouldn't want your site to crash if you experienced a sudden surge of visitors. A cloud-based eCommerce platform, such as one offered by Sekel Tech, is the best choice, as it scales with your business and maintains maximum speed and performance. By choosing an eCommerce platform that can scale with your business needs, you won't have any issues when it comes time for growth or change.

SEO: When customers can find your store in search engines when searching for products like the ones you offer, only then will they visit your website. SEO (Search Engine Optimization) ensures that your site ranks higher and is clearly visible in search engines. Consequently, you should choose a platform that offers SEO-related features such as the ability to write meta descriptions for products, add blogs to your website, use your own domain name, allow customers to leave reviews, and support Google site maps. The presence of these features will have a direct impact on your site's SEO rankings. Sekel Tech is an eCommerce platform that is SEO-friendly. Sekel Tech provides all of the tools needed to optimize your store's SEO from within one single platform: custom pages and blog posts with meta descriptions written by you; ability to add popular social networks such as Facebook and Instagram; Google site map support; ability to use your own domain name; and much more! With Sekel Tech you will get all these benefits as standard with no additional costs!

Support: If you're using an eCommerce platform, you know that things can go wrong. You could get a technical issue and not know how to fix it, or you could have a question about your store and not know who to ask. It's frustrating when you have no one to turn to in these situations, but luckily there are options available today that make it easier than ever before to get in touch with a real person at your provider. When choosing your provider, it's important to consider what communication methods they offer so that if something goes wrong or you need help with something, you can reach out with ease. For example, some providers only offer live chat or email support while others may also provide phone support or even a ticket system where customers submit questions via an online form instead of having to wait in line for hours just so they can talk to someone over the phone (which we've all done). The more options available for communicating with your provider, the better!

Security : Your eCommerce site needs to protect customers' information. If you don't, they won't buy your products. It's that simple. You need a platform that includes essential security features such as PCI compliance, SSL certificates, fraud prevention, and data backups to meet these requirements. As a result of security audits, the platform can identify potential security risks so that necessary changes can be made to protect customers.

Reporting & Analytics: The best eCommerce platform should be able to give you the information you need to make informed decisions at the right time. For example, it should allow you to monitor the performance of your eCommerce store by tracking things like the number of sales, payment methods, order amounts, inventory, traffic source, UTM, AOV, Traffic, New Vs repeat customers allow you to set up collections, manage tags and so on. You will be able to analyze the performance of your business over time if the stats are presented in a clear and understandable format

Checkout: Don't make your customers work hard to buy from you. The process of buying online has changed quite a bit in recent years, with more and more people expecting quick and easy checkout procedures. This means that if your site doesn't have the right tools in place, you could be missing out on thousands of dollars in sales every day. One critical element of seamless checkout is not having to re-enter information each time an individual shops. This helps save time, improve customer satisfaction and increase convenience. Meanwhile, when shoppers don't have to fill lengthy forms or deal with a complicated checkout process, the chances of them completing the purchase and converting into paying customers increase exponentially. The experience of paying is more than just the payment itself. It's how the product makes you feel, and how you feel about the brand. When it comes to D2C brands, payment experiences can impact every aspect of your brand's experience: from winning customers and driving loyalty, to even lowering operational costs. "Payment experiences in the product-customer journey have completely transformed the D2C space,". "In the nascent years of DTC, the biggest problem was not bringing the consumer on your platform—it was making them transact on your platform."There has been an explosion of payment options and sheer ease of payments," he said. "Today transactions that take place with a single swipe or click used to take up to four steps to complete in the last two or three years."

Options for D2C Platforms

1. Shopify: Known for its user-friendly interface and extensive app ecosystem, Shopify is a versatile platform suitable for businesses of all sizes. It offers a range of customizable templates and built-in tools, making it easy for users to set up and manage their online stores without extensive technical knowledge.
2. Magento: is an open-source platform that provides a high level of customization for larger enterprises. It's known for its scalability and flexibility, allowing businesses to tailor their online stores to specific needs. Magento is suitable for businesses with a larger budget and technical resources.
3. WooCommerce: A WordPress plugin, WooCommerce seamlessly integrates with existing WordPress websites, turning them into fully functional e-commerce stores. It's an excellent choice for businesses already utilizing WordPress, offering flexibility and a range of extensions for added functionality.
4. BigCommerce: is a hosted e-commerce solution that provides a robust set of features out of the box. It's particularly known for its scalability and performance, making it suitable for growing businesses. BigCommerce also offers a user-friendly interface, making it accessible to users with varying levels of technical expertise.
5. Wix eCommerce: is a website builder that includes e-commerce functionality. Its drag-and-drop interface makes it easy for users to create visually appealing online stores without coding. Wix is suitable for small to medium-sized businesses looking for an all-in-one solution for their website and e-commerce needs.
6. Squarespace: is a website builder that includes integrated e-commerce features. It is known for its elegant and visually appealing templates, making it an excellent choice for businesses with a focus on design. Squarespace offers an intuitive interface, making it easy for users to create and manage their online stores.
7. Volusion: is a user-friendly e-commerce platform that provides a range of built-in tools for managing online stores. It offers features like inventory management and marketing tools, making it suitable for small to medium-sized businesses. Volusion is known for its simplicity and ease of use.
8. Ecwid:is unique in that it allows users to add e-commerce functionality to an existing website or social media platform. It's known for its simplicity and seamless integration capabilities. Ecwid is suitable for small businesses or individuals looking for a quick and easy way to start selling online.

When choosing an e-commerce platform, it's crucial to consider factors such as the size of your business, budget, technical expertise, and specific feature requirements. Each platform has its strengths, and the best choice depends on the individual needs and goals of the commerce brand. It's important to note that the landscape of e-commerce platforms can evolve, and new platforms may emerge

CHAPTER THIRTY-THREE

DISCOVERY

Crafting Unique Product Experiences: The Tesla Approach

Have you ever looked at your product lineup and wondered if each item stands out or if they all blend together? It's a critical consideration. Do they serve the same purpose, look and feel the same, or are some of them exceptional? If your answer is "yes" to any of these questions, it's time to think about making your products as distinct as a Tesla. You've probably heard that word-of-mouth marketing is the most effective kind, but what does that really mean? It means ensuring that each of your products possesses its unique personality, setting it apart from the rest and becoming a topic of conversation. It involves giving each item a compelling story, an origin tale that people want to share, whether on social media or over dinner. It means making every item feel like a luxury, offering a sense of exclusivity and uniqueness to those who use it. By curating your product offerings into a more concise selection, you provide customers with a manageable and enticing array of options. They won't be overwhelmed by choices; instead, they'll be excited because what's available is presented as something exceptional. Let's put this concept into perspective. Imagine you have 100 products listed on your website, with each having its dedicated page. When a visitor lands on one of these pages, they see all 100 products at once, which can be overwhelming and unhelpful when making a decision. Now, let's change the scenario. Instead of presenting 100 products individually, we curate them into an 8-product package, featuring the best from your entire range. This shift transforms the customer experience significantly.

The Digital Revolution is Upon Us, and It's Growing: We all recognize that people are spending increasing amounts of time online and are increasingly choosing to make purchases there. But how much more significant will this trend become? According to a Google/Ipsos study, people actively shop for over six product categories online simultaneously. Not only are consumers shifting towards online shopping, but they've also altered the way they shop. They are now consistently in a shopping mindset, always on the lookout for exciting products during their online journeys. The advent of mobile devices has further enhanced the convenience of online shopping, enabling consumers to place orders from virtually anywhere, at any time.

Maximizing Discovery with Snackable Content: To ensure your brand is discovered by the right customers, it's vital to leverage snackable content thoughtfully sprinkled throughout your website. Invest in collecting and producing this content just as you would invest in enhancing the physical appearance of a brick-and-mortar store. Rich and informative product pages engage and captivate shoppers, drawing them deeper into your brand. You might be thinking, "I don't have the time for this!" But building a successful e-commerce business requires harnessing all the features at your disposal. Allocate time regularly to compile and write about the products you intend to purchase, treating it as if you were contributing to a blog or magazine. This approach not only fosters familiarity between your brand and visitors but also helps them grasp how your products can enrich their lives, making informed purchasing decisions when they are ready to buy.

Unlocking Discovery in Three Steps

- Step 1: Increase Reach – Leverage popular media channels to reach your target audience efficiently. Utilize data and signals to connect with people who are more likely to engage with your brand, enhancing ad relevance.
- Step 2: Curate Collection – Embrace the digital era by offering a personalized shopping experience that blends content, catalogs, and comparison shopping. Create storefronts tailored to your audience to facilitate seamless and enjoyable purchases.
- Step 3: Make an Impression – Product-aware ads represent the future of advertising. They help consumers discover your brand and inspire consideration for the featured products. The more product-aware your ads are, the more effective they become.

In essence, making your products unique and engaging, optimizing the digital landscape, and adopting modern advertising techniques are pivotal steps towards enhancing brand recognition and expanding your customer base

CHAPTER THIRTY-FOUR

Consumer Types by Generation

Placing consumers into different buckets based on their generation is a valuable marketing and brand strategy for several compelling reasons. It allows businesses to tailor their messaging, product offerings, and overall brand experience to resonate with each generational segment. Here's why this approach is essential and its impact on the brand:

Each generation has distinct preferences, values, and communication styles. By categorizing consumers into generational buckets, brands can create highly targeted marketing campaigns. This ensures that the message reaches the right audience in a way that speaks to their unique interests and needs. Targeted marketing fosters a sense of relatability. When consumers feel that a brand understands their specific challenges and desires, it establishes a stronger emotional connection. This connection, in turn, enhances brand loyalty and advocacy.

Different generations have different cultural touchpoints and reference points. By segmenting consumers by generation, brands can tap into these references to make their messaging more relevant and resonant. This relevance captures the attention of the audience and makes the brand stand out in a crowded marketplace. Being able to relate to consumers on a generational level positions the brand as culturally aware and in touch with the times. It signals that the brand is not stagnant but evolving to meet the needs of today's consumers, which enhances its credibility and appeal.

Generations often have varying preferences when it comes to product features, design, and functionality. Understanding these preferences allows brands to customize their products to cater to each generational group. This customization can lead to increased sales and customer satisfaction. Offering customized products demonstrates that the brand values the unique requirements of its consumers. It positions the brand as adaptable and consumer-centric, enhancing its reputation and driving brand loyalty. By acknowledging the generational differences and adapting strategies accordingly, brands can build stronger, longer-lasting relationships with their consumers. When consumers feel that a brand "gets" them, they are more likely to remain loyal and advocate for the brand within their generational circles. Impact on Brand: High brand loyalty within specific generational segments not only leads to repeat business but also encourages word-of-mouth marketing within those groups, which can significantly boost the brand's reputation and reach. While segmenting by generation is crucial, brands can also leverage the appeal of certain products or messages across generational lines. This approach can maximize market reach and draw in consumers from various age groups. Impact on Brand:The ability to bridge generational gaps demonstrates the brand's versatility and broad appeal. It positions the brand as one that can be enjoyed by consumers of all ages, expanding its customer base and market share. Segmenting consumers by generation is a strategic approach that allows brands to connect more deeply with their audience. It fosters targeted marketing, relevance, and customization, leading to higher brand loyalty and multigenerational appeal. By understanding and embracing generational differences, brands can position themselves as adaptable, culturally relevant, and consumer-centric, ultimately enhancing their brand's reputation and success in the marketplace.

Maturists (Born before 1945):

Maturists, also known as the Silent Generation, are individuals born before 1945, offering a rich reservoir of life experiences and wisdom. Having lived through World War II and the Great Depression, they tend to exhibit conservative spending habits, emphasizing the importance of financial security and savings. Maturists often uphold traditional values, seeking reliability in products and services.

They may not be as digitally connected as younger generations, valuing in-person shopping experiences where they can engage directly with brands.

Baby Boomers (Born 1946-1964):

Baby Boomers represent a generation born after World War II, characterized by a strong work ethic and brand loyalty. They tend to favor established products and services, valuing a sense of familiarity and trustworthiness. Face-to-face communication holds a special place in their hearts, and while they adapt to technology, they may not be as tech-savvy as younger counterparts.

Prioritizing savings, homeownership, and retirement planning, Baby Boomers appreciate brands that align with their long-term financial goals.

Generation X (Born 1965-1980):

Generation X, or Gen X, emerged during a period of significant societal and economic shifts, making them adaptable and independent. They approach traditional advertising with a degree of skepticism and value authentic brand interactions. Seeking a work-life balance, Gen Xers prioritize experiences over material possessions and appreciate brands that align with their lifestyle choices.

While comfortable with technology, they may not be as digitally native as younger generations, making them receptive to brands offering a seamless blend of online and offline experiences.

Generation Y (Born 1981-1996):

Generation Y, also known as Millennials, came of age during the internet and technology boom, shaping them into tech-savvy, socially connected consumers. Authenticity and social connections are paramount for Millennials, who value brands that demonstrate genuine care and ethical responsibility. Prioritizing experiences, sustainability, and social responsibility, they often make purchasing decisions that reflect these values. Highly connected through social media and online platforms, Millennials engage with brands that offer personalized, relevant content and experiences.

Generation Z (Born 1997-Present):

Generation Z, the youngest cohort, are true digital natives, having grown up in an age of smartphones and internet ubiquity. Personalization, diversity, and authenticity hold great importance for Gen Z, making them discerning consumers who favor brands that reflect these qualities. Their entrepreneurial spirit is evident, and they exhibit a preference for online shopping and social commerce platforms. Brands that resonate with Gen Z embrace innovation and a seamless digital experience, acknowledging their unique preferences and expectations.

Understanding these generational characteristics enables brands to tailor their marketing strategies and brand narratives, forging deeper connections and resonating with each segment effectively. It's important to note that these generational characteristics are generalizations, and individual consumer behavior can vary widely within each generation. Understanding these generational trends can help businesses tailor their marketing strategies and products to better resonate with different age groups of consumers.

Understanding diverse customer segments for D2C brands: Direct-to-Consumer (D2C) brands have the advantage of appealing to a range of customer segments, each with unique preferences and characteristics. Some of the prominent customer segments include:

Millennial Enthusiasts:

Millennials constitute a significant and progressively influential demographic for D2C brands. They exhibit a strong inclination toward purchasing directly from brands. Tech-savvy by nature, they value seamless online experiences and prioritize convenience. D2C brands that prioritize user-friendly digital interfaces and efficient shopping processes can effectively capture this audience's attention.

Gen Z Advocates:

Gen Z, another substantial consumer group, demonstrates a growing interest in direct brand interactions. With a strong emphasis on social consciousness and authenticity, Gen Z consumers are drawn to D2C brands that champion sustainability and ethical practices. Brands that authentically align with these values are well-positioned to resonate with and engage this generation.

Affluent Connoisseurs:

D2C brands often find favor with affluent consumers who possess disposable income to invest in premium products. These consumers typically embrace the latest technologies and trends, positioning them as early adopters. D2C brands known for continuous innovation and premium offerings can effectively attract this segment.

Loyal Brand Supporters: Building a community of loyal customers is a strategic asset for any brand, and D2C brands can excel in this endeavor. By providing exceptional customer service, exclusive promotions, and cultivating a sense of belonging within their community, D2C brands can nurture enduring brand loyalty. Understanding the unique characteristics and preferences of these customer segments allows D2C brands to tailor their strategies, create relevant brand experiences, and foster deeper connections. This customer-centric approach contributes to the sustained success and growth of D2C brands in a competitive market landscape.

Characteristics	**Maturists (pre 1945)**	**Baby Boomers (1945 - 1960)**	**Generation X (1961 - 1980)**	**Generation Y (1981 - 1995)**	**Generation Z (Born After 1995)**
Formative experience	Second world war Rationing Fixed- gender roles Rock n Roll Nuclear Families Defined gender roles mostly for women	Cold War Post war boom Swinging Sixties Apollo moon landings Youth Culture Woodstock Family Oriented Rise of the teenager	End of cold war Fall of Berlin War Live Aid The 1st PC Early Mobile technology Latch key kids Rising level of divorce	911 Terrorist attacks Playstation Social Media Invasion of Iraq Reality TV Google earth	Economic Downturn Global focus, Mobile devices Energy crisis Arab Spring Produce own media Cloud computing Wiki Leaks
Aspiration	Home ownership	Job Security	Work Life Balance	Freedom	Security & Stability
Attitude towards technology	Largely Disengaged	Early Information technology (IT Adopters)	Digital Immigrants	Digital Natives	Technoholics-Dependant on tech. Ltd grasp of alternatives
Attitude towards career	Jobs for life	Organisational Careers are defined by employers	Early portfolio careers loyal to profession, notemployer	Digital entrepreneurs work with orgn's not "for	Career multitaskers will move seamlessly between organ's an pop up businesses
Signature product		Television	Personal Computer		
Communication media		Telephone	E-mail and text message		
Communication Preference		Face-to-face ideally, but telephone or e-mail if required	Text messaging or e-mail		Facetime
Preference when making financial decesions		Face-to-face ideally, but increasingly will go online	Online – would prefer face-to-face if time permitting		

Breaking down the generational appeal

CHAPTER THIRTY-FIVE

Develop a solid Marketing Strategy

When a direct-to-consumer (D2C) brand embarks on a market entry with a distinct approach, it signifies their commitment to providing unparalleled products, services, or a novel methodology that distinguishes them from established industry leaders. This strategic pursuit is often embraced by companies with a vision to disrupt conventional business models, challenge industry conventions, and carve out their share of the market. According to marketing expert Sattar Khan, there lies an unexplored treasure in the realm of anticipatory excitement within marketing. It's intriguing to note that our brains produce as much dopamine when we anticipate something pleasurable as when we actually experience it or reminisce about it later. This phenomenon is known as anticipatory utility, where we derive mental and physiological pleasure in the present moment while looking forward to future consumption. The value of a consumer's choice encompasses the pleasure derived from the anticipation of consumption, the experience during consumption, the recollection of the experience, and the act of sharing that experience. While many marketers concentrate on creating value during the consumption and sharing phases of their brands, the significant opportunity lies in stimulating and enhancing anticipatory utility.

> "*As highlighted by Sattar Khan, "**Anticipation is excitement. Anticipation is value. Anticipation is opportunity.**"*"

In the world of marketing and brand strategy, understanding and harnessing the power of anticipation can unlock new dimensions of value creation and customer engagement, paving the way for innovative and successful D2C brand journeys. In 1878, Thomas Hardy wrote in The Return of the Native: "Pleasure not known beforehand is half-wasted; to anticipate is to double it." For the consumer, that's true; for the marketer, that's a clue: Why not double the consumer's pleasure instead of wasting the opportunity to do so? So while you construct you marketing plan its important to answer How can I instigate and intensify anticipatory value for my brand?

Here's a breakdown of the situation:

A D2C brand sells its products or services directly to consumers without relying on traditional retail channels. By cutting out middlemen, they can often offer competitive pricing, maintain closer customer relationships, and have more control over their brand image. The D2C brand intends to differentiate itself from the established leaders in the market. This can be achieved through various means, such as offering innovative products, providing exceptional customer experiences, leveraging technology, adopting sustainable practices, or focusing on a niche segment that is underserved or overlooked by the established players. These are the companies that currently dominate the market and have a strong presence, market share, and brand recognition. They have likely built a loyal customer base, established distribution networks, and possess significant resources and industry experience.

Challenges the D2C brand may face

Brand Recognition: The established leaders already have a well-known brand, making it challenging for the new D2C brand to gain visibility and build awareness among consumers. Extensive marketing efforts and strategic positioning will be essential to stand out. Customers may have established preferences and loyalty towards the existing leaders. Convincing them to switch to a new brand requires offering compelling value propositions, superior quality, competitive pricing, or other incentives that resonate with the target audience. The established leaders likely have well-established distribution networks, partnerships, and shelf space in physical retail stores. The D2C brand will need to focus on efficient and reliable delivery options, optimize their e-commerce platform, and explore partnerships or collaborations to ensure broad product availability. The established leaders may have significant financial resources, manufacturing capabilities, and economies of scale. The D2C brand will need to carefully manage their resources, streamline operations, and seek opportunities for cost optimization to compete effectively.

Strategies for the D2C brand:

1. Innovation and Uniqueness: By introducing novel products, disruptive business models, or differentiated features, the D2C brand can capture the attention of consumers looking for something new and exciting.
2. Exceptional Customer Experience: Offering personalized, seamless, and convenient experiences can help the D2C brand develop a loyal customer base. This can include responsive customer support, hassle-free returns, or interactive online platforms.
3. Target Niche Markets: Focusing on specific customer segments or underserved markets allows the D2C brand to carve out a space where the established leaders may have less dominance. By understanding the unique needs of these segments, the brand can tailor its offerings accordingly.
4. Digital Marketing and Social Media: Leveraging digital platforms for targeted marketing campaigns, influencer collaborations, and social media engagement can help the D2C brand reach its intended audience effectively and build brand awareness.
5. Partnerships and Collaborations: Forming strategic partnerships with complementary brands or influencers can enhance the D2C brand's visibility, credibility, and access to new customer segments.
6. Focus on a specific niche. Don't try to be everything to everyone. Instead, focus on a specific niche and become the go-to brand for that particular audience. This will help you stand out from the competition and build a loyal customer base.
7. Focus on personalization. D2C brands have the advantage of being able to collect a wealth of data about their customers. This data can be used to personalize marketing messages and offers, which can lead to increased conversions.
8. Offer high-quality products or services. This goes without saying, but it's worth repeating. If you want customers to keep coming back, you need to offer them products or services that are of the highest quality.
9. Provide excellent customer service. This is another key factor in building customer loyalty. Make sure you are responsive to customer inquiries and concerns, and that you go above and beyond to make sure they are satisfied with their purchase.
10. Use unique marketing and branding strategies. Don't just rely on traditional marketing methods. Get creative and come up with unique ways to reach your target audience and make your brand stand out.
11. Build a community around your brand. Get people talking about your brand and engaging with your content. This will help you create a sense of excitement and anticipation around your products or services.
12. Use storytelling to connect with your customers. People love stories, so use them to tell the story of your brand and your products. This will help you build an emotional connection with your customers and make them more likely to buy from you.
13. Use data to track your results and make adjustments as needed. It's important to track your results so you can see what's working and what's not. This will help you make adjustments to your strategy as needed.
14. Be creative and experiment. There's no one-size-fits-all D2C marketing strategy. What works for one brand might not work for another. Be creative and experiment with different marketing channels and strategies to see what works best for your audience.

15. Stay up-to-date on the latest trends. The D2C marketing landscape is constantly evolving. It's important to stay up-to-date on the latest trends so you can keep your marketing strategy fresh and effective.

> "*Entering a market as a D2C brand against established leaders requires a combination of differentiation, customer-centricity, strategic marketing, and a focus on innovation to disrupt the status quo and gain market share.*"

By following these tips, you can make your D2C offering unique and stand out from the competition. This will give you a better chance of success in today's crowded marketplace.

Use ad placements creatively

Utilizing ad placement creativity can indeed be an effective strategy, especially for direct-to-consumer (D2C) brands. By exploring additional advertising spaces beyond the traditional ones, you can reach your target audience in unexpected ways and gain a competitive edge. Here are a few ideas to consider:

- Native advertising: Native ads blend seamlessly with the content on a platform, making them less intrusive and more engaging. This form of advertising allows you to deliver your message in a way that resonates with the platform's users, increasing the chances of capturing their attention.
- Influencer collaborations: Partnering with influencers who align with your brand values and have a strong following can significantly expand your reach. Instead of relying solely on traditional ad placements, leveraging influencers' platforms and creativity can help you tap into new audiences.
- Sponsored content: Consider sponsoring relevant articles, videos, or podcasts that your target audience is likely to consume. By aligning your brand with high-quality content, you can establish trust and credibility while subtly promoting your products or services.
- Contextual targeting: Identify websites, blogs, or social media pages that attract your target audience and explore advertising opportunities on these platforms. Rather than relying solely on keywords, focus on the context and themes of the content to ensure your ads appear in relevant and engaging environments.
- Creative keyword usage: Instead of sticking only to direct keywords related to your product or service, experiment with tangentially related or off-topic keywords that still resonate with your target audience. This approach can help you reach potential customers who might not have been exposed to your brand otherwise.
- Location-based advertising: Use geotargeting to display your ads to people in specific locations where your target audience is likely to be present. This can be particularly useful for brick-and-mortar businesses or local events, allowing you to maximize your ad spend and increase the chances of conversion.

Remember, creativity and intuition are key when implementing these strategies. Experiment, analyze results, and refine your approach based on what works best for your brand. By thinking outside the box and exploring new ad placement opportunities, you can effectively disrupt the market and connect with your target audience in unique ways.

Leveraging heuristics to influence decision-making

Research has helped us understand that consumers tend to look for cognitive shortcuts when making buying decisions. Though rational and emotional elements figure into making purchases like the complexity of the purchase, the price of the item, or emotional triggers such as nostalgia, there are powerful cognitive biases at play as well. Category heuristics are rules of thumb or mental shortcuts that consumers use to make quick decisions when evaluating and choosing products within a particular category. In the case of direct-to-consumer (D2C) brands, which sell products directly to consumers without intermediaries, category heuristics can play a crucial role in shaping consumer perceptions and purchase decisions. Here are some examples of category heuristics commonly observed in D2C brands:

1. Packaging: D2C brands often use distinctive, eye-catching packaging to stand out from traditional retail products. Category heuristics may lead consumers to associate specific packaging styles or colors with certain product attributes or qualities. For example, minimalistic packaging with clean lines and neutral colors may be associated with natural or organic products, while bold, vibrant packaging might signal a trendy or innovative product.
2. Brand Storytelling: D2C brands often rely on compelling brand stories to engage consumers and create emotional connections. Category heuristics can lead consumers to associate certain types of narratives or values with different product categories. For example, a skincare brand may emphasize its use of natural ingredients and sustainability practices to tap into category heuristics associated with eco-friendly and ethical products.
3. Social Proof: D2C brands frequently leverage social proof, such as customer reviews, testimonials, or user-generated content, to establish credibility and trust. Consumers often use social proof as a category heuristic to gauge product quality and reliability. Positive reviews, high ratings, or endorsements from influencers can reinforce consumers' perceptions and increase their likelihood of making a purchase.
4. Value Proposition: D2C brands often focus on offering unique value propositions that differentiate them from traditional retail brands. Category heuristics can lead consumers to associate specific benefits or features with different product categories. For instance, a D2C mattress brand may emphasize factors like comfort, durability, or customization options to align with category heuristics related to bedding products.
5. Pricing Transparency: D2C brands often promote transparency in pricing, providing detailed breakdowns of costs and eliminating hidden fees. Category heuristics may lead consumers to associate transparent pricing models with fairness, value, and trust. This can differentiate D2C brands from traditional retail brands known for complex pricing structures.
6. Personalization: D2C brands frequently offer personalized product experiences, leveraging data and technology to tailor offerings to individual preferences. Category heuristics can lead consumers to expect customization and personalization in certain product categories. For example, a D2C clothing brand may offer personalized style recommendations or allow customers to customize their garments, aligning with category heuristics associated with fashion and self-expression.

These examples demonstrate how category heuristics can influence consumer perceptions and decision-making within the context of D2C brands. By understanding and strategically leveraging these heuristics, D2C brands can effectively communicate their value propositions and engage with their target audience.

- **Bais 1 - Representativeness Heuristic** Making judgments based upon the similarity of one thing to its archetype. In social situations, this leads to prejudice. Example we might see a tree and immediately assume it's in the oak family based on the color of its bark or size of its leaves. Our stereotypical assumptions about others can lead to bias, prejudice and even discrimination.
- **Bais 2 - Anchoring Heuristic:** We often make decisions based upon a subjective anchoring point that influences all subsequent thinking on a topic Example: An anchoring point is often the original piece of information that we are given. Based upon this information, all future thinking and decisions look good or bad eg. is when a company sets the cost of their goods high before setting a discount in such a case when a discount is applied, the people would see the price as a bargain rather than high
- **Bais 3 - Base Rate Heuristic:** We neglect the base statistics in favor of other more proximate statistics when making a judgment Example: Base rate neglect occurs when someone forgets the base rate , or a basic fact about information, and instead makes decisions based upon other information that they place too much importance upon
- **Bais 4 - Effort Heuristic:** Assuming the quality of something correlates with the amount of effort put into it. Example: Advertisements might talk about the amount of hours spent testing products , the research and

development money put into it, and soon, in order to show that a lot of effort was put into it. The insinuation here is that the effort has led to a higher quality product eg. travel .

- **Bais 5 - Familiarity Heuristic** We can often take mental shortcuts where we decide things that are most familiar to us are better than things that are less familiar. Example: We may look to a country overseas and see it as potentially dangerous. But , looking at data , our hometown may be far more dangerous ! Similarly, we are much more likely to die in a car crash than a plane crash . Nevertheless , fear may overcome you getting on a plane despite the fact that you didn't put a moment's thought into the drive to the airport.
- **Bais 6 - Fluency Heuristic** If an idea is communicated more fluently or skill-fully then it is given more credence than an idea that is clumsily communicated, regardless of the ment of the idea. Example: The fluency with which an idea is communicated can directly impact how we perceive the idea. This mental shortcut allows us to bypass direct assessment of the merits of a case instead , we rely more on the charisma of the communicator.
- **Bais 7 - Gaze Heuristic:**Humans have developed the ability to fixate on an estimated position rather than conducting complex calculations. Generally, this is in relation to motion. Example: Gaze heuristic is the process humans go through to estimate when a ball will land. We don't do all the calculations to understand trajectory and angle. Instead, we've developed an uncanny ability to identify where the ball will land through mental shortcuts based on previous experience
- **Bais 8 - Recognition Heuristic:** We assume that things we recognize have more value than things we do not recognize. Example: Recognition is an important facet of product marketing. Brand recognition alone can help a brand to thrive among a field of other products on a shelf. The recognition heuristic states that we take mental shortcuts when looking at a range of options by assuming that the most recognizable option holds greater value. Thus, we assume a well- known household brand is high - quality than lesser - known brands.
- **Bais 9 - Scarcity Heuristic**: When something is scarce , we see it as more valuable. False scarcity is a widely - utilized method in marketing psychology because it encourages consumers to see a product as having that really does. Example: One way marketers use false scarcity is that they create limited time discounts . In this case , the low price is a point of scarcity Another way they can create false scarcity is to have open and closed cart periods so the product is only available for a short period of time
- **Bais 10 - Similarity Heuristic**: Similarity between past and present situations impacts decision - making , allowing people to bypass making objective comparisons of two alternatives. Example: Netflix may show you shows and movies similar to previous ones you watched to the end, because Netflix knows that you are going to be partisan toward a similar experience to the ones you obviously enjoyed.
- **Bais 11 - Simulation Heuristic** - We tend to overestimate the likelihood of an event based upon how easy it is to visualize it. Example: Simulation heuristic occurs in relation to regret or near misses . A great example of this is buying a lottery ticket . If you found out that someone bought a winning lottery ticket one hour after you bought your ticket, then you'd easily be able to visualize the potentiality that if you had not been stuck in traffic that day things would have been different.
- **Bais 12 - Social Proof Heuristic**: Use social proof as a mental shortcut to verify the quality or veracity of something instead of investigating it ourselves. Example: People rely on broader society's views (i.e. social proof) as an anchoring point for their own thinking on the topi . Similarly, in marketing, marketers often go to great lengths to get quotes from "average joes" who have used a product in order to provide social proof in their advertisements.
- **Bais 13 - Authority Heuristic:** The thinking and research we tend to defer to authorities as a shortcut rather than doing the thinking and research to validate it. Example: we refer to doctors on medical issues, engineers when building bridges, and lawyers on legal issues.
- **Bais 14 - Naive Diversification:** Longer - term planning tends to involve more diversification than shorter - term planning. Example: Consider a situation where you are asked to purchase 5 weeks ' worth of groceries at once . In this situation , you're more likely to buy a diverse range of fruit and vegetables for the forthcoming five weeks. By contrast, if you were to go shopping once a week for five weeks , you're less likely to diversify. Rather, you would buy a narrow range of products that you want in the short term .

- **Bais 15 - Affect/Availability heuristic.** We often make decisions based on emotions, moods, and "gut feelings " rather than logic. Salient memories override normative reasoning. Example: Overly trusting a friendly seller, exaggerating the performance quality of a product due to its external appeal (e.g. a freshly painted used car) A consumer rejects all Sony products because of an early bad experience with one cheap Sony product
- **Bais 16 - Confirmation bias:** The tendency to seek out opinions and facts that support one's own beliefs and hypotheses. Example: Tendency to take into account product reviews that laud an item you want to purchase, while ignoring negative reviews.
- **Bais 17 - False consensus effect:** Inclination to assume that one's beliefs are more widely held than they actually are. Example: Assuming that others will be satisfied with the same brands and service providers that you prefer
- **Bais 18 - Gambler's fallacy:** Pervasive false beliefs about the nature of random sequences. Example: Lottery players who play the same numbers every time. assuming the number is "due" to win

A brilliant Example is Amazon Recommendations

Amazon, the online retailer, is well-known for its recommendation engine (e.g., Iskold, 2007); as of 2006, 35 per cent of the company's sales came via recommendation elements on the website (Marshall, 2006). Users (potential customers) browsing for products, such as books, are–in addition to basic product information–presented with a number of page elements using variants of 'social proof' (Anderson, 2010; Cialdini, 2007) to influence their decision-making, based on extensive, ongoing background analysis of shopping habits by Amazon. These can include "Frequently bought together", "Customers who bought this item also bought", "What other items do customers buy after viewing this item?", "Customers also bought items by", "Customers who bought items in your recent history also bought" and "Listmania" (which features customer-curated recommended lists of items with similar characteristics), as well as reviews of the item by other customers, who can give one to five stars and write comments (in turn, users can rate the reviews as being helpful or not, and the 'most helpful' reviews are promoted in page position; frequent and well-regarded reviewers receive 'flair' next to their names).

Each of these many elements–in a slightly different way–uses the behaviour and opinions of other users, individually or as a 'community' to attempt to influence the behaviour of the potential customer. They could all be classified as using 'social proof' as a design principle, but this misses the nuances of the approach. The fact that Amazon uses so many variants–and presumably tracks closely the effectiveness of each with different customers and market segments–suggests that slightly different models of behaviour underlie each element, and what 'works' for some users does not work for everyone in terms of influencing behaviour (Kaptein & Eckles, 2010). Each variant makes slightly different assumptions about how people will respond the heuristics that are being followed. What might glibly be classified as 'social proof' comprises assumptions such as:

1. People will do what they see other people doing.
2. People will value or do what seems to be most popular.
3. People value or respect others' opinions and actions.
4. People want to learn more about a subject.
5. People will buy multiple items at the same time.

CHAPTER THIRTY-SIX

Customer Journey Mapping: A Strategic Guide to Enhancing Customer Experiences

Customer journey mapping is a vital tool for businesses to understand and improve the customer experience. This strategic approach involves visualizing and analyzing a customer's interactions with a company throughout their entire journey, from initial awareness to post-purchase support. By mapping these interactions and understanding customer emotions, expectations, pain points, and opportunities for improvement, businesses can create satisfying and seamless journeys. Let's explore the various stages of a customer journey with examples at each stage.

Stage 1: Awareness
Example: A Fashion E-commerce Brand
Touchpoint: Social Media Ad
Emotions/Expectations: A customer sees an ad on Instagram for a fashion e-commerce brand offering trendy clothing.
Pain Points: The customer wants to know more about the brand's reliability.
Opportunities: The brand can link the ad to customer reviews and testimonials to build trust.

Stage 2: Consideration
Example: Online Travel Booking Platform
Touchpoint: Customer Searches "Best International Flights
Emotions/Expectations**: The customer is seeking information on international flights.
Pain Points: Too many options, and they are unsure about the best deals.
Opportunities: The platform provides a "Top 10 Destinations" section and filters for "Best Deals."

Stage 3: Purchase
Example: Consumer Electronics Store
Touchpoint: Online Shopping Cart
Emotions/Expectations**: The customer adds a smartphone to their cart.
Pain Points: Concerns about shipping costs and return policy.
Opportunities: The store provides free shipping above a certain purchase amount and a no-questions-asked return policy.

Stage 4: Post-Purchase
Example: Online Grocery Delivery Service

Touchpoint: Delivery Confirmation Email
Emotions/Expectations: The customer receives an email confirming their grocery delivery.
Pain Points: Worries about missing items or delivery delays.
Opportunities: The email includes a detailed receipt and contact information for customer support.

Stage 5: Loyalty and Advocacy

Example: Coffee Chain
Touchpoint: Mobile App Notification for Loyalty Reward
Emotions/Expectations: The customer receives a notification about a free coffee as a loyalty reward.
Pain Points: None; the customer is delighted.
Opportunities*: The app encourages the customer to refer friends for additional rewards.

Customer journey mapping is an invaluable approach for businesses to create and optimize the customer experience. By addressing each stage of the journey with a deep understanding of customer emotions, expectations, pain points, and opportunities, companies can develop strategies that enhance satisfaction, build loyalty, and promote advocacy. Whether it's the initial awareness or post-purchase support, every touchpoint plays a crucial role in the overall journey, impacting the customer's perception of the brand.

Each of these stages offers multiple opportunities for the brand to engage with the customer, gather feedback, and create a positive experience. Mapping this journey enables companies to identify pain points and areas for improvement and to tailor their strategies, communications, and services to meet customer needs effectively. A well-crafted customer journey, focused on a satisfying and seamless experience, can lead to increased customer satisfaction, loyalty, and advocacy, ultimately benefiting the brand's success. Many commerce brands have successfully built customer journey maps to enhance their understanding of the customer experience. Here are a few examples:

Amazon: The e-commerce giant, Amazon, is known for its comprehensive customer journey mapping. They have identified various customer personas, analyzed touchpoints, and gathered extensive data to understand their customers better. Amazon has mapped the customer journey from the initial product search to checkout and post-purchase support. This mapping has allowed them to personalize recommendations, optimize their website's user experience, and offer efficient customer service.

Zappos: Zappos, an online shoe and clothing retailer, is renowned for its customer-centric approach. They've created detailed customer personas, analyzed touchpoints, and focused on understanding customer emotions. For example, they emphasize emotions such as happiness, ease, and satisfaction throughout the customer journey. Zappos has mapped out the journey from the moment a customer visits their website, selects products, to the delivery and returns process. This detailed mapping has enabled them to create a brand known for superior customer service.

Starbucks: Although not a traditional e-commerce brand, Starbucks has utilized customer journey mapping in their mobile app experience. They've analyzed touchpoints in the customer journey, including mobile ordering, payment, and rewards. Starbucks ensures a seamless experience by personalizing the app, enabling easy payments, and offering rewards that engage and retain customers.

Airbnb: Airbnb, a platform for short-term lodging rentals, has an extensive customer journey map. They have identified various customer segments, including hosts and guests, and mapped out their interactions on the platform. From the initial property search to booking, staying, and leaving a review, Airbnb has focused on personalizing the journey and ensuring trust and transparency between hosts and guests.

Nordstrom: Nordstrom, a high-end fashion retailer, has taken a customer-centric approach to their journey mapping. They've created customer personas and analyzed touchpoints in the in-store and online shopping experience. Nordstrom aims to provide a seamless and personalized journey, offering services like personal stylists, easy returns, and an exceptional in store experience.

These brands demonstrate the diverse ways in which customer journey mapping can be applied to improve the customer experience. Whether it's through personalization, analyzing emotions, or ensuring consistency across touchpoints, successful commerce brands have harnessed the power of customer journey mapping to build stronger, more satisfying relationships with their customers. Indian e-commerce brands have recognized the importance of customer journey mapping in enhancing the customer experience. Here are a few examples of how some of these brands have implemented customer journey mapping:

Flipkart: Understanding User Behavior: Flipkart, one of India's largest e-commerce platforms, utilizes customer journey mapping to analyze user behavior on their website and mobile app. They track how customers move from product discovery to the checkout process, identifying drop-off points and areas for improvement.

Customized Recommendations: Through the mapping process, Flipkart segments customers based on their browsing and purchase history. This allows them to offer personalized product recommendations and target customers with relevant marketing campaigns.

Amazon India: Seamless Multichannel Experience: Amazon India leverages customer journey maps to ensure a seamless experience across its website and mobile app. They focus on unifying the shopping journey, making it easy for customers to transition from one channel to another without disruptions. Improving Delivery and Customer Service: Amazon tracks the customer journey from order placement to delivery. They use these maps to optimize delivery times and enhance customer service interactions to reduce friction points.

Myntra: Personalized Fashion Experience: As a prominent fashion e-commerce brand, Myntra uses customer journey mapping to create personalized fashion experiences. They study user interactions and preferences to curate personalized fashion collections for their customers. Style Quiz: Myntra has integrated a style quiz into their journey mapping process. By asking customers about their style preferences, they can deliver customized product recommendations that align with individual tastes.

MakeMyTrip: End-to-End Travel Experience**: MakeMyTrip employs customer journey mapping to visualize the entire travel planning and booking process. They cater to different segments, such as leisure travelers, business travelers, and international tourists, and create unique journey maps for each. Customer Support Optimization: The company analyzes the customer support journey, identifying areas where travelers might face issues. This helps them improve customer support and ensures that any problems are addressed promptly.

Nykaa: Personalized Beauty Regimens: Nykaa, an e-commerce platform for cosmetics and beauty products, creates customer journey maps that focus on beauty regimens. They guide customers through their beauty journey, offering personalized advice and product recommendations. Content-Driven Engagement: Nykaa uses journey mapping to tailor content for beauty enthusiasts. They offer blog posts, video tutorials, and other resources to engage customers at different stages of their beauty routines.

These Indian e-commerce brands understand that effective customer journey mapping is key to offering personalized, seamless, and value-driven experiences. By using data and insights gained from these maps, they not only optimize their customers' journeys but also create strong, long-lasting relationships with their audiences.

Brand Tracking Customer Journeys vs. Brands Not Tracking Customer Journeys: Brands that actively track customer journeys have a deep understanding of how customers interact with their products and services. They collect data at various touchpoints, allowing them to analyze customer behavior, preferences, and pain points. For example, an e-commerce brand may use website analytics to track the customer's path from product discovery to purchase. With insights gathered from tracking customer journeys, brands can offer personalized experiences. They can recommend products, send targeted marketing messages, and tailor their services to individual customer preferences. An example is Amazon's product recommendation engine, which suggests items based on a customer's browsing and purchasing history. When brands track customer journeys, they can identify pain points and address them proactively. This leads to improved customer satisfaction and loyalty. For instance, a hotel chain might use guest feedback data to resolve issues promptly, ensuring a pleasant stay for future guests. Data from customer journey tracking helps brands optimize their marketing efforts. They can allocate resources more effectively by focusing on channels and touchpoints that generate the most engagement and conversions. A fitness app might analyze user data to determine which marketing channels bring in the most sign-ups.

Brands that track customer journeys make data-driven decisions. They can adjust their strategies based on real customer behavior and market trends. A social media platform might monitor user engagement metrics to decide which new features to introduce.

Brands Not Tracking Customer Journeys: Brands that don't track customer journeys have a limited understanding of their customers. They might make assumptions about customer behavior, but these may not reflect the reality. For example, a retail store without tracking data might guess at its most popular products rather than relying on actual sales data. Without insights into individual customer behavior, brands can only offer generic interactions. This results in mass marketing efforts that may not resonate with most customers. An email marketing campaign that sends the same content to everyone is an example of this approach. Brands not tracking customer journeys are likely to miss valuable opportunities for improvement. They might not even be aware of pain points experienced by customers, which can lead to customer churn. An airline that doesn't track customer feedback might not address recurring complaints about long wait times.

Without data on which touchpoints and channels are most effective, brands may allocate resources inefficiently. This can lead to wasted marketing spend and efforts in the wrong areas. A tech startup that doesn't analyze customer acquisition metrics might continue investing in underperforming ad campaigns. Brands not tracking customer journeys risk being outpaced by competitors who are leveraging data to refine their strategies. They may lose market share and fail to adapt to changing customer preferences. An online bookstore without data tracking might struggle to compete with a rival offering personalized book recommendations. The impact of tracking vs. not tracking customer journeys on a brand is significant. Brands that track journeys enjoy higher customer satisfaction, greater loyalty, and improved marketing efficiency. They adapt to changing market conditions and make informed decisions. On the other hand, brands not tracking journeys risk stagnation, inefficiency, and customer dissatisfaction, ultimately leading to weaker market positioning and reduced competitiveness. Customer journey tracking is a valuable tool for brands seeking to thrive in today's data-driven and customer-centric business landscape.

CHAPTER THIRTY-SEVEN

Customer Retention Journeys

Setting up customer journeys in retention marketing involves creating a series of automated and personalized touchpoints that guide customers through various stages of their relationship with the brand. Each journey is designed to engage, nurture, and retain customers, leading to increased loyalty and repeat business. Here are some key customer journeys in retention marketing, along with details and examples for each:

1. **Welcome Journey:** The welcome journey aims to make a positive first impression on new customers and set the foundation for a long-lasting relationship. Upon a customer's initial sign-up or purchase, the welcome journey triggers a series of personalized welcome emails or messages that introduce the brand, its values, and the benefits of being a customer. Example: The first email can be a warm welcome message, followed by subsequent emails that highlight different product categories, user guides, and exclusive offers to encourage further exploration of the brand. The period starts immediately after a customer signs up or makes their first purchase.
2. **Onboarding Journey:** The onboarding journey focuses on ensuring that new customers are successfully introduced to the brand's products or services, leading to a higher likelihood of continued engagement. The onboarding journey consists of educational content, tutorials, and tips to help customers get the most value from their purchase and build confidence in using the product. Example: For a subscription-based D2C brand, the onboarding journey can include a series of tutorials on how to use the product effectively, personalized recommendations based on customer preferences, and guidance on customizing their subscription. The journey starts once the consumer has demonstrated seriousness and the potential to purchase This kicks into effect during the initial days or weeks after a customer's first purchase or sign-up.
3. **Abandoned Cart Journey:** The abandoned cart journey aims to recover lost sales by reminding customers about items left in their cart and encouraging them to complete the purchase. When a customer abandons their cart, an automated series of reminder emails or messages is triggered to entice them back to the website. Example: The first email can serve as a friendly reminder, the second can offer a limited-time discount, and the third can highlight social proof or product reviews to instill confidence in the purchase decision. This is triggered when a customer leaves items in their shopping cart without completing the purchase.
4. **Re-engagement Journey:** The re-engagement journey targets inactive or lapsed customers to bring them back to the brand and increase their involvement. The re-engagement journey includes targeted messages with personalized offers or incentives to motivate customers to re-engage with the brand. Example: A D2C brand may send a re-engagement email offering a discount or an exclusive product preview to customers who have been inactive for a certain period, encouraging them to return and make a purchase. This is activated when a customer becomes inactive or shows a decline in engagement.
5. **Loyalty Journey:** The loyalty journey focuses on rewarding and retaining existing loyal customers to foster long-term brand loyalty and advocacy. The loyalty journey includes personalized offers, rewards, and exclusive perks for customers who have reached specific milestones or have exhibited strong engagement and loyalty. Example: A loyalty journey may involve sending exclusive offers or sneak peeks of upcoming products to customers who

have been with the brand for a certain period or have achieved a specific purchase frequency. This is ongoing as customers participate in the loyalty program.

6. **Post-Purchase Journey:** The post-purchase journey aims to continue engaging and delighting customers after their initial purchase to encourage repeat business and advocacy. The post-purchase journey includes follow-up emails or messages that express gratitude, request feedback, and provide post-purchase support. Example: A D2C brand can send a post-purchase email thanking the customer for their purchase, asking for a product review, and including a personalized discount for their next order. The period begins after a customer completes a purchase.
7. **Win-back Journey:** The win-back journey targets customers who have churned or have been inactive for an extended period, with the goal of reactivating their interest and bringing them back as active customers. The win-back journey involves a series of re-engagement messages with enticing offers or incentives to motivate inactive customers to return and make a purchase. Example: A win-back email may offer a significant discount or an exclusive offer to customers who have been inactive for a certain number of months, encouraging them to re-engage with the brand.
8. **Birthday/Anniversary Journey:** This is automated and triggered around the customer's birthday or the anniversary of their first purchase. Example: Send a birthday or anniversary email with a special discount or gift to celebrate the occasion. Personalize the message to make the customer feel valued and appreciated.
9. **Engagement Journey**: These journeys ate set up to keep customers actively using the product and engaged with the brand. To nurture a relationship with your customers it important to regular communicate with them, send them product updates, feature highlights, Taylor personalized content. The strategy in this case is to encourage consistent interaction, showcase new features, and offer tips for maximizing value.
10. **Customer Support Journey**: To address customer issues promptly and effectively.
11. The key elements of this journey is to set up an active helpdesk, live chat, customer support portals, and proactive issue resolution. Timely addressing customers concerns and providing excellent customer service and proactively address potential concerns not only resolves problems efficiently but also forms a bond with your customers who will believe you truly care.
12. **Community Building Journey:** To foster a sense of community among customers. The key elements include Forums, social media groups, and user meetups. Encourage customers to connect with each other, share experiences, and become advocates for the brand.
13. **Personalization Journey:** To create personalized experiences based on individual customer preferences. Personalized content, recommendations, and targeted communications. Leverage data to understand customer preferences and tailor interactions to enhance their overall experience.
14. **Feedback and Improvement Journey**: To continuously improve based on customer feedback. automate surveys, feedback forms, and continuous improvement initiatives based on the actions of consumers with different touch points with your brand. post receiving the feedback its imperative to Act and communicate the changes, and show customers that their input drives positive changes.
15. **Upsell/Cross-Sell Journey:** This journey is automated and triggered based on customer behavior and purchase history. Example: Send personalized product recommendations based on the customer's previous purchases or browsing behavior. Offer upsell opportunities for complementary products or cross-sell items that align with their interests.
16. **Reactivation Journey:** To win back customers who have become inactive or churned. This journey is activated for customers who have not purchased over a period of 90 days. The Key Elements: Re-engagement emails, special offers, and targeted campaigns. The strategy is to Identify reasons for inactivity, address concerns, and provide compelling reasons for customers to return.
17. **VIP/Exclusive Journey:** This is an ongoing journey for high-value or loyal customers. Example: Segment high-value customers and provide them with exclusive access to new products, early sales, or VIP events. Send personalized communications to make them feel like valued insiders.

Market automation and Customer Relationship Management (CRM) play pivotal roles in designing and executing effective customer retention journeys. Market automation involves leveraging technology to streamline, automate, and measure marketing tasks and workflows. Through targeted communication, personalized content, and timely interactions, market automation helps nurture customer relationships and enhance brand loyalty. By integrating CRM into the process, businesses gain a comprehensive understanding of their customers, tracking their preferences, behaviors, and purchase history. This data empowers marketers to create highly tailored and relevant retention strategies. CRM systems facilitate the segmentation of customer bases, allowing for the delivery of personalized messages and offers to specific groups. Furthermore, the combination of market automation and CRM enables businesses to automate responses to customer interactions, ensuring timely engagement and satisfaction. Through these tools, businesses can design intricate customer retention journeys that anticipate needs, address concerns, and provide ongoing value, fostering long-term relationships and maximizing customer lifetime value. The synergy between market automation and CRM not only streamlines marketing efforts but also enhances the overall customer experience, ultimately contributing to sustained customer loyalty and increased profitability.

CHAPTER THIRTY-EIGHT

"PRICE" IS NOT THE ONLY WAY TO STAND OUT

Customer experience has become a crucial factor in today's business landscape, and its significance is only expected to increase in the future. With access to abundant information and numerous options, modern customers are more discerning and have higher expectations from the brands they engage with. Here are a few reasons why customer experience is such a deciding factor and its importance will continue to grow:

- Competitive differentiation: In a crowded marketplace, where products and services can be easily replicated, customer experience sets businesses apart. A positive and memorable customer experience creates a competitive advantage, making customers more likely to choose and remain loyal to a particular brand.
- Customer loyalty and advocacy: Satisfied customers are more likely to become loyal advocates for a brand. They share their positive experiences with others, both online and offline, leading to increased brand awareness and organic growth. Conversely, a negative customer experience can lead to dissatisfied customers sharing their grievances, potentially damaging a brand's reputation.
- Repeat business and revenue growth: Customers who have a great experience are more likely to return and make repeat purchases. By focusing on delivering seamless experiences and meeting customer needs, businesses can increase customer retention rates and drive revenue growth over time.
- Positive brand perception: Customer experience plays a significant role in shaping a brand's perception in the minds of consumers. A consistently positive experience builds trust, enhances brand reputation, and positions a business as customer-centric, leading to greater customer satisfaction and loyalty.
- Increased customer expectations: As customers become more informed and tech-savvy, their expectations continue to rise. They expect personalized interactions, convenience, quick problem resolution, and proactive engagement from the brands they interact with. Businesses that fail to meet these expectations may lose customers to competitors who can deliver on these demands.
- Data-driven insights: Customer experience provides valuable insights into customer preferences, pain points, and behavior. By leveraging customer feedback and data analytics, businesses can identify areas for improvement, refine their offerings, and provide tailored experiences that align with customer needs.

To thrive in today's competitive landscape, businesses must prioritize customer experience and invest in strategies and technologies that enable them to deliver seamless, personalized, and memorable interactions. By doing so, they can build stronger customer relationships, foster loyalty, and drive sustainable business growth.

CHAPTER THIRTY-NINE

Pricing Strategy

Pricing is a critical aspect and a unique opportunity for D2C (Direct-to-Consumer) brands to differentiate themselves, drive sales, and build a loyal customer base. D2C brands have direct control over their pricing, unlike traditional retail models where pricing decisions may be influenced by intermediaries like wholesalers or retailers. This control allows D2C brands to be more flexible and responsive to market trends, customer behavior, and competition. With direct interactions between the brand and consumers, D2C brands can maintain pricing transparency. Customers appreciate this level of transparency, which fosters trust and loyalty. Being open about product costs and value proposition can help build a strong brand-customer relationship. D2C brands can leverage data analytics to set prices strategically. They can gather insights on customer behavior, preferences, and purchase patterns, enabling dynamic pricing strategies based on real-time market conditions. Personalization is a powerful tool for D2C brands, and pricing can be part of this strategy. Tailoring prices based on individual customer preferences, purchase history, or loyalty can enhance the overall customer experience and boost customer satisfaction. By offering unique and competitively-priced products, D2C brands can differentiate themselves from traditional retail channels and even from other D2C competitors. Being able to showcase their value proposition through pricing can give them a competitive edge in the market. D2C brands can quickly adapt their pricing strategies in response to market changes, product launches, seasonal trends, or special promotions. This agility allows them to stay relevant and competitive in a fast-paced market. Pricing can influence how customers perceive a brand. D2C brands that strategically price their products can convey a sense of exclusivity, quality, or affordability, depending on their positioning in the market. D2C brands can create bundled offers or upsell complementary products directly to customers, thereby increasing the average order value and maximizing revenue opportunities. By employing smart pricing strategies like subscription models, loyalty programs, or VIP pricing tiers, D2C brands can foster long-term customer loyalty and repeat purchases. Pricing also plays a crucial role in D2C brands' international expansion efforts. They can adjust prices to cater to different markets, considering factors like purchasing power, local competition, and regulatory requirements.

Pricing is not just about setting a cost for products; it represents an opportunity for D2C brands to strategically position themselves, connect with customers, and drive growth and profitability. Through data-driven decision-making and a customer-centric approach, D2C brands can capitalize on pricing as a unique opportunity in the ecommerce landscape. Pricing a product goes beyond the producer's perspective; it involves understanding how buyers perceive the product's price. To gain insight into this, it's valuable to categorize customers into different types:

- Value-Seekers - These individuals seek long-term value from their purchases. They may invest more initially, but they aim for maximum value over time, approaching pricing with a rational mindset.
- Image-Conscious Shoppers - Some consumers opt for higher-priced products simply because of their exclusivity. They aim to stand out by choosing more expensive options.
- Hedonistic Shoppers - Hedonists purchase items for enjoyment or because they can afford to do so, without the intention of showcasing their purchases.
- Frugal Buyers - In contrast to hedonists, frugal buyers prioritize lower-priced products, even if the value proposition is not particularly high.

- Novelty Enthusiasts - Novelty buyers are willing to pay extra for unique experiences. They aren't concerned with flaunting their purchases but are willing to invest more for a fresh encounter.
- Impulsive Shoppers - These customers make spontaneous purchases, often attracted to products with attractive price points like Rs. 99/-. Companies carefully design pricing strategies to appeal to impulsive shoppers.
- Indecisive Consumers - Overwhelmed by decision-making, these customers may opt for well-known brands at a higher price, finding comfort in familiarity rather than rationally evaluating value.
- Loyal Customers - Loyal shoppers repeatedly choose the same products due to the comfort of familiarity. Unlike indecisive buyers, they approach pricing with a rational perspective and don't shy away from making decisions.

This approach allows companies to tailor their pricing strategies to different customer segments effectively. Choosing the right price within your customer's acceptable range is a critical aspect of pricing strategy for D2C ecommerce brands. To achieve this, consider the following main factors that can influence your pricing decisions. Understanding your total operating costs is essential in setting a sustainable price. This includes expenses related to production, raw materials, labor, overhead, marketing, and other fixed and variable costs. By accurately assessing your costs, you can determine the minimum price needed to cover expenses and achieve profitability. The availability of your product can impact pricing decisions. If your product is in high demand and limited supply (scarcity), you may be able to command higher prices. On the other hand, if you have excess inventory (abundance), you might consider discounting prices to move inventory quickly. For D2C ecommerce brands, shipping costs are a crucial consideration. Customers often appreciate transparent and reasonable shipping fees. Integrating shipping costs into your pricing strategy can help you avoid surprise charges at checkout and improve customer satisfaction. Consumer demand can vary due to factors like seasonality, trends, or economic conditions. Understanding demand patterns can help you adjust your prices accordingly. For example, during peak demand periods, you might consider raising prices, and during slower times, you could offer promotions to stimulate sales. Analyze your unique selling points and competitive positioning. If you offer distinct features, superior quality, or excellent customer service, you may justify higher prices than your competitors. Highlighting your competitive advantages can support premium pricing.

The way customers perceive your pricing is critical. Price perception is influenced by various factors, such as the perceived value of your product, your brand reputation, and the context in which the price is presented. Communicate the value proposition effectively to align the perceived value with the price you set. To effectively determine the right price within your customer's acceptable range, consider employing the following strategies:

- Value-Based Pricing: Set prices based on the perceived value your product brings to customers. Focus on the benefits and unique features that set your product apart, rather than solely on cost-based pricing.
- Dynamic Pricing: Leverage real-time data and market insights to adjust prices dynamically. This allows you to respond to fluctuations in demand, competitor pricing, and other market conditions.
- A/B Testing Conduct pricing experiments to gauge customer responses to different price points. This can help you identify the optimal price that resonates with your target audience.
- Tiered Pricing: Offer multiple pricing tiers with varying features or services to cater to different customer segments. This allows customers to choose the level of product and service that best suits their needs and budget.

Pricing is a complex and dynamic aspect of your D2C ecommerce strategy. By considering factors like operating costs, inventory, shipping, demand, competitive advantage, and price perception, you can make informed pricing decisions that align with your customers' acceptable range and contribute to the success of your D2C brand. A winning pricing strategy goes beyond simply setting a price for your products; it effectively communicates the value of your offerings to customers, convinces them to make a purchase, and instills confidence in the quality and benefits of your products. Here's how a well-crafted pricing strategy achieves these objectives, along with examples for better understanding:

- Portrays Value: Value-Based Pricing: This approach focuses on setting prices based on the perceived value your product delivers to customers. By highlighting the unique features, benefits, and solutions your product offers, customers will understand why your product is worth the price. For example, a smartphone with innovative features, exceptional camera capabilities, and outstanding performance may command a premium price due to its perceived value.
- Bundling and Upselling: Offering product bundles or upselling complementary items can enhance value perception. For instance, a gaming console bundled with popular game titles and extra controllers at a slightly higher price may entice customers with the added value of the package.
- Promotional Pricing-: Temporary discounts or limited-time offers create a sense of urgency and drive customers to make a purchase decision. For instance, a "Buy One, Get One Free" promotion or a limited-time discount during a holiday sale can encourage customers to take advantage of the deal.
- Free Trials and Samples-: Offering free trials or product samples can help customers experience your product's benefits before committing to a full purchase. This strategy is often used for software subscriptions, streaming services, or beauty products.
- Money-Back Guarantees-: Providing a risk-free money-back guarantee reassures customers that they can get a refund if they are not satisfied with the product's performance or quality. This reduces perceived risk and increases customer confidence in making the purchase.
- Customer Reviews and Testimonials-: Positive reviews and testimonials from satisfied customers serve as social proof of your product's value and quality. Displaying these on your website or product pages can build trust and confidence in potential buyers.
- Quality Packaging and Branding-: Investing in high-quality packaging and branding communicates a sense of professionalism and attention to detail. Customers often associate better packaging with higher product quality.
- Warranty and Customer Support-: Offering a robust warranty and excellent customer support demonstrates your commitment to customer satisfaction and product reliability. This fosters trust and confidence in your brand.

Example Scenario: Imagine you are a D2C brand selling premium noise-canceling headphones. Your target market comprises music enthusiasts, frequent travelers, and professionals seeking top-notch audio experiences. To portray value, you emphasize the superior sound quality, cutting-edge noise-canceling technology, and long-lasting battery life of your headphones. You set a price that reflects the premium features and benefits your product offers, positioning it as a high-end audio solution. To convince customers to buy, you run a limited-time promotion offering a 20% discount and free shipping for the next 48 hours. Additionally, you offer a 30-day money-back guarantee, allowing customers to try the headphones risk-free. To give customers confidence in your product, you prominently display glowing customer reviews and testimonials on your website. Your headphones come with a 2-year warranty, and your customer support team is readily available to assist with any inquiries or issues. By implementing this pricing strategy, you effectively communicate the value of your headphones, motivate customers to make a purchase during the promotion, and instill confidence in the quality and performance of your product, ultimately driving sales and building customer loyalty. A winning pricing strategy should be aligned with your brand positioning, target audience, and overall business goals. It should continuously evolve based on market trends, customer feedback, and competitive insights to maintain a competitive edge in the D2C ecommerce landscape.

its important to use price as a strategic weapon rather than a tactical response. To set up a pricing system that allows you to utilize pricing as a strategic weapon rather than a tactical response, consider the following steps and examples from D2C brands that have successfully employed strategic pricing. Conduct thorough market research to understand customer needs, preferences, and price sensitivity. Analyze competitor pricing strategies to identify gaps and opportunities. Example: A D2C clothing brand uses data analytics to identify popular fashion trends and sets prices for its clothing line accordingly, staying ahead of competitors with up-to-date, trendy offerings. Segment your customer base and tailor pricing to cater to different customer groups. Personalize offers based on customer behavior and preferences. Example: An online skincare brand offers personalized subscription plans based on individual skin concerns, adjusting prices according to the specific products needed by each customer. Implement dynamic pricing algorithms that respond to real-time market changes, demand fluctuations, and customer behavior. Example: An online travel booking platform adjusts hotel prices based on factors such as seasonal demand, availability, and booking trends, ensuring optimal revenue generation. Focus on communicating the unique value proposition of your products and services. Price according to the perceived value to customers rather than solely on cost. Example: A D2C electronics brand emphasizes the cutting-edge features and performance of its smartphones, setting premium prices that reflect the devices' advanced technology. Offer subscription-based services or membership programs that provide ongoing value to customers, encouraging loyalty and recurring revenue. Example: A D2C fitness brand provides customers with access to exclusive workout programs, personalized training, and nutrition plans through a monthly membership fee. Use promotions strategically to drive specific business objectives, such as increasing sales, clearing excess inventory, or attracting new customers. Example: An online grocery delivery service offers limited-time discounts on specific product categories during slow shopping hours to boost sales during off-peak periods. Bundle complementary products or services together to create attractive offers that encourage customers to spend more. Example: A D2C home furniture brand offers discounted furniture bundles for entire room setups, enticing customers to purchase multiple items at once. Utilize psychological pricing techniques, such as setting prices just below round numbers (Rs.999 instead of Rs.1000), to create the perception of a better deal. Example: An online beauty brand prices its skincare products at Rs.199 instead of Rs.200 to create the impression of affordability while maintaining a premium image.

Ensure that your pricing strategy aligns with your brand positioning and identity. Consistent pricing reinforces brand image and customer trust. Example: A D2C sustainable fashion brand prices its products slightly higher than fast fashion competitors, appealing to eco-conscious consumers who value ethically-made products. Continuously monitor market dynamics, customer feedback, and competitor moves. Adapt your pricing strategy accordingly to stay relevant and competitive. Example: A D2C electronics company frequently adjusts pricing based on customer reviews, feedback, and competitive offerings, ensuring they meet customer expectations. By implementing a well-designed pricing system that considers market data, customer preferences, and competitive dynamics, D2C brands can utilize pricing as a strategic tool to differentiate themselves, drive sales, and achieve long-term success in the ecommerce landscape.

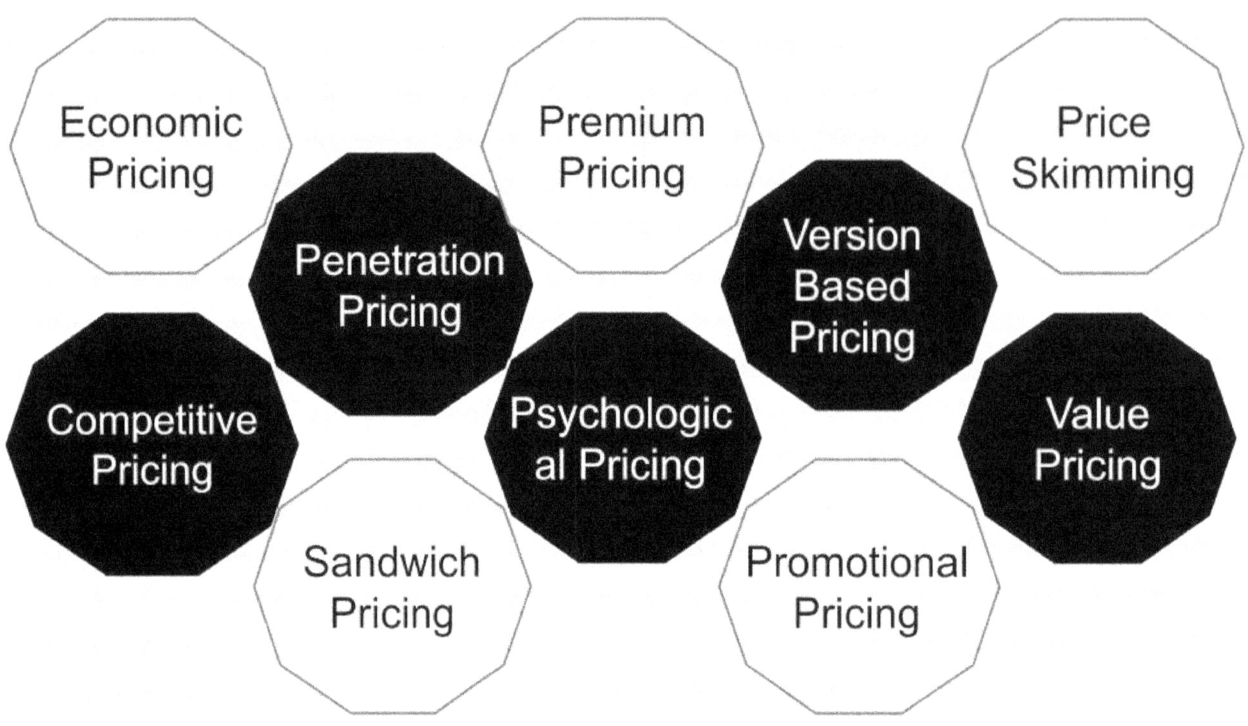

Strategic pricing and Types of pricing strategies

D2C brands have a variety of pricing strategies at their disposal to optimize revenue and achieve their business objectives. Here are some common types of pricing strategies for D2C brands:

1. Competition-Based Pricing-: Setting prices based on competitor prices to remain competitive in the market. This strategy involves monitoring rivals' pricing and adjusting your own accordingly.
2. Cost-Plus Pricing-: Adding a markup to the cost of production to ensure that all costs are covered and a desired profit margin is achieved.
3. Dynamic Pricing-: Adjusting prices in real-time based on factors like demand, inventory levels, time of day, or customer behavior. This allows brands to optimize revenue based on market conditions.
4. Freemium Pricing-: Offering a basic version of the product or service for free and charging for premium features or upgrades. This allows for wider product adoption and upselling to a paying customer base.
5. High-Low Pricing-: Offering regular prices for most products but occasionally running promotions or discounts to create a sense of urgency and attract customers during sales periods.
6. Economy Pricing-: Setting prices at a low and affordable level to target price-sensitive customers and gain a competitive advantage through cost leadership.
7. Skimming Pricing-: Setting high initial prices for new or innovative products to capitalize on early adopters and recoup development costs quickly. Prices are then gradually reduced to reach a broader market.
8. Penetration Pricing-: Setting low initial prices to quickly gain market share and attract new customers. Once market presence is established, prices may be increased.
9. Premium Pricing-: Positioning products as high-end or luxurious and charging premium prices to convey exclusivity and high quality.
10. Customization / Personalization Pricing-: Offering personalized product configurations or experiences at different price points to cater to individual customer preferences.

11. Value-Based Pricing-: Setting prices based on the perceived value of the product to the customer, rather than solely on cost or competition.
12. Bundle Pricing-: Offering multiple products or services together as a package at a discounted price compared to buying them individually. This encourages customers to purchase more items at once.
13. Psychological Pricing-: Using pricing tactics that exploit customers‘ psychological perceptions, such as setting prices just below a whole number (e.g., $9.99 instead of $10) to make them appear lower.
14. Geographic Pricing-: Adjusting prices based on geographic location, considering factors like shipping costs, taxes, and local market conditions.

These pricing strategies can be combined or adapted to suit a D2C brand's specific goals, target audience, and market dynamics. Implementing the right pricing strategy can significantly impact a brand's revenue, profitability, and overall success in the competitive D2C ecommerce landscape.

What happens when you have a weak Pricing Strategy ?

A weak pricing strategy can have several negative consequences for a D2C ecommerce brand. Let's explore how each aspect can impact the brand and its customers: If your pricing strategy does not align with the perceived value of your product, customers may feel that your offering is overpriced or lacking in quality. Overpricing a product that does not deliver on its promised value can lead to disappointed customers, negative reviews, and a damaged brand reputation. Example: A D2C brand sells basic, entry-level smartphones at premium prices, misrepresenting them as high-end devices with advanced features. Customers who buy these phones expecting top-notch performance will be disappointed and may not return for future purchases. Inconsistent or unclear pricing can create uncertainty and distrust among customers, making them hesitant to make a purchase. Hidden fees, unexpected charges during checkout, or constantly changing prices can lead to a negative customer experience and high cart abandonment rates. Example: An online retailer initially advertises a product at a discounted price, but during the checkout process, additional fees are added, making the final price significantly higher than expected. Customers who encounter this may feel misled and abandon the purchase. If your pricing strategy is not aligned with your target customer's budget or preferences, you may miss out on potential sales and fail to attract the right audience. Underpricing may attract bargain hunters who are not loyal to your brand and may switch to competitors offering even lower prices. Overpricing may alienate your target customers and push them toward more affordable alternatives. Example: A luxury skincare brand targets budget-conscious consumers by offering premium-priced products, but this pricing strategy attracts customers who are not willing to spend significantly on skincare. As a result, the brand fails to reach its intended audience of customers seeking high-end skincare solutions. A weak pricing strategy can lead to a mismatch between your product's perceived value and its price, create uncertainty and doubt among customers, and attract the wrong audience. This can have detrimental effects on your brand's reputation, customer loyalty, and overall profitability. To avoid these pitfalls, it's crucial for D2C ecommerce brands to invest time and effort in crafting a strategic pricing approach that accurately portrays the value of their products, instills confidence in customers, and targets the right audience for sustained growth and success.

A few more examples of pricing strategies gone wrong:

1. Example 1 - Tech Gadgets Brand-: This D2C brand launched a line of high-end smartwatches with advanced features and health monitoring capabilities. However, they priced the smartwatches significantly lower than other competing brands in the market. As a result:

    1. Perception of Lower Quality: The low pricing led customers to question the quality and reliability of the smartwatches. Customers perceived them as cheap and less technologically advanced compared to higher-priced competitors.
    2. Inadequate Profit Margins: By underpricing their products, the brand faced challenges in maintaining profitability, especially considering the sophisticated technology and research that went into developing the smartwatches.

2. Example 2 - Luxury Fashion Brand A D2C luxury fashion brand launched a new line of designer handbags with premium materials and craftsmanship. However, they opted for aggressive discounting and frequent sales promotions:

    1. Devaluation of the Brand: Constant discounts created a perception that the brand's products were not as exclusive or high-end as they claimed. Customers began to wait for sales instead of purchasing at full price, undermining the brand's premium image.
    2. Loss of Customer Trust: The brand's pricing inconsistency eroded customer trust and loyalty. Customers questioned the authenticity of the luxury experience and felt uncertain about the true value of the products.

3. Example 3 - Subscription Box Service-: A D2C subscription box service offered a range of niche products at a fixed monthly rate, but their pricing was set too high for the perceived value of the items included:

    1. Customer Churn and Dissatisfaction: Subscribers felt that the subscription cost exceeded the value of the products they received. Many customers canceled their subscriptions after the first few months, leading to high churn rates and negative reviews.
    2. Missed Target Audience: The brand's pricing strategy failed to attract the target audience effectively. The higher price point limited their appeal to potential customers interested in trying out new products without significant commitment.

In all these examples, the weak pricing strategies negatively impacted the brands' reputations, customer satisfaction, and profitability. It is essential for D2C brands to conduct thorough market research, understand their customer base, and accurately assess the value their products offer. Pricing should be aligned with the brand's positioning and the value proposition it aims to convey. By avoiding underpricing or overpricing products and targeting the right customer segments, D2C brands can create a strong foundation for success and long-term growth in the competitive ecommerce market.

CHAPTER FORTY

MARKET SIZE

Total Addressable Market (TAM) is a term used in business and marketing to represent the entire revenue opportunity available for a particular product or service within a specific market. It represents the maximum achievable revenue if a business were to capture 100% market share, assuming perfect market conditions and no competition.

Elaborating on the concept of TAM:

TAM begins with defining the target market segment that a business is interested in. This segment can be defined by factors such as demographics, geographic location, industry, or any other relevant criteria. It's important to be as specific as possible to accurately estimate the market size.TAM is based on several variables that determine the size of the market. These variables typically include:

1. Number of Potential Customers:- This is the total count of individuals or organizations that fit the defined market segment.
2. Average Revenue per Customer:- The average amount of revenue that a business can generate from each customer within the market segment.
3. Frequency of Purchase:- How often customers are likely to buy the product or service.

TAM calculations are often adjusted to account for factors like market growth rate, seasonal variations, and geographic differences. For example, if a market is expected to grow over the next five years, you might factor in that growth to estimate the TAM for the future. TAM is a valuable metric used for various purposes, including business planning, investment decisions, and marketing strategies. It helps businesses understand the revenue potential of their products or services and guides them in setting realistic goals and strategies for market penetration. TAM represents the total market size, but businesses usually do not capture the entire market. They target a specific portion of the market, known as the Serviceable Addressable Market (SAM), and then further narrow it down to the actual achievable market share, known as the Share of Market (SOM). TAM calculations can vary significantly depending on the industry and product. For example, the TAM for a niche product might be much smaller than that for a widely used consumer product. To estimate TAM, businesses rely on various data sources, including market research reports, industry statistics, government data, surveys, and customer databases. TAM is a fundamental concept in market analysis and strategic planning. It helps businesses assess the size of the opportunity, evaluate market potential, and make informed decisions about resource allocation and growth strategies. However, it's essential to remember that TAM is an estimate, and real market conditions can be influenced by many unpredictable factors.

Total Addressable Market (TAM), Serviceable Addressable Market (SAM), and Share of Market (SOM) are three related concepts used in market analysis to understand the potential market for a product or service. They are interconnected but represent different aspects of the market opportunity:

TAM is the total market demand for a specific product or service, assuming there are no constraints or limitations on market reach. It represents the maximum revenue a business could generate if it captured 100% of the market share. TAM is calculated by multiplying the number of potential customers by the average revenue per customer and the frequency of purchase. TAM provides a broad view of the market's potential size and is often used for strategic planning, investment decisions, and assessing the attractiveness of entering a market. The formula is:

TAM = Number of Potential Customers × Average Revenue per Customer × Frequency of Purchase

Different ways to calculate TAM: Top-Down Approach: The top down method of calculating. TAM is called so because it is shown as an inverted pyramid. In this approach, you use different industry research to narrow down a large market to your specific TAM. Bottom up approach: In the bottom up approach to calculating your TAM tends to be more accurate and reliable than the top-down approach because it uses firsthand market data instead of secondary research To calculate your TAM using the bottom-up approach, multiply the total number of potential customers in your industry by the average annual spending on your product or service.

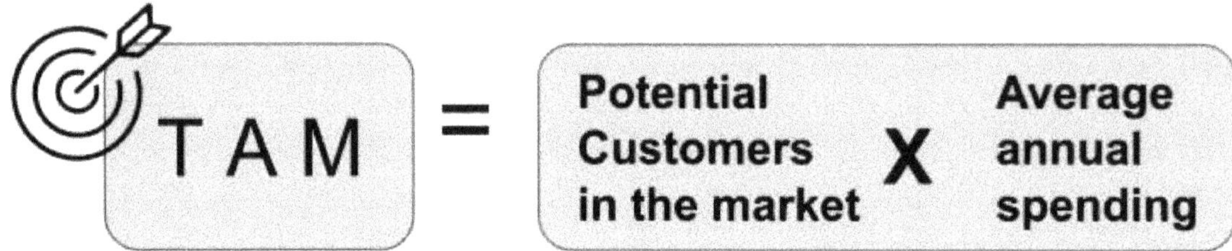

Formula to calculate total addressable market

2. Serviceable Addressable Market (SAM) SAM is a subset of TAM that represents the portion of the market that a business can realistically target with its product or service. SAM considers factors such as geographical limitations, regulatory restrictions, and the business's capabilities. SAM is calculated by identifying the specific market segment or segments that the business intends to serve and estimating the market size within those segments.

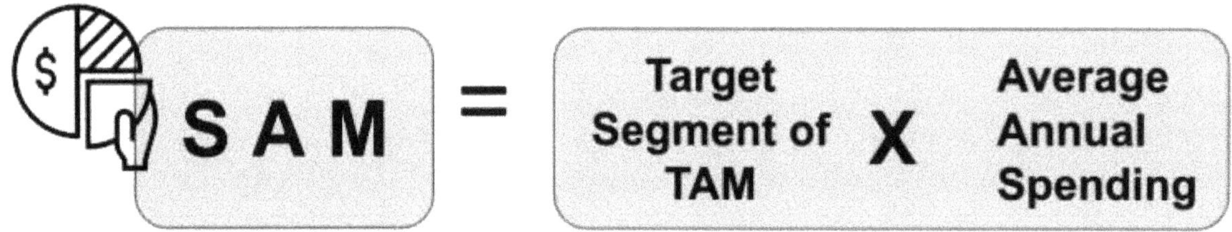

Formula to calculate serviceable addressable market

SAM helps businesses narrow down their target audience and focus on the portion of the market that aligns with their resources and capabilities. It is essential for refining marketing and sales strategies.

3. Share of Market (SOM): also known as Market Share, represents the portion of the market that a business or product has actually captured in terms of revenue or sales. It is a measure of a company's performance within its target market. SOM is calculated by dividing a company's revenue or sales within a specific market by the TAM or SAM for that market. The formula is:

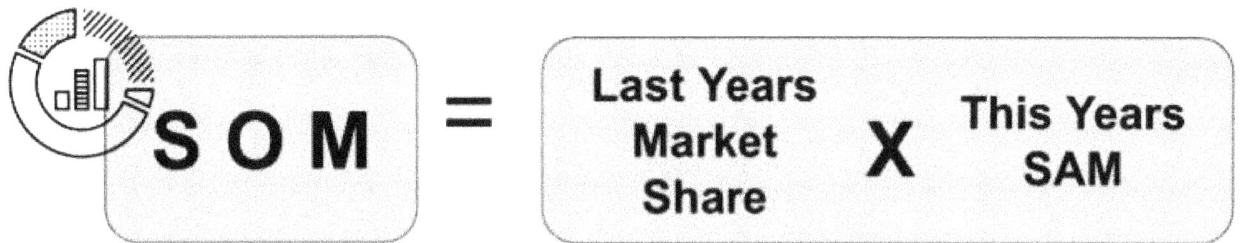

Formula to calculate your share of marlet

SOM = (Company's Revenue or Sales in the Market) / (TAM or SAM for the Market)

SOM assesses a company's market performance and competitiveness. It helps track progress toward market penetration goals and can guide resource allocation and marketing strategies.

Correlation and Relationship:-TAM, SAM, and SOM are interrelated but represent different stages in market analysis.SAM is a subset of TAM, as it focuses on the portion of the market that is realistically reachable by the business. SOM is a measure of a company's market performance relative to the total market size (TAM) or the serviceable market size (SAM). The goal is to increase SOM over time by capturing a larger share of the market through effective marketing, sales, and product development strategies. While TAM provides a high-level estimate of market potential, SAM and SOM offer more practical insights into targeting and market share. TAM represents the entire market opportunity, SAM represents the portion a business can realistically target, and SOM measures the company's share of that market. Understanding these concepts is essential for effective market analysis and strategic decision-making.

Using the TAM SAM SOM example, we can express the ROI calculation as follows:

- TAM = $2 billion
- SAM = $100 million
- SOM = $5 million in 2 years and $12 million in 4 years
- Initial Investment = $250,000 for 20% equity

When the company reaches $5 million in revenue, it generates an EBITDA of $5 million x 25% margin = $1.25 million. At this point, the company's valuation is 8 times the EBITDA, which equals $10 million. The ROI for an investor holding 20% ownership at this stage is calculated as follows:. ROI = ($10 million x 20% ownership) / $250,000 investment = 8.0x If the company achieves the target of $12 million in revenue, its EBITDA becomes $12 million x 25% margin = $3 million. This increases the company's valuation to 8 times the EBITDA, resulting in a valuation of $24 million. The investor's ROI under these circumstances is calculated as follows: ROI = ($24 million x 20% ownership) / $250,000 investment = 19.2x. This ROI calculation demonstrates the potential return on investment for an investor based on the company's growth and valuation at different revenue milestones.

To determine your market value, you'll follow these steps:

1. Estimate Market Potential:- Begin by estimating the market volume or market potential, which represents the total potential sales for your product or service within a defined timeframe.
2. Calculate Market Penetration Rate:- Your market penetration rate indicates the percentage of the total target market to which you've successfully sold your product or service at least once during that specific period. Market Penetration Rate = (Number of Customers Sold to / Market Size) x 100. For instance, if you've sold to 1000 customers out of a target market with a size of 2000, your market penetration rate is calculated as: (1000 / 2000) x 100 = 50%.

3. Determine Market Value:- To find your market value, multiply the number of sales by the average value of each sale to a customer.
4. Understand Revenue Potential:- With both your market penetration rate and market value revenue in hand, you gain insights into your potential for revenue growth as you scale and expand your business over specific time periods.

By following these steps, you can assess your market value and make informed decisions about scaling and growing your business within your target market.

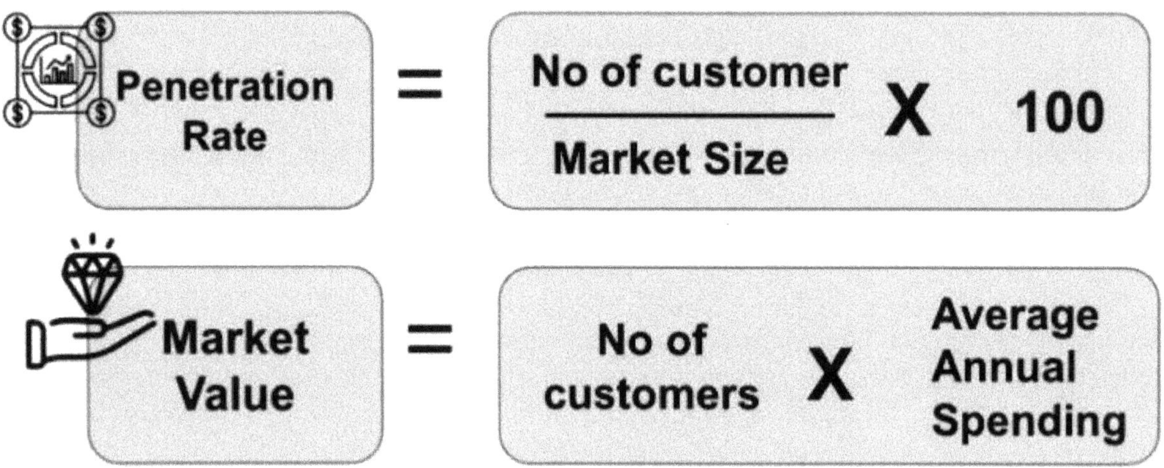

Define your growth trajectory

CHAPTER FORTY-ONE

THE GOST FRAMEWORK FOR GOAL SETTING

The GOST model is a structured approach that helps organizations and marketing teams align their efforts and make data-driven decisions throughout the product development and marketing process. It ensures that there is a clear understanding of what needs to be achieved, how it will be done, and the actions required to reach those goals and objectives. This model promotes a systematic and organized approach to product development and marketing planning. The GOST model is a framework for goal setting that helps individuals and organizations define clear and achievable objectives. The acronym GOST stands for Goals, Objectives, Strategies, and Tactics. Here's a breakdown of each component of the GOST model:

1. Goals:- Goals are broad, overarching statements that outline what you want to achieve in the long term. They provide direction and purpose. Goals should be specific, measurable, achievable, relevant, and time-bound (SMART). Goals answer the question, "What are we trying to accomplish?" Examples of goals include "Increase annual revenue by 20% in the next three years" or "Become a market leader in our industry."
2. Objectives:- Objectives are specific, quantifiable targets that support the achievement of goals. They break down the goals into smaller, manageable steps. Objectives provide a clear path to follow and help measure progress. Objectives answer the question, "How will we achieve our goals?" Using the examples above, objectives could be "Increase monthly sales by 10%," "Expand our product line by Q2," or "Enter three new markets by the end of the year."
3. Strategies:- Strategies are the high-level plans or approaches that outline how you intend to achieve your objectives. They are the broad methods or tactics you will employ. Strategies answer the question, "What approach will we take to achieve our objectives?" For instance, if the objective is to "Increase monthly sales by 10%," the strategy might involve "Launching a targeted marketing campaign" or "Expanding our sales team."
4. Tactics:- Tactics are the specific actions or steps you will take to implement your strategies. They are the practical, day-to-day activities that help execute your plan. Tactics answer the question, "What specific actions will we take to implement our strategies?" Continuing with the example, if the strategy is to "Launch a targeted marketing campaign," the tactics might include "Creating social media ads," "Sending email newsletters," or "Running online promotions."

The GOST model is a structured approach to goal setting that ensures clarity and alignment within an organization or for an individual. It starts with defining clear and specific goals, breaks them down into measurable objectives, outlines the strategies to achieve those objectives, and finally, specifies the practical tactics that will be executed to implement the strategies. This model helps in effective planning, execution, and measurement of progress toward desired outcomes.

	Goals	Objectives	Strategies	tactics
Corporate Level Business unit level Program level (Marketing)	Desired Outcome The qualitative essence of what you aspire to attain. Comprehensive and Enduring Encompassing a wide scope and focusing on the long-term perspective. Setting the Course Providing a guiding compass to determine the path forward.	Qualitative Objectives": These represent the measurable outcomes essential for reaching the overarching goal. "Numerical Targets": incorporate specific numerical targets on revenue growth, profit margins, expanding the customer base, market penetration, revenue increase. etc	Long-Term Bets & Trade-Offs vs Competition Specific Strategic Areas of Focus Key Plan for Achieving Goals & Objectives Ownable & Differentiated Create unique and distinctive brand elements. Focus on intangible qualities that evoke emotions.	Short-term actions aligned with strategies Details that expand on the "how" of achieving objectives Sufficient information to instill confidence in strategy execution Tangible and specific, pointing to concrete activities

GOSTFramework element defination

Sunscreen SPF50 & SPF 30 GOST model (Simplified version)

The GOST model for sunscreen in India is a framework for setting goals, objectives, strategies, and tactics to effectively market and promote sunscreen products in the Indian market. Here's a simplified example of how the GOST model can be applied to a sunscreen brand in India:

1. Goals:

    1. Goal 1: Become a leading sunscreen brand in India within the next five years.
    2. Goal 2: Increase awareness about the importance of sun protection in the Indian population.

2. Objectives:

    1. Objective 1: Achieve a 15% market share in the Indian sunscreen industry by the end of year three.
    2. Objective 2: Educate 1 million Indians about the risks of sun exposure and the benefits of using sunscreen in the first year.

3. Strategies:

    1. Strategy 1: Product Diversification - Develop a range of sunscreen products suitable for various skin types and sun protection needs, including SPF 30, SPF 50, and water-resistant options.

2. Strategy 2: Marketing and Education Campaign - Launch an extensive marketing campaign that includes television, social media, and outdoor advertising to raise awareness about the brand and the importance of sun protection.
3. Strategy 3: Distribution Expansion - Increase the distribution network by partnering with major retail chains, pharmacies, and online platforms to make the sunscreen products readily available across India.

4. Tactics:

   1. Tactic 1: Product Development: Research and formulate sunscreen products that cater to the specific skin types prevalent in India, such as products for oily skin, dry skin, and sensitive skin.
   2. Tactic 2: Social Media Advertising. Create engaging and informative social media content that educates consumers about the harmful effects of UV rays and encourages sunscreen use. Run targeted ad campaigns on platforms like Facebook and Instagram.
   3. Tactic 3: Collaborations with Dermatologists - Partner with dermatologists and skincare experts to endorse the brand's products and provide expert advice on sun protection through webinars, workshops, and content collaborations.
   4. Tactic 4: Retail Display and Promotions - Work with retail partners to secure prominent in-store displays and offer special promotions and discounts to incentivize customers to try the products.

This simplified GOST model outlines the overarching goals and objectives for a sunscreen brand in India, the high-level strategies to achieve them, and specific tactics to implement those strategies. Of course, in a real-world scenario, each of these components would require detailed planning, market research, and execution to succeed in the highly competitive Indian sunscreen market. The first step is estimating market volume, or market potential. This refers to the total amount of potential sales you could make for your product or service within a set period of time. To find your market volume for a specific period, you must calculate what your market penetration rate is. Market penetration is represented by a percentage that is equal to the portion of the total target market that you have sold your product or service to one or more times within the specific period.

To calculate your market penetration rate, use the following equation: penetration rate = (number of customers sold to /market size) x 100. So, if you have sold to 1000 customers out of a target market with a size of 2000, the equation would be: (1000 / 2000) x100 = 50%. In other words, your current market penetration rate is 50%. Now, to calculate your market value, multiply your number of sales by the average value of a sale to each customer. Once you get both your market penetration and market value revenue you can better understand your potential for increasing revenue as you scale and grow your business over specific periods of time

About Ravneesh

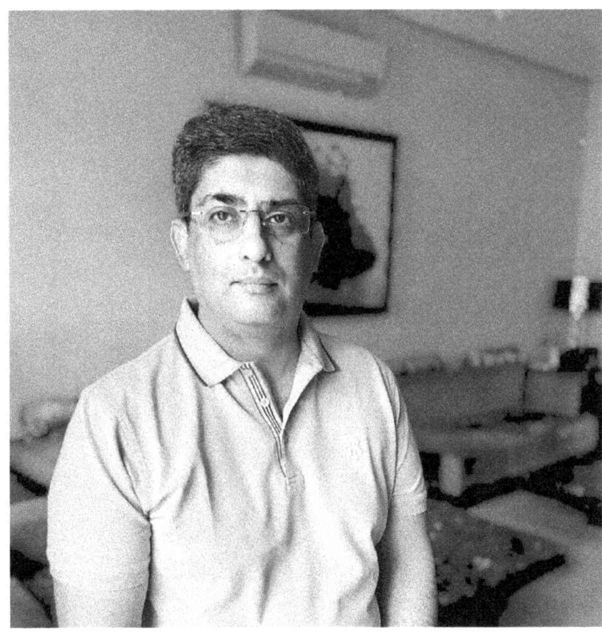

Ravneesh Suresh Dhaneshwar

Ravneesh Suresh Dhaneshwar is a seasoned professional with over 18 years of invaluable experience in the intricate world of scaling digital-first brands. With an impressive track record spanning across India and Singapore, Ravneesh has left his indelible mark on the e-commerce landscape, operating on both the agency and brand sides of the spectrum. Having navigated the complex and ever-changing terrain of e-commerce, his wealth of experience extends to a multitude of product segments, including fashion, jewelry, home & accessories, nutraceuticals, beauty, and personal care, to name but a few. His journey has been marked by one constant theme - strategizing for brand growth and fiercely protecting market share from the relentless strategies of competitors.

The book " Confidential Ecommerce Strategies & Tactics for Success " is the culmination of Ravneesh's vast experience and business intelligence, carefully gathered and honed over the years. It is a treasure trove of insights, born from the crucible of real-world experience. Within its pages, you'll find a blueprint for success, with a clear understanding of how stakeholders should define their business objectives, engage with the right partners, and deploy effective scaling strategies. Most importantly, it reveals how to safeguard your strengths once you've discovered them. At its core, the book delves into every aspect that influences a consumer's perception of value and, ultimately, drives them to make a purchase. This is where the worlds of strategy, innovation, disruption, brand building frameworks, and marketing tactics converge, all under Ravneesh's expert guidance.

On the educational front, Ravneesh holds a postgraduate degree with a specialization in growth strategies from the prestigious Indian Institute of Management Calcutta (IIM Calcutta). This academic foundation enhances his already profound understanding of the business world, allowing him to approach complex challenges with both analytical rigor and innovative creativity. Beyond the realm of business, Ravneesh's interests in travel, art, and music further exemplify his creative mindset, a valuable asset when tackling the dynamic e-commerce landscape. His dedication to strategically aligning marketing efforts with business objectives has consistently yielded remarkable ROI for his clients and employers. With "Confidentail Ecommerce Strategies and tactics," Ravneesh Dhaneshwar opens the door to the world of direct-to-consumer success, sharing insights, strategies, and wisdom honed by years of experience. It's a must-read for anyone seeking to thrive in the digital commerce arena.

Stay Tuned

In my capacity as a practicing growth strategist and the author behind "Confidential - Ecommerce Strategies & Tactics for Success," I am excited to present to you a resource that transcends the ordinary, offering more than just surface-level insights into the realm of digital marketing. Instead, this book takes a deep dive, providing you with the clandestine ingredients required to craft a thriving ecommerce and D2C business. To optimize your journey, I have meticulously organized this guide into two distinct segments. This strategic arrangement is designed to enable you, the reader, to immerse yourself wholly in the art of constructing a flourishing brand.

Part 1: Strategy, Planning & Goal Setting

In Part 1, we will delve into the crucial foundation of strategy and planning. You can expect to gain a comprehensive understanding of the core elements necessary for brand success, from defining your vision to crafting a laser-focused strategy. This section will equip you with the knowledge and insights required to set the stage for a thriving brand in the ever-evolving digital landscape.

Part 2: Tactical Implementation, measuring outcome and path iteration

In Part 2, we will shift our focus to the essential role of goal setting and the tactical steps necessary to holistically build and scale a profitable brand. You'll discover a wealth of tactics, tips, and strategies to achieve your objectives and make your brand not just a presence but a thriving force in the market. By breaking the content into these two distinct parts, I aim to ensure that you not only grasp these crucial concepts but also have the time and space to reflect and apply them effectively. Your journey towards D2C success begins with a strong foundation in strategy and unfolds into the dynamic world of goal-oriented, tactical execution. Let's embark on this transformative journey together! ?

www.ingramcontent.com/pod-product-compliance
Lightning Source LLC
LaVergne TN
LVHW070228170826
845679LV00035B/1868

9798891862678